"I've worked with many companies on digital transformations, and it is refreshing to see Sunil Gupta's tight framework for what drives success. He makes clear the challenges involved, the deep underlying issues you need to attack, and the case for going big. In health care right now, I personally see the reality of everything Gupta is describing and the importance of taking his all-in approach."

—**DAVID EDELMAN,** Chief Marketing Officer, Aetna

"Highly interesting and extremely relevant, *Driving Digital Strategy* is an essential book for leaders struggling with the many challenges and opportunities of digitization."

—**HÅVARD S. ABRAHAMSEN,** CEO, PwC Norway

"Sunil Gupta delivers a world-class guided tour on how to understand, design, and drive a digital strategy—an intelligent, inspiring, and intriguing call for action!"

—**SØREN RØSSEL,** Head, PwC's Executive Education Global Centre of Excellence

"In a world where technology and new age companies have already disrupted most of the industries and businesses, it is imperative for every business to go all-in on digitization in order to compete and succeed. *Driving Digital Strategy* is the quintessential guide for achieving that transformation."

—**VIJAY SHEKHAR SHARMA,** founder and CEO, Paytm

Driving Digital Strategy

Sunil Gupta

Driving Digital Strategy

A Guide to Reimagining Your Business

Harvard Business Review Press

Boston, Massachusetts

Library of Congress Cataloging-in-Publication Data is forthcoming.

The paper used in this publication meets the requirements of the American National Standard for Permanence of Paper for Publications and Documents in Libraries and Archives Z39.48-1992.

ISBN: 9781633692688
eISBN: 9781633692695

To
Kamal for your love and inspiration
and
Tarun and Kunal for bringing so much joy
and happiness to my life

Contents

PART FOUR
Rebuild Your Organization

Introduction

Framework for Reinventing Your Business

Disruption and transformation get a lot of hype, and for good reason. Digital technologies have had a profound impact on the world, disrupting entire industries while also enabling companies such as Facebook and Amazon to achieve exponential growth. There's no doubt that incumbents have struggled as new and nimble players have emerged with innovative business models. But there's also a more important story to tell: as much as digital has posed a threat to the old guard, and continues to do so, it also presents an endless number of opportunities for companies from traditional industries.

The Weather Company is a case in point. When consumers moved away from TV to mobile phones but did not stay long enough to generate ad revenues, the company execs pivoted and created a service called WeatherFX, which uses data from its app to help retailers predict how the weather will affect consumer purchasing behavior. And other companies are finding success, too. Faced with declining print subscriptions and the loss of revenue from classified ads, the *New York Times* built a highly successful digital-subscription business with over 2.5 million subscribers, and the company is on track to generate $800 million in digital revenue by 2020. Car companies such as Cadillac are experimenting with subscription services, Sephora and other retailers are using apps to enhance the in-store experience, and Goldman Sachs has created an online platform (and asked its competitors to join in as well).

As a business leader, you've no doubt had "digital" on your mind for quite some time, and you've probably started new initiatives and run experiments in an effort to "digitize" your business. Some of these have probably been fruitful. But if you're like the executives I interact with, you're looking to make a more transformative impact. But how? If your company lacks the digital DNA and agility of a startup, how can you take full advantage of the unique opportunities that the digital era provides?

For over ten years, as a professor at Harvard Business School, I've studied digital strategy and have worked with scores of companies on their digital transformations. While doing so, I have seen firsthand what works best and what doesn't, and what I've learned is that the leaders who achieve transformative results go all-in on digital. That is, they don't treat digital strategy as separate from their overall strategy. Instead, they lead with a digital-first mentality and make sure their digital strategy touches *all* aspects of their organizations. Digital transformation requires strengthening the core and building for the future at the same time.

This is what this book, using a broad range of examples, will show how to do. It compiles case studies and best practices from companies who have reinvented their businesses, and provides a framework that will help you create an all-encompassing digital strategy while leading your entire organization through the transformation process.

Where Companies Go Wrong

To mitigate the effects of digital disruption while also exploring new opportunities, companies have typically followed some combination of these three strategies—creating small, independent units or startups within the larger organization; doing a series of digital experiments;

and/or leveraging technology to cut costs and improve efficiency. However, in most cases these initiatives have led to limited success.

Almost every large company launches independent digital units or has outposts in Silicon Valley, with the hope that a handful of young entrepreneurs will spark innovation for the firm. The Spanish telecom giant Telefónica, for example, launched an independent unit, Telefónica Digital, in September 2011. While the parent company had its headquarters in Madrid, the new Digital unit was housed in London with a separate CEO and an independent budget. Like most telecom companies, Telefónica had failed to benefit from the mobile revolution. Instead, new players such as Skype and WhatsApp were beginning to threaten the very core of its business. Telefónica's management hoped that the Digital group would come up with new and innovative ideas for products and services that would provide a future direction for the company.

With an ambitious agenda, the freedom to operate independently, and a large budget, the Telefónica Digital team started coming up with just such ideas. As expected, many of these ideas were quite new for a telecom company at the time. After developing, testing, and piloting them, the Digital group sent the promising ideas to the Madrid headquarters for potential global launch. However, Telefónica faced resistance from country heads who were neither convinced about these ideas nor had the capabilities to implement them. After three years of this experiment, the company shut down its Digital unit in London and moved all activities back to Madrid.

Creating an independent unit is like launching a speedboat to turn around a large ship. Often the speedboat takes off but does little to move the ship.

Next, companies tend to run experiments, which makes a lot of sense given the rapidly changing environment and uncertainty about the future. This journey often begins with a few tactical experiments, typically in marketing departments, where employees are quick to try new social media tools or new mobile platforms. As the excitement around digital spreads throughout the organization, new initiatives start emerging all over the company, leading to a proliferation. In 2012, Kasper Rørsted, CEO of Henkel at the time, realized this when he asked a team of senior leaders to catalog all of Henkel's digital initiatives. He was shocked to find over 150 separate digital initiatives throughout the company. Many of these started as small experiments designed to solve a specific problem faced by one department or country. Soon new and varied digital initiatives began to pop up all over the company: "hundreds of flowers," as Rørsted described them.[1]

Realizing that this proliferation does not lead to any synergy, companies often start consolidating these disparate initiatives. A team of leaders takes inventory of various digital projects in different functions, brands, business units, and regions, to figure out a way to rationalize and combine them. Often, a governance body is created to approve future digital projects. At this stage, projects that used to be regional might become global, and single-brand initiatives might be scaled up to include multiple brands.

Each stage of the journey may be useful, and even essential, at a certain point in time. Experiments help a company test novel ideas and explore future trends. Proliferation of ideas across business units is a sign of entrepreneurship and enthusiasm. Consolidation is a necessary and effective way to rationalize processes and allocate resources. However, doing experiments without a road map or a sense of direction may give the illusion of success in the short run without making any impact in the long run, and ideas that proliferate without scaling may only waste valuable time and resources. More important, this bottom-up approach tends to be tactical in nature and does not address fundamental strategic issues that the company should be debating.

A third approach is to leverage technology to reduce costs and improve the efficiency of operations. For instance, banks close branches as consumers move to online and mobile banking. Retail stores reduce their real estate footprint and close marginal stores. Processes are digitized and streamlined to minimize overlap and increase efficiency. Many of the internal tasks are redesigned to allow customers to self-serve, thereby reducing labor costs.

Companies should always try to improve efficiency and minimize cost. However, if you rely solely on this approach, you are implicitly assuming that technology will not fundamentally change your business. Effectively you are assuming that banks, for instance, will still operate as before and that fintech companies won't have a major impact on their business. In many cases this may be a flawed assumption. For example, Alibaba's four-year-old Yu'e Bao fund, set up as a repository for consumers' leftover cash from online spending, has become the world's largest money-market fund, with $165.6 billion under management, overtaking JPMorgan's $150 billion money-market fund.

Essentially, through initiatives like these, managers are using a Band-Aid for a deeper problem. In order to be successful, you can't just create a separate digital unit, or run experiments, or use technology to improve efficiency. Instead, you must make digital strategy an integral part of your overall business strategy. That is, rather than treating digital strategy as a separate exercise, you must embed it into the operations and DNA of your organization, in a way that touches all aspects of your business.

Crafting a Strategic View: A Framework for Reinventing Business

Using numerous examples across a variety of industries, this book provides a framework for reinventing your business that will help you leverage existing assets and pinpoint areas where new capabilities must be developed.

The framework consists of four key components:

1. Reimagining your business

2. Reevaluating your value chain

3. Reconnecting with customers

4. Rebuilding your organization

Throughout the book, I'll go into detail about the four parts of this framework. You'll need to face each part head-on. To achieve success,

FIGURE I-1

A framework for digital leadership

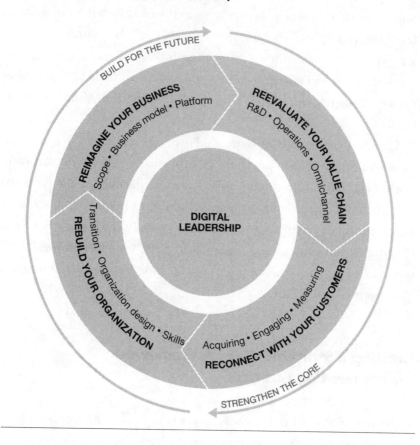

you can't tackle one part and not the others. But as you'll see from the wide range of case studies that we'll explore, the options for how you transform your business can be varied, flexible, and open-ended. Knowing that there is no one, magic solution, the book provides instead a systematic approach for digital transformation.

Let's take a brief look at the framework, one part at a time.

Reimagine Your Business

Given the dramatic changes that digital has caused, you'll need to sit back and reflect on the core essence of your business, examining three components: scope, business model, and ecosystem.

When considering scope, you'll need to ask yourself this fundamental question: "What business are we in?" Think about Amazon. It started as an online retailer, but it is no longer just an online retailer. In 2017, Amazon is expected to generate more than $3.5 billion from advertising alone, and its hardware devices, such as Echo, are making significant inroads in homes. Google is moving into autonomous vehicles, and Apple, for years primarily a hardware company, is now investing heavily in original content. What should you be investing in?

Competition in the digital age usually comes laterally, from new players, and redefining the scope of your business is essential to ensuring future success. This requires a careful balance of broadening the scope of your business while staying within your core competencies. Chapter 1 discusses business scope and shows how the rules of competition are changing and what you need to do to stay competitive in the digital age.

Technological changes also require you to rethink your business model: how you create and capture value. For example, when iTunes unbundled the music industry, leading to a significant decline in revenues from recorded music, the industry had to shift its focus to live performances as a major source of income. With the decline in its classified ads, the entire publishing and print-media industry has been forced to consider if its focus on an ad-based model is appropriate for the future. Chapter 2 describes innovation in business models and what your company can learn from these best practices.

As business models change and new competition from different industries starts affecting your business, you may realize that you can't succeed alone. In this case, you may need to evolve into a platform, which will require you to manage an ecosystem of players—both partners and competitors, or "frenemies." Companies have found great success creating platforms, which also led them to redefine how they think about competition.

When Goldman Sachs launched its structured-notes business, SIMON, it shocked the world by inviting its competitors to sell their products on it. This strategy led to Goldman Sachs's becoming the second-largest issuer of structured notes within a few years. A shift from selling products to creating a platform requires a very different mindset and strategy, as described in chapter 3.

Reevaluate Your Value Chain

Digital technology can significantly improve the efficiency and effectiveness of various parts of your value chain, especially as new models of R&D and innovation have emerged. Companies such as GE, P&G, and Siemens have leveraged open innovation to redefine their R&D process. Chapter 4 describes why and when open innovation works, how you should design open innovation in your organization, and what prevents organizations from being successful with this new approach.

Digital technology has also ushered in a new era of Industry 4.0. Innovations such as digital manufacturing, virtual and augmented reality, 3-D printing, and digital supply chains are improving operational excellence. Chapter 5 describes how firms around the globe are leveraging these new technologies to improve productivity, reduce failure rate, and create competitive advantage.

New entrants often use digital technology to disrupt the existing value chain, especially distribution. In the first wave of the internet, new entrants disintermediated several industries—for example, travel agencies. This process has continued, and now auto dealers and brick-and-mortar stores have come under increasing pressure as manufacturers have started their own e-commerce channels. The challenge for manufacturers is to manage the inherent channel conflict that this situation creates. Every company now has to think about its omnichannel strategy, which creates a synergy between its online and offline channels—a topic discussed in chapter 6.

Reconnect with Your Customers

Digital technology has changed the way consumers search for information and buy products, and technology is enabling firms to collect information about the entire consumer decision journey or path to purchase, which will open up new ways for you to acquire customers. Long before a consumer buys a car, she searches for information on Google, which provides an opportunity for auto manufacturers to understand her preferences and influence her behavior. Sensors in washing machines will soon allow Whirlpool to understand consumers' usage behavior and even provide valuable consumption data about laundry detergent to P&G. And as consumers increasingly rely on online reviews and friends' advice, you can monitor social media to understand how those friends and reviewers might be converted into brand advocates. Chapter 7 discusses how digital technology has opened new channels for customer acquisition.

Despite all the developments in digital marketing, the click-through rates of ads remain less than 1 percent. Every brand wants to engage consumers, but consumers don't find any compelling reason to engage with, say, a bar of soap, a can of soda, or a bottle of beer. How can you engage consumers in this cluttered environment? Chapter 8 shows that the answer does not lie in technology and data alone but—more generally—in finding new ways to provide unique value to consumers, as done by Tesco in South Korea, Unilever in India, and Mastercard in Singapore.

Digital technology was supposed to make advertising more measurable and accountable. Yet many challenges, such as attribution, remain—making it difficult to measure the effectiveness of ads. How can you measure and optimize marketing spend? Chapter 9 describes new research that points to some useful directions to help companies in this important task.

Rebuild Your Organization

Managing the digital transition in a large organization is a nontrivial task. As you try to strengthen your core business and build for the future at the same time, you'll face the challenge of running two organizations in parallel. As a result, revenues and profits often decline during the transition period before they go back up, which can shake the resolve of even the most confident CEO. Chapter 10 discusses the challenges in managing the digital transition and highlights how companies like Adobe have successfully navigated this passage.

How do you design an organization for innovation? As I mentioned earlier, creating a separate entrepreneurial group to bring digital innovation into a legacy company is like launching a speedboat to help maneuver a large ship. So instead of launching a speedboat, you must create a "landing dock" where new initiatives, or speedboats, can dock, leverage the power of the mothership, and help change its course over time. We'll cover this in chapter 11.

Data, artificial intelligence, and machine learning are automating tasks and having a significant impact on jobs and the skills and capabilities that companies will need in the future. Technology is also allowing firms to move to a more data-driven and less subjective approach to talent management. New and innovative ways of hiring and managing talent are emerging. Chapter 12 discusses these topics and describes how Knack, a San Francisco–based company, uses mobile games to help its clients recruit talent. Each ten-minute game provides Knack thousands of data points—pertaining to such things as how people process information, how they handle challenges, and how they learn from their mistakes. Knack's innovative approach has won the company ardent fans and influential clients, including AXA, BCG, Nestlé, and Citigroup.

The rest of the book will discuss further the four major areas of digital transformation shown in figure I-1. Each chapter will describe in detail the three topics within each of these areas, highlight best practices, and address some of the questions raised above.

PART ONE

Reimagine Your Business

**REIMAGINE
YOUR BUSINESS**
Scope
Business model
Platform

Chapter 1

Business Scope

In 1960, Theodore Levitt, a Harvard Business School professor, published a provocative paper in *Harvard Business Review* in which he argued that companies were too focused on products and not enough on customer needs. To help managers address this problem, he asked, "What business are you really in?"[1] More than five decades later this fundamental question has become even more important, as companies are moving from products to platforms and as industry boundaries are getting blurred. Yet even though the majority of firms are trying to become customer-centric, it is not uncommon to hear senior executives, be it from General Motors or Walmart, define their businesses, their industries, and their competition by the products they produce and sell.

Let's look to Amazon to see the advantage of heeding Levitt's advice.

What Business Is Amazon In?

When Amazon first launched its website, in July 1995, founder Jeff Bezos's goal was to use the internet to sell books at low prices. He created a virtual store with lower fixed costs and a larger inventory than those of most brick-and-mortar bookstores. The concept quickly became popular, and Bezos realized that consumers shopping for other types of goods might also appreciate this concept. So he began adding dozens of categories to Amazon's online assortment, including music, DVDs, electronics, toys, software, home goods, and many more. Amazon's low prices and large selection, and the convenience online retailing provided consumers, posed a significant threat to traditional retailers like Best Buy, Toys "R" Us, and Walmart.

Five years later Amazon opened its site to third-party sellers, who could post their products on Amazon's site for a modest service fee. This move was a win-win: third-party sellers increased Amazon's assortment without Amazon having to stock extra inventory, and sellers got access to the ever-increasing pool of consumers who enjoyed shopping on Amazon's site. Adding third-party sellers also transformed Amazon from an online *retailer* to an online *platform*, which required Amazon to develop new capabilities of acquiring, training, and managing sellers on its sites without losing control or damaging customer experience. And its competitive set expanded to include eBay, Craigslist, and others.

Other online retailers, such as Flipkart in India, are undergoing a similar transition and realizing that this seemingly simple move from an inventory-based model to a marketplace model requires a significant shift in the capabilities and operations of the company.[2]

The introduction of iTunes, in 2001, dramatically changed consumers' behavior as they started downloading digital music instead of buying CDs in a store. Recognizing this trend, Amazon launched its video-on-demand service, initially called Unbox and later renamed as Amazon Instant Video, almost a year before Netflix introduced video streaming. Once again Amazon followed its customers and shifted from selling CDs and DVDs to offering streaming services that required it to develop new capabilities and pitted it against a new set of competitors, such as Apple and Netflix.

In 2011, in partnership with Warner Bros., Amazon launched Amazon Studios to produce original motion-picture content. Suddenly it was competing against Hollywood studios. Why does it make sense for Amazon, which started as an online retailer, to move in this direction?

Because video content helps Amazon convert viewers into shoppers. In a 2016 technology conference near Los Angeles, Jeff Bezos said, "When we win a Golden Globe, it helps us sell more shoes."[3] According to Bezos, the original content of Amazon Studios also encourages Prime members to renew their subscription "at higher rates, and they convert from free trials at higher rates" than Prime members who do not stream videos.[4] Launched in 2005, Prime offers free two-day shipping for a subscription fee, which started at $79 a year and was later increased to $99 a year. By 2017, Amazon had almost 75 million Prime members worldwide.[5] Not only does the subscription fee generate almost $7.5 billion in annual revenue for Amazon, but Prime members also spend almost twice the amount of money than other Amazon customers do.[6] In addition to creating loyalty among Prime members, original content is also a means of attracting new customers. In 2015, Amazon's CFO Tom Szkutak credited Amazon's $1.3 billion investment in original content as a key driver for attracting new customers to other parts of Amazon's business, including Prime.[7] In 2017, Amazon spent almost $4.5 billion on original video content.[8]

But Amazon's business scope did not end with retailing and content. In 2007, Amazon released the Kindle, almost three years ahead of the iPad. Now Amazon, which started as an online retailer, was in the hardware business. The Kindle was designed to sell ebooks as consumers shifted from physical products to digital goods. It is important to recognize that Amazon's strategy for the Kindle is quite different from Apple's strategy for the iPad. Apple makes most of its money from hardware, whereas Amazon treats the Kindle as a "razor," selling it at a low (or even break-even) price in order to make money on the ebooks, which would be akin to the "blades." As consumers started spending more and more time on their mobile devices, Amazon launched its own Fire phone in July 2014. It failed to gain traction, but was pursuing that market a mistake? Perhaps. However, the upside from a successful launch would have been enormous.

More recently, Amazon launched additional devices: Dash buttons, which let users order products from over a hundred brands when users' supplies get low, and Echo, a voice-activated virtual assistant, which can be used to stream music, get information, and of course, order products from Amazon in an even more convenient fashion.[9] Echo was launched in November 2014, and within two years Amazon had sold almost eleven million Echo devices in the United States and developers had built over twelve thousand apps or "skills" for this device. As voice increasingly becomes the computing interface for consumers, Amazon is well positioned with Echo.

Amazon also started its own advertising network, which put the company squarely in competition with Google. Amazon's large customer base, and more specifically the company's knowledge of consumers' purchasing and browsing habits, provides Amazon with a rich source of data for targeting its customers with relevant ads. While Google only knows a consumer's intention to buy a product, Amazon has information on whether or not a consumer actually bought a product on its site—highly valuable information for product manufacturers, which is encouraging them to shift digital advertising dollars to Amazon. This shift has allowed Amazon to generate almost $3.5 billion of ad revenue in 2017.[10] But an even bigger goal for Amazon is to replace Google as a search engine for products, so that customers start their product search on Amazon rather than on Google. This would not only reduce Amazon's ad spend on Google but would also give Amazon tremendous market power. In October 2015, a survey of two thousand US consumers revealed that 44 percent go directly to Amazon for a product search, compared with 34 percent who use search engines such as Google or Yahoo.[11] Eric Schmidt, Google's executive chairman, acknowledged this shift. "People don't think of Amazon as search," said Schmidt, "but if you are looking for something to buy, you are more often than not looking for it on Amazon."[12]

Perhaps the most controversial choice was Bezos's decision to enter the cloud-computing market with the launch of Amazon Web Services (AWS). Suddenly a completely new set of companies—for instance, IBM—became Amazon's competitors. What is an online retailer doing in cloud computing? AWS helps Amazon scale its technology for future growth. It allows Amazon to learn from other e-commerce players who use its platform. And it enables Amazon to leverage and monetize its excess web capacity. Effectively AWS is a way for Amazon to build its technology capability to become one of the largest online players and monetize that capability at the same time.

However, this was certainly a risky move and many experts questioned Bezos's decision. A 2008 *Wired* magazine article criticized this decision. "For years, Wall Street and Silicon Valley alike have rolled their eyes at the legendary Bezos attention disorder," wrote *Wired*. "What's the secret pet project? Spaceships! Earth to Jeff: You're a retailer. Why swap pricey stuff in boxes for cheap clouds of bits?"[13] Bezos had a pithy response to AWS critics: "We're very comfortable being misunderstood. We've had lots of practice."[14] In the fourth quarter of 2017, AWS generated over $5 billion in revenue, representing annual revenue of more than $17 billion and 43 percent year-over-year growth.[15]

Amazon's success in broadening the scope of its business while continuing to focus on consumer needs is undeniable: Since its inception, Amazon has grown at a staggering pace, with almost a 60,000 percent increase in its stock price.

Define Your Business Around Your Customers, Not Your Products or Competitors

Amazon's varied products and services, and the company's correspondingly numerous and varied competitors, can be seen at a glance in figure 1-1. As an online retailer, Amazon competes with Barnes & Noble, Best Buy, and Walmart. As an online platform, Amazon competes with eBay. In cloud computing, it battles for market share with IBM, Google, and Microsoft. In streaming services, it has Netflix and Hulu as formidable competitors. Amazon Studios puts the company up against Disney and NBC Universal Studios. Its entry into mobile phones put it in the crosshairs of Apple, HTC, and Samsung. Its ad network made it Google's rival.

FIGURE 1-1

Amazon's business and its competitors

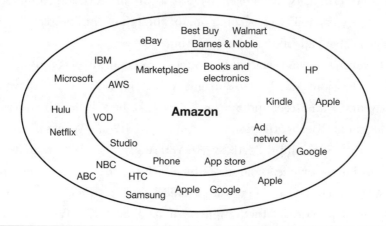

Most companies define their business by either their products or their competitors—for example, you may consider yourself in the banking business or the automobile industry. But it is hard to define Amazon in this traditional fashion. Amazon expanded its scope around its customers.

Redefining your business around customers is not limited to technology companies. John Deere, the heavy-machinery and farming-supply company, was founded in 1837 by a blacksmith who sold steel plows to farmers.[16] By 2014, the company had $36 billion in sales worldwide and employed nearly 60,000 people.[17] For decades, John Deere had been very successful selling its heavy machinery to farmers and construction companies, but in the early 2000s the company began adding software and sensors to its products. Its newest farming equipment includes guided-steering features so accurate that the equipment can stay within a preset track without wavering more than the width of a thumbprint.[18] Later, John Deere formed two new divisions: a mobile-technology group and an agricultural-services group.

By the mid-2000s, John Deere had collected data from over 300,000 acres to help farmers optimize their fertilizer use.[19] Soon the company transitioned from a farm-equipment manufacturer to a farm-management company that provided predictive maintenance, weather information, seed optimization, and irrigation through remote sensors (see figure 1-2). The company is planning to open the platform's application programming interfaces (APIs) to outside developers, so that the information can be used in new ways.[20]

Automobile companies, which used to see themselves as being strictly in the business of manufacturing and selling vehicles, have to wake up to the new competition from ride-sharing companies like Uber, which are providing mobility without the need to own or even lease a car. Now, as a defensive move, all automakers are positioning themselves within the "mobility" business and offering their own ride-sharing services, even though these services have the potential to reduce the demand for cars, a concern shared by most auto manufacturers. However, these services, such as Mercedes car2go and BMW DriveNow, also have the potential to

FIGURE 1-2

John Deere's transformation

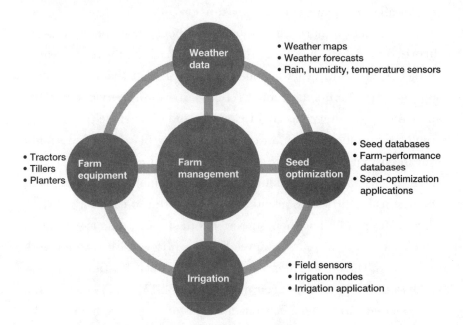

Source: Adapted from Michael E. Porter and James E. Heppelman, "How Smart, Connected Products Are Transforming Competition," *Harvard Business Review,* November 2014.

generate interest among millennials, who may not have considered these brands otherwise but who will do so on a low-cost, trial basis, possibly leading to greater brand loyalty in the future.

Competition Is No Longer Defined by Traditional Industry Boundaries

It should be clear from the discussion so far that competition is no longer defined by traditional product or industry boundaries. The rapid development of technology is making data and software integral to almost all businesses, which is blurring industry boundaries faster than ever before. In a 2014 *Harvard Business Review* article, Michael E. Porter and James E. Heppelmann suggested that smart, connected devices—or the internet of things—shift the basis of competition from the functionality of a single product to the performance of a broad system, in which the firm is often one of many players.[21]

Typically new players, either startups or companies from different industries, enter a market and catch incumbents by surprise. Amazon surprised Google by becoming the dominant competitor in the search market. Apple is hiring automobile engineers at a rate that is scaring the auto industry. Netflix and, more recently, streaming services by HBO and CBS are causing concern for Comcast and other cable players.

Often incumbents leave an opening for new players by ignoring a shift in customer needs in response to changes in technology. Netflix changed customers' expectations about on-demand streaming, and although cable providers eventually pursued the so-called TV Everywhere concept to allow their subscribers to stream content anywhere, it took them several years to develop this service, and it is still a work in progress. During a conference in late 2015, Reed Hastings, Netflix's CEO, said, "We've always been most scared of TV Everywhere as the fundamental threat. That is, you get all this incredible content that the ecosystem presents, now on demand, for the same [price] a month. And yet the inability of that ecosystem to execute on that, for a variety of reasons, has been troubling."[22] Had Comcast understood the shift in customer needs and transformed its business around those needs, it might have prevented the threat of cord-cutting (which is cable customers canceling their subscriptions in favor of such streaming services as Netflix, Hulu, and HBO Now). Similarly, Uber might not have been so successful had taxi companies kept in touch with consumer needs and provided consumers a convenient way to order and pay for taxi rides.

Competitive Advantage No Longer Comes from Low Cost or Product Differentiation

In 1979, Michael Porter, one of my colleagues at Harvard Business School, published a landmark paper in which he argued that a company could follow one of two potential strategies for competitive advantage: either by being cheaper (that is, as a low-cost producer) or by being different (with differentiated products that command higher prices).[23] This view suggested that the core competencies required to become a low-cost producer include scale and operational efficiency, whereas a differentiation strategy requires the ability to create innovative products and services. As the scope of a business expands and both its competition and its industry boundaries are defined more broadly than before, a company needs to rethink its core competencies and its competitive advantage.

What is Amazon's core competency that allows it to enter into such disparate business areas as online retailing, cloud computing, hardware, digital advertising, media streaming, and content creation? Although Amazon started as a low-cost player without the fixed cost of stores, it is not product-centric knowledge that gives it an advantage of differentiation or low cost. Instead, Amazon has mastered three skills:

- Deep knowledge of *customers* obtained from mining customer data. This is embedded in the recommendation system for books and movies as well as in the introduction of new products and services.

- Back-end *logistics* for warehousing and shipping that could rival the logistics systems of FedEx and UPS. With its investment in drones and now its own trucking business, Amazon is further strengthening this part of its competency.

- Knowledge of and ability to manage *technology* infrastructure. This has allowed it to become not only one of the largest online retailers but also a dominant player in cloud computing.

These skills provide a unique advantage to Amazon, an advantage that makes it difficult for Amazon's rivals to compete. For example, a deep understanding of customers and their demand patterns allows Amazon to have a cash conversion cycle of minus fourteen days, in contrast to the cash conversion cycle of ten days for Walmart and twenty-seven days for Target.[24] (The cash conversion cycle is calculated by adding the number of inventory days and accounts-receivable days and subtracting accounts-payable days. Amazon reduces its inventory days by accurately forecasting consumer demand. Its accounts-receivable days are low since it gets payment from consumers almost immediately, and it pays its suppliers in thirty to sixty days. With a cash conversion cycle of minus fourteen days, Amazon is effectively letting its suppliers fund its growth.) An accurate estimation of demand also allows Amazon to prestock the right products in a particular warehouse and promise delivery of these items within two hours in that geography through its recently launched Prime Now service.

Complementary Products and Network Effects Provide Strong Competitive Advantage

In today's connected world, sustainable competitive advantage comes from offering a system of connected and complementary products, and from creating a platform with strong network effects that increase consumers' switching costs. Mobile-phone companies such as Nokia were product-based until smartphone players such as Apple moved to a platform-based model whereby the value of the iPhone increased with the development of new apps. The iPhone's product advantage over Samsung's Galaxy phones has lessened dramatically over time, yet the iPhone has managed to maintain its leadership position largely due to complementary services, such as iTunes and FaceTime, that make it harder for consumers to switch.

Traditional retailers like Walmart and Best Buy have started their own e-commerce operations and often find it frustrating that their operations have not gotten the needed traction even though Walmart and Best Buy prices are not only comparable but, in many cases, lower than those of Amazon. Although Amazon started as a low-cost player, over time it has built a series of complementary services (e.g., free music and video to Prime members) that have redefined its competitive advantage.

Paytm, an Indian startup backed by Alibaba, illustrates the idea of complementary products very well. Paytm began its operations as an online mobile-recharge company that offered consumers the convenience of adding money to their prepaid mobile phones. It charged mobile operators a small fee for this service. Soon it added new complementary services: Consumers could use money from their Paytm wallet to buy bus and train tickets. They could use it to pay for Uber and other online-to-offline (O2O) services. They could use it for peer-to-peer payments. They could use it to pay offline merchants, including millions of mom-and-pop shops, who put QR codes in their shops for consumers to scan with their mobile phones, instead of installing expensive POS machines to accept credit cards. (Unlike credit-card companies, Paytm did not charge any fee to small merchants for accepting Paytm money. Paytm did charge large merchants, and consumers were charged a fee if they took money out of the Paytm system. This encouraged consumers to keep the money within the Paytm network.) And, finally, consumers could use money from their Paytm wallet to buy products online. In 2015, Reserve Bank of India, the country's central bank, gave banking licenses to Paytm and several mobile operators to provide mobile banking services to millions of consumers who did not have access to banking services in India. By adding these complementary services, Paytm made its wallet increasingly valuable to consumers. By mid-2017, Paytm had more than 200 million wallets. In the process of adding these new services, Paytm expanded the scope of its business, developed new capabilities (e.g., running an online marketplace, becoming a bank), and started competing with a diverse set of players.

In many cases the value of a product (e.g., WhatsApp) increases as more consumers use it, without any change in the product's features or functionality. This is the *direct network effect*. In addition, as a product becomes a *platform* that connects, say, buyers and sellers (e.g., eBay), it gains from *indirect network effect*. That is, as buyers join the platform in increasing numbers, more sellers have an incentive to be part of it. This virtuous circle leads to a winner-take-all environment that makes it harder for any other player—even those with better products or lower costs—to compete effectively. Companies enjoying strong indirect network effects include Uber, Airbnb, Match.com, Flipkart, and others.

Figure 1-3 shows how the traditional way of providing value to customers has changed dramatically in the digital age. In the last several decades companies have been organized by products, and each business unit's goal has been to provide product value for every single target customer, effectively focusing on a single product and a single customer (the bottom left quadrant of figure 1-3). The traditional strategic framework espoused by Michael Porter worked well here, and companies focused on making their products cheaper or better. Automobiles, consumer products, banking products, all have used this traditional approach.

However, companies like Amazon exploit the synergy between complementary products by using the razor-blade strategy, in which the razor (e.g., Kindle) can be sold almost at a loss in order to make money on the blades (e.g., ebooks). Note that for this strategy to work, an organization's structure and its incentive systems have to move away from one built around traditional product units. The performance of a Kindle manager cannot be measured and evaluated based on the profitability of his business unit.

FIGURE 1-3

New ways to provide value to customers and create competitive advantage

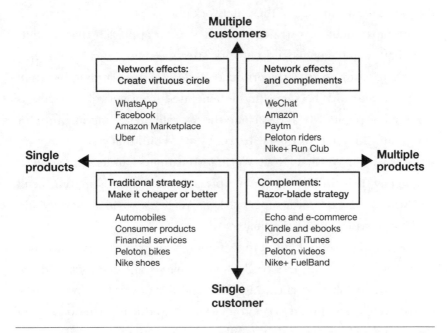

His goal is not to make money on the Kindle but to help sell more ebooks. It can become very hard for a rival to compete with a firm whose strategy is based on complementary products. In 2016, Amazon made over $1 billion in small-business loans to more than 20,000 merchants who sell products on its platform.[25] Amazon could easily decide to offer these loans at a much lower rate than traditional banks, because Amazon can use these loans as a razor to make money on the merchant transactions on its platform. If the core product of banks were to become a complement for Amazon, banks would find it very hard to compete.

In the connected world, the value of a product such as WhatsApp or Uber increases as more people use it, without any changes in the product features. This creates a winner-take-all scenario that makes it very hard for competitors who are competing solely on the basis of low cost or product differentiation. Amazon was an online retailer without any network effects until it added the marketplace that allowed third-party sellers to join. In chapter 3 we will discuss how traditional companies like GE are rethinking their strategy by moving from products to platforms to take advantage of these network effects.

The most ambitious strategy is to devise an approach that benefits from both complements and network effects. When Tencent launched WeChat in China in 2011, the product was designed as a messaging application, similar to WhatsApp, and it benefitted from network effects. As it gained in popularity and became the favorite messaging medium for almost all Chinese consumers, Tencent started building complementary services within WeChat. Now, WeChat consumers can use the application to pay their utility bills, order a pizza, book a doctor's appointment, and scan a QR code at a supermarket. WeChat's payment service has become a serious threat to Alibaba's Alipay.

This strategy is not limited to technology companies. Nike launched FuelBand to help runners track their activities and later created the Nike+ Run Club that encouraged people to run and train with the global Nike+ community. Peloton, when introducing a new exercise bike, didn't simply claim that its bike was better than competing products. It launched a series of exercise videos that users subscribe to on a monthly basis. Peloton also introduced live classes that users can stream from the comfort of their own homes, and as part of the streaming, the user's performance metrics—exertion level, heart rate, rank in the class—are displayed at the bottom of the screen. It is not uncommon for a few hundred people to be participating in a live class. This not only creates a sense of community but also, for many, creates a competitive environment that gives them an additional incentive to put in that extra effort in their exercise routine. US Foods, a company that distributes food to restaurants, provides complementary services to its clients to help them manage inventory, reduce waste, and optimize labor. It is also building a platform to connect several smaller suppliers to its large client base, similar to what Amazon did when it added third-party sellers on its platform.

Data and Customers Become Critical Assets of a Company

The two most valuable assets of a company today are its data and its customer base, yet they don't show up in the balance sheet. The financial reporting system, which reflects how companies have traditionally managed their business, focuses on physical assets instead.

Customers create a powerful network effect, and they also provide an opportunity for introducing complementary services. Amazon has used this strategy very effectively. It is not hard to imagine how Amazon may leverage its large base of Prime customers to introduce new services. In May 2017 Amazon was rumored to be exploring a move into the $465 billion US pharmaceutical market. If the company can deliver books and other products to its trusted Prime customers, why couldn't it also deliver prescription drugs to those very same customers? T-Mobile, a wireless service provider in the United States, has over seventy million customers. The company started offering its customers free pizza on Tuesdays, which soon expanded to include offerings of free movie tickets and magazine subscriptions and discounts on gas. The exchange is mutually advantageous. Providers of these free products get access to T-Mobile's customer base in order to generate trial offerings and acquire new customers, and T-Mobile gets to offer additional value to its customers at no cost.

"Data is the new oil" is the often-quoted mantra these days, and for good reason. Unlike physical assets, data does not get "used up." It can be replicated and used in multiple applications without diminishing its value. In fact, the value of data increases as more data is collected—sort of a "data network effect." Amazon's Echo gets better as people use it more and as Amazon refines its functions. Tesla improves its self-driving algorithms and updates its software regularly as it gets more data from its cars. Artificial intelligence and the internet of things are creating products with the ability to learn and improve the more the products are used, because the more they're used, the more data they collect, and the more data they collect, the more refined their functioning becomes. These data network effects also create a powerful competitive advantage. Even if General Motors and Ford can create cars with better physical product features, Tesla's wealth of data from its autonomous vehicles, which fuels the development of its algorithms, will continue to give the company a strong competitive advantage for a long time.

A Broader Business Scope Requires Building New Capabilities

During the launch of the Kindle 2, Jeff Bezos explained how Amazon shifted from selling electronics to manufacturing them: "There are two ways to extend a business … Take inventory of what you're good at and extend out from your skills. Or determine what your customers need and work backward, even if it requires learning new skills. Kindle is an example of working backward."[26] Traditionally companies expand into adjacent businesses where they can leverage their existing core capabilities. However, a customer-centric view requires a firm to follow shifts in customer needs and to develop new capabilities to meet those needs.

By 2006, half of John Deere's employees were engineers and the company planned to hire even more engineering talent to support new capabilities, such as artificial intelligence and satellite navigation. "We're known as a company that provides great tractors or great lawn mowers. What many don't know is that we have a great focus on innovations in information technology," said Larry Brewer, John Deere's global infrastructure services manager.[27]

As John Deere moved into value-added services such as predictive maintenance, analytics, and crop optimization, it had to build significant internal capabilities around data science and analytics. In 2015, Charles Schleusner, who worked in John Deere's Intelligent Solutions Group, shared that fewer than 40 percent of farmers in North America documented their harvests and even fewer captured their planting of crops or field applications of fertilizers and pesticides.[28] John Deere saw an increasingly important role for the company to help harness data for farmers to use in making better decisions, and was willing to invest in building new capabilities in pursuit of that goal.

How Far Should You Extend Your Business?

At this point, some of you may be wondering if broadening the scope of the company would lead to a lack of focus. Isn't the success of Apple due to its laser-sharp focus on a handful of products that can fit on a table? Can a company do everything and be good at all of them? Didn't the strategy books teach us to focus on our core competencies lest we spread ourselves too thin?

The tension between focus and broad scope is reasonable and healthy. It's best to think about your consumers' point of view and how your core competencies can help serve those consumer needs. Apple is hiring hundreds of automobile engineers, and there is a lot of speculation that Apple may build its own car. Is Apple losing focus? If we think a little broadly, an automobile is the ultimate mobile device, and the core skill of Apple—creating superb user interface—is becoming increasingly important in cars, where consumers want a seamless integration of their mobile devices. If automobiles become software on wheels, Apple may have a strong role to play in this industry. And the company's strategy of tightly integrating its hardware and software would suggest that it better invest in the hardware: the automobile.

Industry leaders are beginning to recognize this new reality. Speaking at the Consumer Electronics Show in Las Vegas in January 2016, Mark Fields, then the CEO of Ford Motor Co., said, "[Y]ou are going to see us change pretty dramatically, becoming an auto and mobility company. You will see us focus more attention on the transportation-services sector, even as we maintain our emphasis on our core automotive business."[29] In May 2017, Jim Hackett, chairman of Ford Smart Mobility, replaced Mark Fields as CEO, signaling a major shift in Ford's strategy.

Chapter 2

Business Model

A business model defines the way a firm creates, delivers, and captures value. Often, technological innovations lead to changes in consumer behavior and to the emergence of new competitors, requiring a company to radically transform its business model. In this chapter, we'll discuss some of the tough situations faced by companies and highlight the basic principles of new business models that firms should embrace to survive and thrive in the digital era.

Convert Razor into Blade

For a long time the music industry enjoyed significant growth by selling music in physical formats: vinyl, tapes, and CDs. Remember the days when you used to buy a CD with twelve to fifteen songs, even though you really wanted to listen only to one or two songs? Why did the music industry force you to buy twelve to fifteen songs? The cost of producing, shipping, and selling a CD did not change significantly whether a CD had one song or twelve songs, so it made sense for the industry to bundle multiple songs and charge a higher price to cover these costs. However, digital technology changed all this. The cost of reproducing and distributing music dropped significantly in the digital world and allowed iTunes to sell singles.

While the unbundling of music was good for consumers, it wreaked havoc on the music industry, which saw a significant drop in its revenues. The sale of digital singles (and albums) and even revenue from streaming services did not come close to equaling that which came from selling bundled music on CDs. Music piracy exacerbated the problem for the industry. As a result of these dramatic shifts, those in the business of making music (songwriters, musicians, sound engineers, etc.) also saw their incomes take a nosedive. The industry had arrived at a kind of paradox: while the popularity of music among consumers reached record highs, the music studios and artists suffered a dramatic drop in their income (see figure 2-1).

FIGURE 2-1

Revenue from the sale of recorded music in the United States, 2000–2017 ($ millions)

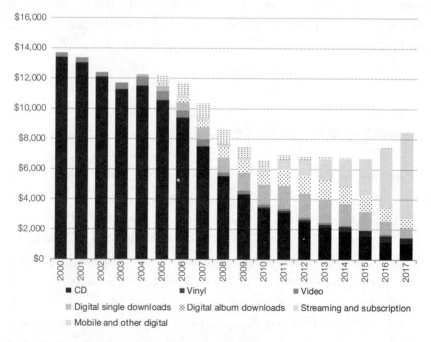

Source: Recording Industry Association of America.

Music studios and artists had traditionally used concerts to generate awareness and excitement among fans in order to sell and make money on music albums. In other words, concerts were the razors to sell music albums—the blades.

Companies have used the razor-blade strategy for a long time: sell razors cheap to make money on the blades. HP sells its printers cheap in order to make money on the ink cartridges. As the income from the selling of recorded music (the blades) declined, studios and artists converted the razor (i.e., the concerts) into blades, or the money-making part of their business. Suddenly free and even pirated music became the cheap razor to drive fans to the expensive concerts (see figure 2-2).

FIGURE 2-2

Revenue from concerts and from the sale of recorded music in the United States, 2000–2017 ($ millions)

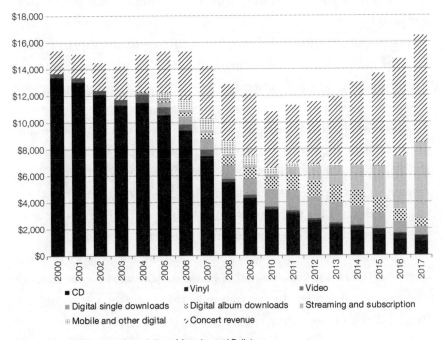

Source: Recording Industry Association of America and Pollstar.

Artists have benefitted from this shift, since the percentage they generally receive on concert revenues exceeds the royalties they receive from the sale of music albums.

Artists have also been able to exploit the popularity of their music by entering into direct partnerships with brands. Companies such as Mastercard offer their customers unique experiences by inviting music artists to perform at special events that have become a lucrative source of income for the artists. Global revenue from live music performances is expected to be more than $28 billion by 2020.[1]

Most companies have multiple sources of revenue, often from complementary products. As we discussed in chapter 1, complements provide a new source of competitive advantage in the connected digital world by increasing consumers' switching cost. Even if you think your iPhone is similar in its product features to a smartphone from Samsung, you will find it hard to switch to Samsung if you use Apple's complementary products and services, such as iTunes, FaceTime, and Apple Pay. And complements offer another key advantage: as technology affects a company's profitability, it can transform the company's business model by shifting revenue sources from one product/service to another, effectively converting a razor into a blade.

The *New York Times* (NYT) went through a similar transformation. Like the music industry, newspapers witnessed unbundling due to digital technology, which resulted in the loss of a large portion of their classified advertising revenue to Craigslist, Monster.com, and others. To compensate for the losses in print, every newspaper built an online presence with the hope of reaching a much larger audience around the globe and of generating lots of money in online advertising. While newspapers did reach a large global audience—in 2012 NYT had thirty million unique visitors per month on its website—the online ad revenue was not enough to compensate for the loss of print advertising.

Newspapers like NYT were facing a dilemma. For decades they had sold subscriptions at a low price (the razor) to generate revenue through advertising (the blade). In the online world the razor was completely free, and the blades weren't selling like they used to. Was it time to convert this razor into a blade? In March 2011, NYT decided to create

FIGURE 2-3

Digital subscribers to the *New York Times*

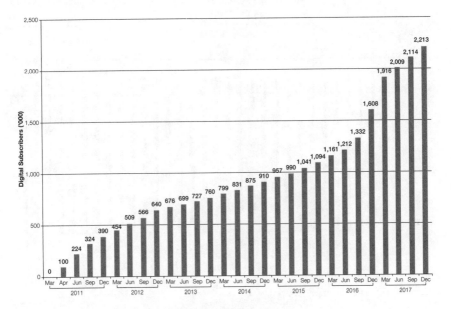

Source: Compiled from NYT press releases and financial reports.

Note: The numbers show digital news subscribers only and do not include subscribers to other digital products such as cooking and crosswords, and print subscribers who have digital access to the NYT.

a paywall and made its website restricted. Users would get free access to twenty articles per month, after which they had to pay. This was a bold move in an era when everyone believed that information should be free. Critics wondered why anyone would pay for access to the NYT's website when they could get free news through Google. However, NYT believed that consumers still cared about reliable journalism of high quality. The value of a newspaper is not simply in information—anyone can tweet or blog and create information, fake or real. The value is in the curation of that information. Through careful design and pricing, NYT successfully launched its paywall, and by June 2017 it had over two million digital news subscribers (see figure 2-3). In 2000, advertising accounted for almost 70 percent of NYT revenue. During the first half of 2017, over 70 percent of NYT revenue came from subscriptions, a large portion from digital subscribers. The razor has become the blade!

FIGURE 2-4

Number and type of Comcast subscribers, 2010–2017 ($ millions)

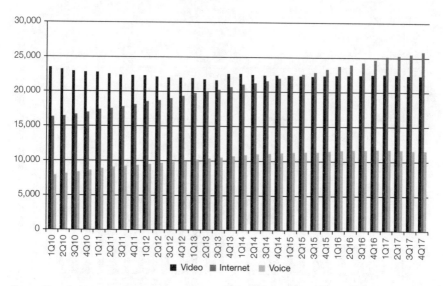

Source: Compiled from company reports.

Cable companies such as Comcast are facing similar pressures, as consumers are willing to cut the cord and subscribe to streaming services like Netflix and Hulu. Once again the bundled offering is falling apart in the digital world. New competitors such as Sling TV are offering skinny bundles at low prices to entice consumers. While cord cutting is a topic of significant debate among experts who disagree if this is a relatively limited phenomenon or one that is destined to grow, it is nonetheless a major concern for Comcast, which derives the bulk of its revenue from cable. However, even as cable TV revenue comes under threat from streaming, broadband services provide Comcast a new blade (see figure 2-4).

Shifting the sources of income among complementary products, or converting a razor into a blade or vice versa, is a powerful way not only to manage your own profitability but also to disrupt another industry. For example, Amazon can help its sellers grow by offering them loans at a much lower rate than banks can, since Amazon can use these loans as a razor to make money on the seller transactions (the blades) on its platform. This disrupts the market for small-business loans and makes it difficult for banks to compete.

So, what are your razor and your blade?

Find New Ways to Capture Value

As technology disrupts a company's business model, the company needs to find new ways to capture value, as demonstrated by The Weather Company and Best Buy.

Turbulent Times for The Weather Channel Company

When David Kenny joined The Weather Channel Company (TWCC) as CEO in January 2012, he inherited an organization that was facing significant challenges. For decades, the company had steadily grown its revenues by selling advertising on its twenty-four-hour cable weather TV channel. Hitching its business model to the ever-increasing American appetite for cable TV had been a sure bet for TWCC . . . until suddenly it wasn't.

In 2010, the number of cable TV subscriptions in the United States began to slide downward—and continued to fall lower and lower, even as economic conditions improved following the recession. As the cable-subscriber numbers crept down, TWCC was worried that its business model, which relied heavily on TV advertising, would no longer cut it in a world where consumers used apps, online videos, and websites to get news as easily as, or more easily than, they could by turning on the TV. The company was not blind to digital trends and had launched its own website and mobile app. Following the introduction of the iPhone, in 2007, TWCC developed a mobile app that users could download for $3.99. But by 2009, the mobile revenue was a mere $3.5 million. To jump-start its mobile business, TWCC changed its model to one in which the app was free and revenues would be derived from mobile advertising. Although this made its mobile app the second-most-downloaded app for the iPad, consumers checked the weather app for only a few seconds at any given time, which made ad-based monetization difficult.[2]

With a declining TV audience and a mobile monetization challenge, Kenny faced the task of transforming a company built by the rising tide of cable TV into a modern, weather-oriented media conglomerate.

Landmark Communications had created TWCC in 1982 as the first-ever twenty-four-hour weather channel on cable TV, following in the footsteps of the newly minted twenty-four-hour news channel format started by CNN in 1980. For many years, TWCC made money by selling advertising on its TV channel as well as through subscription fees that cable operators, such as Comcast, paid to TWCC in order to carry its channel in their cable packages. The company also operated a business-to-business, or B2B, subsidiary, Weather Services International (WSI), which provided weather information to businesses such as airlines and insurance companies. In 2008, Landmark sold the company for $3.5 billion to a group consisting of Comcast and two private-equity firms. By 2012, the company's TV business accounted for roughly 60 percent of total revenue, but the channel was suffering from an eight-year decline in ratings.

Reflecting on the situation he faced, Kenny, in a personal interview with the author, said,

> When I joined TWCC, I saw a company that was heavily
> reliant on TV, and although it was active in new media, it was
> moving slowly. We were facing competition from many new
> digital players, including app developers and weather startups.
> Google, with its deep pockets and fast processing speed, could
> use publicly available National Weather Service data to quickly
> become a player in our space. The question that I focused on the
> most was, how do we add value to consumers and our partners in
> this new environment?

Kenny had a key insight that drove the vision for the company: "People use weather, which is inherently local, to plan their day," he said. "What if we provide them relevant information to help them in this critical task?" Suddenly, the company saw itself not simply providing weather forecasts but also helping consumers plan daily activities that may be affected by weather. To reflect this new vision, in September 2012, Kenny proposed to the board that the word *channel* be dropped from the company's name, and so it became The Weather Company. And he set an ambitious goal: to grow from $600 million in revenue in 2012 to more than $1 billion by 2016. To achieve this, Kenny followed a particular philosophy: "Think big, start small, scale fast."

The consumer trend away from TV toward mobile apps was both a challenge and an opportunity. In 40 percent of all smartphones, a weather app is the first app in the morning and the last app at night that people check. However, this daily habit does not last very long since most consumers check weather for only a few seconds. The challenge for The Weather Company was to engage consumers for longer periods.

"We were among the most trusted brands, but we lacked personality," noted Kenny. To attract and engage millennials, Kenny transformed The Weather Company's consumer-facing properties into "platishers," a combination of platforms and content publishers. To lead this effort, he hired Neil Katz—who had previously worked at Huffington Post— as editor in chief of Weather.com. Soon, the company's website began to move away from showing only syndicated content to creating original stories and videos that were weather- or nature-themed. The company began publishing short videos, such as "Virus Hunters" (about super viruses that could threaten humanity), "Grid Breakers" (about explorers in extreme weather), and "What Does Mars Smell Like?" Lots of the newly developed content also found its way into the company's mobile app. Not everything worked (e.g., content featuring exercises for a bikini body), but Kenny's philosophy of learning by experimentation provided new energy and a sense of empowerment to the employees. The new content nearly doubled the amount of time users spent on the site, which in turn led to better advertising partnerships.

Building on his key insight that consumers check local weather to plan their daily activities, Kenny decided to link science with big data to understand consumers' decisions. In May 2012, he hired his former colleague Curt Hecht, from Publicis, to recreate the way ads were sold.

One of Hecht's early insights was that weather affects the sales of many products. So the company built a platform, WeatherFX, to predict demand based on weather and location. Hecht and his team persuaded retailers and manufacturers to share sales data on every product sold, in every store location, over the last five years. Then the team correlated sales with local weather conditions and forecasts at that time of the year. This created a powerful predictive algorithm of how weather drove consumers' purchasing decisions.

The goal was to go beyond predicting the obvious relationships (like increased sales of umbrellas when it is raining), and indeed, Hecht and his team found many surprising correlations. Some were hard to explain, such as that strawberries and raspberries sold far better when it was humid outside! Others made a lot of sense after some reflection. For instance, at a particular dew point, people in Dallas rush to buy bug spray . . . because insects' eggs hatch at that dew point. Yet other insights were intriguing. During bad weather, for example, women worry about logistics, such as getting kids from school or groceries from the market. For men, by contrast, the same inclement weather seems an occasion for watching sports, hosting parties, and buying beer.

The next step was to leverage these insights for commercial purposes. The Weather Company helped retailers decide when to put products on promotion. But just as important, it helped retailers know when no promotion was needed to quickly sell a product. The company then moved on to work with brands like Pantene by showing that consumers buy different types of shampoos based on weather forecasts for the next three days. Pantene started running location-specific ads on The Weather Company's mobile app and offered a custom tool, "Haircast," to tell consumers which hair products to use during different weather conditions. Sales of Pantene's advertised products jumped 28 percent.

The WSI division of the company, as previously mentioned, was already providing weather information to several industries, such as airlines, retailers, and insurance companies. But the new vision that Hecht helped create revealed new possibilities. Just as pilots need weather data to avoid turbulence and make corrections to their flight path, car drivers could also benefit from weather information. The Weather Company struck a deal with BMW to provide weather data in its new cars. In exchange, BMW allowed weather sensors to be placed on the windshield wipers of certain new models so that the motion of the wipers would inform The Weather Company when and where it was raining, which would then further improve the accuracy of The Weather Company's forecasts.

"Weather affects everything," explained Kenny, "and as a result, it offers amazing new opportunities for us." Tesla owners could benefit from the company's forecasts, since weather conditions affect the battery life and the driving range of Tesla's electric cars. A partnership with Nike could link weather data to shoes and running applications. Farmers could better manage their crops by installing irrigation systems with built-in chips that receive weather information.

Kenny also looked to partner with companies that could help expand The Weather Company's global reach. IBM's consulting division licensed The Weather Company's data to sell as a product to its clients, including governments, across the globe. Weather data was a centerpiece of many of IBM's consulting initiatives, including smart cities. The Weather Company also provided weather data to companies like Mahindra, an Indian tractor manufacturer that produces driverless machines that analyze the soil as they move through the field to dispense only as much fertilizer as is needed according to the soil's profile and expected weather patterns.

By July 2015, almost half of The Weather Company's employees had joined after Kenny's arrival. Kenny attracted digital stars, revamped his senior leadership team, and inducted new members into his board. Offices in New York and San Francisco scaled up to bring in talent that could not be recruited into the Atlanta headquarters. A sense of urgency was now palpable in the company. "I am obsessed with velocity," said Kenny. With a clear direction, The Weather Company, on his watch, transformed itself in a short period of time.

In January 2016, IBM acquired The Weather Company for about $2 billion and David Kenny became the head of IBM Watson with the goal of doing for IBM what he had done for The Weather Company.

Best Buy: Managing the Challenge Posed by Amazon

When Hubert Joly joined Best Buy as its CEO in September 2012, he faced a number of challenges: There was a shareholder challenge, as the company's founder was attempting to take the company private. There was an operational challenge regarding how to deliver the best possible customer experience. There was a leadership challenge, as the prior CEO had been hurriedly replaced amid allegations of misconduct. And, finally, there was the strategic challenge of competing with Amazon—as Best Buy was increasingly becoming Amazon's *showroom*, where a consumer would, for example, see a camera in a Best Buy store, get all the information and advice from the salesperson, but later buy the camera on Amazon for a cheaper price. As a result, Best Buy had seen a dramatic decline in its revenues and profits, and its very survival was in question.

To address these challenges, Joly crafted a "Renew Blue" strategy that addressed Best Buy's two biggest problems: declining same-store sales and decreasing operating margin. While "Renew Blue" encompassed many different factors—ranging from investing in price matching and improving the online shopping experience to improving the customer experience in stores and finding $1 billion worth of cost savings by eliminating operational inefficiencies—one of its key pillars was to leverage Best Buy's stores and strengthen the company's relationships with vendors.

"We were the 'last man standing' at the time, since we were the only consumer-electronics store with national presence in the [United States]," said Joly. "We had six hundred million visits to our stores each year—some used to say that our stores would be a liability, but we truly believed those visitors were coming to Best Buy for a reason." These store visits were also critical for Best Buy's vendors, such as Samsung, LG Electronics, Sony, and Hewlett-Packard, companies that did not have a national footprint of stores in which to display their products. Joly saw a win-win opportunity for Best Buy and its vendors, an opportunity for those vendors to showcase their products in Best Buy stores in order to provide the best possible customer experience.

In a 2012 interview, Joly mentioned that Best Buy was seeking to strengthen its partnerships with vendors. Shortly thereafter, the head of Samsung Electronics reached out to Joly to establish a new type of arrangement between the two companies, and as a result Best Buy agreed to install 1,400 Samsung "shops" within Best Buy stores. Since it was typically not cost-effective or strategic for manufacturers like Samsung to open their own stores, this arrangement provided a unique benefit. The branded store-within-a-store, which employed dedicated Samsung sales staff, helped Samsung very quickly gain more visibility and engage directly with customers. In return, Best Buy got a fee for showcasing Samsung's products, similar to the fee paid by consumer packaged-goods firms to supermarket retailers.

Following the success of Samsung Experience Shops, as they were called, Best Buy formed or expanded partnerships with the world's foremost tech companies, including Amazon, Apple, AT&T, Canon, Google, LG, Microsoft, Nikon, Sony, Sprint, and Verizon. Each vendor made an investment to fund its store-within-a-store. The investment covered things like the cost of in-store fixtures, labor, marketing, and training as well as the fee for Best Buy. With such partnerships, Best Buy evolved and augmented its business model to embrace both its strengths and the needs of the company's vendors. Although it still made the bulk of its revenues from product sales and services, these new stores-within-stores offered Best Buy upside potential and a way to capture the value Best Buy had already been creating for consumers and vendors alike.

This new strategy worked: comparable store sales and operating income improved, and total shareholder return during 2012–2017 was 642 percent, placing Best Buy among the top 10 percent of S&P 500 companies in that time period. This is especially impressive given that all major retailers in the United States were (and still are) facing tremendous pressures. Circuit City, Radio Shack, and H. H. Gregg, three large electronics retailers, declared bankruptcy in 2008, 2015, and 2017, respectively, and Toys "R" Us announced bankruptcy in March 2018.

The success of Best Buy's "Renew Blue" strategy shows that physical stores can be great assets and that retail is not a zero-sum game against a single competitor. It also illustrates an often-observed reality: shifts in technology and changes in consumer behavior typically disrupt companies by significantly affecting their source of income even when these companies continue to create tremendous value for their customers. The old ways of capturing value may no longer work, and companies need to find new and often hidden sources of value. When threatened by Amazon, Best Buy partnered with its own vendors to create a win-win situation and found an additional source of revenue while providing consumers great experience.

2018 and Beyond

After the success of "Renew Blue" Hubert Joly and his team embarked on a new growth strategy, called "Best Buy 2020: Building the New Blue." The company has stated that its purpose is to help customers pursue their passion and live their lives with the assistance of technology, a much bigger idea than merely selling products. As such, the company is vastly expanding its addressable market from just hardware products to services and solutions, including subscription services (a topic we will discuss in detail later in this chapter).

This strategy is based on a few key observations. First, the company is operating in an opportunity-rich environment. Consumers are spending more and more on technology products, and Best Buy is well positioned in this market, having captured more than 16 percent of millennials' spending in this category. Second, buying technology products is typically part of a complex decision that involves integration across many different products from various manufacturers. Thus, Joly and his team based the new "Best Buy 2020" strategy on two main pillars: "expand what we sell" and "evolve how we sell."

To expand what it sells, Best Buy is using its strong skills and assets to move into areas such as smart-home management, assisted living (for a population that is aging), and total tech support. In its tech-support pilot, the company is testing a subscription service wherein consumers pay $199 per year or $19.99 per month for unlimited phone, online, and in-store service in addition to discounted in-home service from its tech advisors. As of March 2018, this service was available in all Best Buy stores in Canada and in about two hundred US stores in specific geographies and states. In addition, Best Buy is "evolving how it sells" by continuing to build its online channel and by introducing its in-home channel, through which Best Buy advisors will come meet customers in the comfort of their own homes, free of charge, to listen to their needs and provide recommendations for products and services.

This new strategy highlights the shift in Best Buy's business model from simply selling products to selling solutions and from processing mere transactions to building a deeper relationship with its customers.

Create Value through Experiences

Best Buy is not alone in facing the pressure from Amazon and e-commerce. The future of the entire retailing industry is uncertain, and retailers are declaring bankruptcy at an alarming pace.

In 2015 alone, Body Central Corp. (a women's-clothing retailer), Quiksilver (surfwear retailer), American Apparel (clothing retailer), Wet Seal (teen fashion retailer), and Sports Authority (sporting-goods retailer) declared bankruptcy in the United States. Some of the largest department stores, such as Macy's, are also facing severe financial pressure. As their business shrinks, these retailers are closing stores at a pace that in turn is threatening the very survival of shopping malls. Some retail analysts predict that a third of America's shopping malls are likely to shut down in the coming years.[3]

Supermarkets are also under threat. A&P, the pioneering grocery company that drove independent grocers out of business nearly a hundred years ago, itself declared bankruptcy in 2015. Tesco, the leading supermarket in the United Kingdom, is also showing signs of trouble. Retailers such as Borders bookstore and video-rental giant Blockbuster are gone.

What is the future of retailing and brick-and-mortar establishments in the digital age? Perhaps it is time for them to rethink their business model and shift from selling products to selling experiences. These retailers can learn from Starbucks, which started by selling not just coffee but also an experience, endeavoring to become the "third place" in people's lives (after their homes and their workplaces). But how do you develop an experience-based business?

Reinventing a Grocery Store

In 2007, Oscar Farinetti, an Italian entrepreneur, founded Eataly in Turin, Italy, as a unique, complementary blend of restaurants, a supermarket, and a culinary school—all under one roof—to let customers eat, shop, and learn about Italian food. Essentially, Farinetti reinvented the grocery store.[4] By 2016, Eataly had grown from a single store in Turin to thirty-one stores across the world, in cities such as Milan, Rome, New York, Chicago, Boston, Istanbul, Dubai, Tokyo, Munich, and Seoul. And it had ambitious plans to expand its global reach to cities such as Copenhagen, Moscow, and London. Eataly focused on customer experience by making careful strategic choices.

- **Concept and Store Design.** Supermarkets have traditionally relied on providing convenience, variety, and low prices to consumers. While some newer players, such as Whole Foods, have focused on organic, high-quality fare with fresh food bars, Eataly took this concept to new heights by combining a super-market with several monothematic restaurants and culinary schools about Italian food and cooking.

  Why does Eataly combine restaurants, a marketplace, and a culinary school all in one store? There are several advantages to this concept. First, restaurants create the buzz and traffic that lead people to buy products in the marketplace. No one wants to shop in an empty store. Making fresh cheese or pasta right in front of consumers also creates theater that enhances user experience.

  Second, restaurants create an environment with lots of social interaction in the middle of a supermarket, which provides a unique experience for customers, allowing Eataly to charge higher prices for its products.

Third, Oscar Farinetti realized from an earlier mistake that restaurants alone are not very profitable. They are a risky venture, with a failure rate of almost 80 percent in large cities.

Fourth, restaurants have a capacity limit. You can turn the tables over only so many times per day, after which there is no possibility of growth unless you somehow expand the seating. Finally, restaurants help reduce wastage or shrinkage of fresh food or food with expiration dates. Shrinkage in a typical supermarket is about 2 percent, and for perishable products is as high as 6 percent to 7 percent. Industry experts believe that eliminating shrinkage could easily double the profitability of the industry.

- **Store Size and Location.** Combining restaurants and open displays of food preparation, which are essential ingredients for creating an experience, requires additional space—one of the main reasons Eataly stores tend to be large. Eataly has a 50,000-square-foot store in the middle of Manhattan, and a 63,000-square-foot store in the center of Chicago. A typical grocery store has about half the square footage of an Eataly store but stocks almost three times the number of items. Eataly locates its stores in the heart of big cities in order to generate traffic. In other words, it expects its stores to be destinations, places to which customers come from all over the city in search of a good experience, not convenience.

- **Marketing and Promotions.** Eataly spends almost nothing on marketing. Its marketing consists of in-store displays that tell the origin and story of its products. These displays have a clean and simple design and do not look like typical in-store advertising. Price is almost never mentioned. In-store communication is the main promotional policy, along with events designed and hosted to attract new customers to its stores, and to give food bloggers a reason to continue writing about Eataly—a brilliant form of free advertising. In other words, Eataly leverages social

media to market itself at low cost while also continuously changing the stores to attract repeat customers.

How does Eataly's approach compare with that of traditional
supermarkets? The latter compete largely on the basis of price
and offer weekly discounts on a variety of products to attract
customers to their stores. Manufacturers and suppliers typically
fund these promotions by giving trade allowances to retailers
to pitch their respective brands. This has made supermarkets
heavily reliant on trade allowances and has given immense
negotiating power to suppliers.

- **Metrics.** Retail stores typically measure their performance on the
  basis of sales or revenue per square foot. However, Eataly eschews
  such a metric. Commenting on this, Oscar Farinetti said, "[I]t is
  useless to calculate sales per square meter when we create sales
  points that are totally different."[5] Alex Saper, the general manager of Eataly USA, elaborated on one of those different sales
  points: the fresh pasta station. On Saper's watch, Eataly removed
  shelves of potentially salable goods just to create spaces in which
  shoppers could observe fresh pasta being made by hand. It was a
  bold gamble, but as Saper noted, sales of fresh pasta subsequently
  increased by 15 percent to 20 percent. "And the reason," he said,
  "is that we are selling emotion, we are selling theater here."[6]

Oscar Farinetti wants to bring Italian food and its experience to the
world, the way Howard Schultz, chairman of Starbucks, brought the
Italian coffee experience to everyone. And by 2016, Eataly had built a
global brand with half a billion dollars in revenues, healthy profitability,
and an aggressive plan to grow all around the world.

Starbucks and Eataly provide powerful lessons for many other industries. As consumers move away from products to experiences, creating
value and sustainable advantage will not be based on product features
alone. Just like Blockbuster, movie theaters could have been wiped away by
Netflix and streaming services. But instead of lowering prices and selling

more popcorn, movie theaters in North America are installing reclining chairs akin to business-class seats in an airline, providing seat-side food and wine service, and charging more than double the price they charged before. As a result, movie theaters in the United States and Canada have seen their sales grow from $7.5 billion in 2000 to more than $11.1 billion in 2015, and concession sales in theaters continues to show robust growth.

The move away from products to experiences is evident even in American shopping malls, which were once vast emporiums of products of all types. As the retail environment changes, Simon Property Group, a real-estate giant that operates 108 shopping malls in the United States worth $110 billion, is reinventing the shopping mall for the future. Malls emerged in the 1960s when Melvin Simon (the company's founder) had the brilliant idea of using a department store as an anchor for a shopping center. Department stores used to attract lots of traffic as stand-alone properties in city centers, and to entice them away, Melvin Simon offered them highly subsidized rent. Even today these anchor stores pay about $4 per square foot annually compared with $42 paid by nonanchor stores.[7] But as the fate of department stores has changed due to e-commerce, David Simon, the current CEO of the Simon Property Group, is replacing many of these department stores with restaurants and movie theaters to position malls as a place for experience.

Build an Asset-Light Business

Almost a century ago automobile manufacturers settled on a system of franchising whereby independent dealers would sell mostly a single company's models. Over time these dealerships have become large businesses in their own right, with many boasting sales in billions of dollars. Until recently, the business model of dealers has remained largely unchanged. Dealerships typically stock hundreds of cars on a large lot (away from city centers to reduce real estate costs), and consumers drive several miles to these lots to see and test-drive cars and to negotiate prices.

However, in the last decade consumer buying behavior has changed dramatically. Studies by Google show that most consumers start their search online about two or three months before they actually buy a car. By the time consumers come to the dealer, they know everything about the car and the various options they want to buy. Surveys also show that consumers hate visiting dealers. They find the experience boring, confrontational, and time-consuming. A study by McKinsey found that ten years ago Americans visited an average of five dealers, perhaps to compare and negotiate prices, but now they visit 1.6 dealers on average, because online services such as TrueCar offer price transparency. Today, the only compelling reason for consumers to visit a dealer is to test-drive a car.

But what if a dealer were to send the two cars that you wanted to test drive to your home at a time that was convenient for you? And what if you had to wait only four to six weeks for a car that was made-to-order, with all the features customized to your taste? Studies by Autotrader confirm that as in-car technologies become increasingly important, consumers are willing to wait longer to get specific features in their car.

There is really no need for dealers to follow a capital- and asset-intensive model anymore. Some auto manufacturers are already embracing this new reality. Tesla does not have traditional dealers. Instead it has showrooms in shopping malls. In the last few years, Audi has opened digital showrooms in London, Beijing, and Berlin. These showrooms are much smaller than their traditional counterparts and display only four models. They are located in the heart of the city to make it easy for even casual car buyers to visit and explore cars, and they offer large multimedia screens for consumers to configure and customize their vehicles. In its first year after opening, in 2012, Audi's London City showroom had 50,000 visitors and sold an average of seven cars per week, with 75 percent of the orders placed by first-time Audi buyers. On average, customers paid 120 percent of the car's base price, since the digital showroom encouraged them to configure their cars by adding lots of technology options. Perhaps the most intriguing part is that 50 percent of the customers in the first half of 2013 never bothered to test-drive the car.[8] As virtual reality becomes mainstream, visiting a dealer to test-drive a car may become a thing of the past. And dealers would benefit from this new asset-light business model.

Gas Station of the Future

Let's extend our thinking to reimagine the gas station of the future. For almost a century, gas stations have looked and functioned pretty much the same. Granted, they have become cleaner, made payment easier, and are now often integrated with a convenience store. But the fundamental model of a gas station has remained unchanged. Although electric cars may eventually alter this landscape completely, we will still have gas stations in the near future.

Any business model has to start with solving customers' pain points and then thinking about how to make that solution economically viable for the company. So let's start with the customer pain point. Do consumers enjoy going to the gas station to fill up their cars? The answer is an unequivocal no—it is a necessity that we all have to endure but will be happy to do without if possible.

What if the gas station were to come to you instead of you having to go to the gas station? In other words, what if a fuel truck were to come fill your car while it was parked in the parking lot of your company or a shopping mall (delivery to individual homes would be too expensive and inefficient). Sound impossible? There are several startups, such as Booster Fuels, Purple, Filld, and WeFuel, that are already offering this service. You simply order fuel through their apps, indicating a time and a place. In the future, cars may be equipped with sensors that automatically alert you and your fuel app that your car needs refueling. And you don't even have to pay a premium price for this service. How can these companies make this model work? By delivering gas to you they don't have the high fixed cost of the gas station. Note that gas stations are often sited in prime locations in a city to make it convenient for consumers, but this also leads to very high real estate costs for the stations. By eliminating this fixed cost, the new players can charge the same price as existing gas stations, provide added convenience to consumers, and still be profitable.

Transition to Product-as-a-Service

In April 2015, Amsterdam's Schiphol Airport, Europe's fourth-busiest airport, reached an agreement with Philips, the global leader in lighting, and Cofely, an energy services company, to pay for "lighting as a service" in its terminal buildings. In this so-called pay-per-lux arrangement, Schiphol pays only for the light it uses, while Philips maintains ownership of all light fixtures and remains responsible for their maintenance and upgrade. With this new business model Philips is no longer selling light fixtures and light bulbs (the inputs). Instead, it is being paid for the light (the output) used by its customer. As a result Philips is developing special lighting fixtures that will last 75 percent longer than the conventional fixtures. By using energy-efficient LED bulbs, it hopes to achieve a 50 percent reduction in energy consumption.[9]

Schiphol was not the only Philips customer opting for lighting as a service. A year earlier, Philips signed a ten-year contract with the Washington Metropolitan Area Transit Authority in the United States for its twenty-five parking facilities. This arrangement required no up-front cost for Washington Metro, which expected to fund the entire contract through the $2 million in annual savings in energy consumption and maintenance costs.[10]

Philips is not alone in adopting this new business model. In its "pay-per-copy" model, Xerox retains ownership of its office equipment while customers pay for the copies made on these machines.[11] Atlas Copco, which produces compressors and air-treatment systems, now offers its customers a "contract-air" arrangement whereby they can pay per cubic meter of compressed air.[12] Rolls-Royce offers its airline customers "power-by-the-hour," whereby customers pay engine repair and service costs pegged only to those hours the engine is in use. Michelin has introduced a similar "pay-per-mile" program for the use of its tires. Hilti, the tool manufacturer, introduced a fleet-management system in which customers pay a monthly subscription fee to get tools on-demand instead of buying them. Using RFID chips to track the usage of these tools, Hilti can anticipate problems, do preventive maintenance, and reduce customers' downtime. These chips also significantly reduce tool theft at construction sites. With this program, Hilti's customers benefit from access to the latest tool fleet, less downtime, greater reliability, and an improved cash flow, since there's no need for a large up-front investment. During the global crisis of 2008–2009, the fleet-management system was instrumental in increasing Hilti's sales by 26 percent and its operating profit by 12 percent.[13] In the new partnership between GE Oil and Gas and its customer Diamond Offshore Drilling, GE owns the equipment and is responsible for its maintenance. Diamond pays GE Oil and Gas only for the days when the equipment is working.[14]

Product-as-a-Service for Luxury Products and Automobiles

The product-as-a-service model is not limited to industrial products. Almost any company can rethink its business model in these terms. Consider LVMH, which has prided itself on creating the best-quality products and selling them to exclusive clients at very high prices. A typical LVMH handbag sells for a few thousand dollars, and the company's crocodile-skin City Steamer satchel with engraved padlock and a nametag can fetch $55,000. Similarly, automobile manufacturers like BMW have perfected the engineering of their products, and their mid-size luxury cars would reduce your bank account by $60,000 or more.

These companies have always focused on their products, but can they benefit from reimagining their business model and making those products available the way Philips does its light bulbs or Michelin its tires? What if LVMH were to create a service in which subscribers would pay a low monthly fee to get an LVMH bag from a curated list every month? A consumer who could not buy a dozen (or perhaps even one) of these expensive bags would now have the possibility to possess a different bag every month, and for different occasions. Such a service would open up a large and new customer base for LVMH. Several startups, such as Bag Borrow or Steal, have recognized this consumer need and are already offering such a service. Two of my former MBA students, Jennifer Hyman and Jennifer Fleiss, started Rent the Runway with a similar idea of allowing young women to rent expensive dresses rather than having to buy them.

Car companies could benefit from a similar business model. Why do I have to buy a car for $60,000 and drive the same vehicle for the next five years? What if BMW offered a monthly subscription service that allowed consumers to access any car from a curated list? I could drive a sedan on a weekday and a convertible on the weekend. Again, this subscription service could open up a whole new market of consumers for BMW, people who could never afford to buy a BMW otherwise. Interestingly, in 2017 Cadillac started such a subscription plan. For $1,500 a month, members can trade in and out of Cadillac's ten models up to eighteen times a year. Following Cadillac, Porsche also launched its $2,000 per month subscription service, Porsche Passport, which allows customers to flip between Porsche Cayman, Boxster, Macan, and Cayenne as their needs change. Clutch, a startup in Atlanta, is also offering a monthly subscription service that lets you flip between cars every day.

A New Business Model

As global competition for products intensifies and product differentiation diminishes, it is not surprising that companies are relying more on services for their growth and profitability. Service contracts, replacement parts, and maintenance fees were always an important source of revenue for companies, but product-as-a-service is fundamentally a different business model for the following reasons:

- **Outcome-Based.** As the examples mentioned above show, the focus in this model is on the outputs or the outcomes for customers, not on the input or the product that the company manufactures. Why is this important? Consider the case of Rolls-Royce, which sells jet engines to its airline customers. In the traditional service model, every engine problem and maintenance need was a revenue opportunity for Rolls-Royce, even though this downtime was costing its customers millions of dollars. In other words, the incentives for Rolls-Royce and its airline customers were not aligned. However, under the outcome-based model, Rolls-Royce is paid only for every hour the plane is flying, thus aligning the incentives for both parties.

- **Improved Reliability and Reduced Cost.** When a manufacturer retains ownership of and maintenance responsibility for its products, the incentives of the company and its customers are aligned, because the company is motivated to improve the reliability of its products, extend their life, and reduce their operating cost. Rolls-Royce dramatically improved engine reliability and reduced unplanned downtime for its customers as a result of its power-by-the-hour model. The same motivation drove Philips to design lighting fixtures for Schiphol airport that last 75 percent longer. The pay-per-copy model led Xerox to develop an extensive remanufacturing program that saved raw material and reduced waste. A similar program at Philips not only led to cost savings but also helped the company move toward its goal of sustainability.[15]

- **Expanded Customer Base.** In many B2B settings the capital cost of the product can be prohibitive, especially for small customers. By retaining ownership and maintenance responsibility, a firm can expand its customer base to those who would not be able to afford the product otherwise. It would have been difficult for Washington Metro to replace and upgrade all its lighting fixtures to reduce its operating costs, but the pay-per-lux model allowed it to benefit from the energy savings without the up-front capital investment. By offering car rental by the hour ZipCar expanded the market to students and infrequent users.

- **Customer-Focused Innovation.** An outcome-based model drives a company to become customer-focused and thereby changes the company's innovation process. Ted Levitt, a Harvard Business School professor, once said that people don't buy drills; they buy holes. While a product-focused company would continue to make its drills better, a customer-focused company would think of new technologies, such as laser, which could be used to achieve the outcome (in this case, creating a hole) that the customer is looking for. Michelin's pay-per-mile program led it to find innovative ways to get more out of its tires. Its research showed that a third of all breakdowns are tire related and that 90 percent of these are due to incorrect tire pressure. As a result Michelin launched a suite of connected software solutions that, along with its tire-pressure-monitoring system, is designed to help trucking managers whose fleets ride on Michelin tires to optimize the performance of those fleets. This customer focus also helped Michelin realize that fuel represents 29 percent of the per-kilometer operating cost of a forty-ton tractor trailer. So the company launched a new service to help the managers of trucking fleets reduce their fuel consumption. Since its launch, the service has delivered average savings of 1.5 liters per 100 kilometers to its trucking customers, which for the entire European trucking industry would translate into savings of three billion liters of fuel, nine million tons of CO_2, and €3 billion in operating cost.[16]

- **Organizational Shift.** The product-as-a-service business model leads to significant shifts both within and beyond the organization. The sales force needs to change from selling machines to selling outcomes, and customers who are used to buying products also need to be educated and convinced about this shift. Highlighting the challenge in selling outcome-based services, Bill Ruh, the CEO of GE Digital, noted, "Before we targeted an existing budget line item, but if you are promising to save fuel burn costs, a budget line item does not exist for that, posing a problem for a box-seller."[17] Jim Fowler, GE's chief information officer, elaborated, "Changing to an outcome based model means willing to be [in] an environment where you don't know everything about everything that you're working on. For people who are very risk averse, that's an uncomfortable place to be."[18] The company also needs to build skills to manage customer relationships over long periods of time. BMW's launch of its hourly rental service, BMW DriveNow, requires it to develop both analytical and customer-relationship-management capabilities. This model also has financial implications, since the company does not get the large up-front revenue from the sale of its product. Instead, the revenue trickles in over many years. Customer retention in this approach becomes critical.

According to IDC, a global market-intelligence firm, 40 percent of the top one hundred discrete manufacturers (who produce finished products such as automobiles) and 20 percent of the top process manufacturers (who combine ingredients such as in the chemical and food industries) will offer product-as-a-service by 2018.[19] There's also been significant acceptance of product-as-a-service and pay-per-use pricing among consumers. In a 2012 survey of over 2,200 consumers in the United States and Europe, Accenture found that payment models such as pay-per-use and power-by-the hour were preferred by an overwhelming 70 percent of consumers to the full up-front product purchase (see figure 2-5).[20]

FIGURE 2-5

Why consumers accept service-based payment models

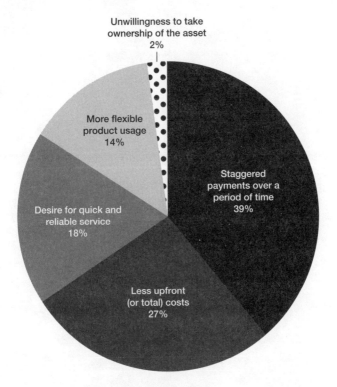

Source: Vivek Agarwal, Vinay Arora, and Kris Renker, *Evolving Service Centric Business Models: Quest for Profitability and Predictability,* Accenture Report, 2013.

As we move toward a demand-based economy, access, not ownership of products, will drive the success of businesses. This shift will make the product-as-a-service model increasingly important in the future.

We will continue to see the emergence of new business models and new rules of engagement. Digital technology is not necessarily a threat to incumbents. It often provides a new set of opportunities if the companies are willing to rethink their business models.

Chapter 3

Platforms
and Ecosystems

When Johannes Gutenberg invented the printing press around 1440, he revolutionized the dissemination of ideas to the masses through books and other printed material. Today the global printing industry is worth over $800 billion, more than fifty times the size of the music industry. While digital printing is replacing offset printing and print volume is declining, shift to higher-value products has led to a growth in print revenues that is expected to continue until 2020.[1]

Although printing technology has evolved in the last six centuries, the printing industry remains highly fragmented. Thousands of small and medium enterprises around the world buy printing machines, which can cost several million dollars apiece, to serve the needs of their local customers. Due to variability in customer demand, the majority of these machines are grossly underutilized. Globally, print capacity exceeds demand by a factor of six to one. Even with this large printing capacity, the process remains inefficient and costly for customers. Large multinational retailers often print the entirety of their catalog supply with a centralized printing company and then ship these catalogs to their stores around the world. However, this process is inefficient due to high shipping costs, the inability to produce localized content (e.g., catalogs in a local language), and oversupply of printed material, which gets outdated quickly and is often discarded by the local stores.

Gelato, a startup based in Norway, decided to reinvent the printing industry to solve the problems of buyers and suppliers by building a platform that connects the two parties. Customers can upload their print design on Gelato's cloud and order any quantity of the print material to be delivered anywhere in the forty countries where Gelato currently operates. Gelato matches this demand with the unused capacity of a supplier who is closest to the local delivery address. Since its inception in 2007, Gelato has grown rapidly and is cash-flow positive. Henrik Müller-Hansen, its CEO and cofounder, has aspirations to make Gelato into a multibillion-dollar company and, in the process, transform the centuries-old printing industry.

The Platform Revolution

Gelato is one of the many companies that are building platform-based businesses to transform established industries. In recent years we have witnessed the explosion of platform businesses that connect multiple parties such as buyers and sellers (e.g., eBay), or consumers and developers (e.g., Apple's app store). Alibaba, Amazon's marketplace, and eBay are all e-commerce platforms. Uber has revolutionized transportation by connecting drivers with riders on its platform. Airbnb built a platform to connect homeowners with travelers who need a place to stay. Upwork connects businesses with freelancers who can perform a variety of tasks.

Why is there a sudden explosion of platforms? To understand this it is useful to go back to 1776 when Adam Smith published his classic book *The Wealth of Nations*. The main thesis of Smith's economic theory is that people act in their own self-interest and that in a free market an invisible hand allocates resources efficiently. If the free market is supposed to efficiently match workers with tasks, then why do firms exist? Why don't we sell our skills in an open market instead of working for a company?

In 1937, the economist Ronald Coase published a paper titled "The Nature of the Firm" to address this very question, a paper for which, in 1991, he received the Nobel Prize in economics. Coase argued that firms exist because of transaction costs. Simply put, it would be too difficult and costly for you to get up every morning and find a day's work that was suitable to your skill.

Today digital technology has dramatically reduced the transaction cost of finding and selling goods and services. Two decades ago it would have been hard for you to sell your old bike except in your immediate locale through a garage sale, but now internet-based platforms such as eBay allow buyers and sellers around the world to connect with one another, thereby reducing the transaction cost of selling (and buying) goods beyond your immediate locale. Similarly, platforms like Upwork reduce the transaction cost of freelancers seeking suitable work that doesn't require working for a company permanently.

Advantages and Challenges of a Platform

Platforms provide unique advantages compared with traditional business models.

- **Greater Access to Sellers.** The platform model works best in fragmented markets by aggregating dispersed supply and demand. This aggregation provides tremendous reach to suppliers, on a scale they could not imagine before. Jack Ma, the founder of Alibaba, recognized this opportunity in China when he said, "There are more than 40 million small businesses in China. Many of them operate in fragmented markets, with limited access to communication channels and information sources that would help them market and promote their products."[2] This insight led to the creation of Alibaba, a platform that sells goods from millions of third-party suppliers.

- **Better Value to Consumers.** Platforms also provide better value to consumers by offering them convenience and a greater variety of products and services at competitive prices, since a large number of suppliers compete for a buyer's business. A 2015 study of European consumers found that almost all of them (97 percent of internet users) derive significant value from online platforms.[3] Through its platform Gelato's customers have seen a 90 percent reduction in transportation costs and a 50 percent reduction in paper waste.[4]

- **Market Growth.** By lowering transaction costs, platforms open up whole new areas of supply and demand. Uber created a completely new supply of cars and drivers by reducing the transaction cost of finding riders, and riders' demand grew because of an increase in supply that made it easy to find a car on demand. Platforms also break down geographical barriers, greatly expanding the physical reach of both buyers and suppliers.

- **Asset-light.** Platform businesses facilitate the transactions of third-party players without owning many assets. As indicated in chapter 2, an asset-light model lowers the capital requirement and allows for a business to rapidly expand. Gelato connects $300 million in print assets without owning a single printing machine.

- **Scalability.** In addition to having a low capital requirement, platform businesses scale quickly due to network effects—more buyers on a platform attract more sellers, and more sellers in turn draw in more buyers. This creates a virtuous circle that often leads to a winner-take-all situation. Not surprisingly we see companies like Facebook, Uber, Alibaba, and Airbnb dominate and effectively become the standard in their markets.

- **Innovation.** By attracting large numbers of sellers and developers, a platform creates an implicit incentive for them to innovate and improve their product and service to remain competitive. Research on crowdsourcing and open innovation also shows that—in contrast to dynamics within a company-led team—innovation is more likely to thrive in an environment where thousands or even millions of sellers or software developers are creating new products and services on a platform. Platforms also provide a natural lab for these sellers to test new ideas and services.

In spite of these advantages, a company should carefully consider some the challenges it may encounter as it moves to a platform model. Flipkart, an e-commerce player in India valued at over $15 billion, illustrates these challenges.

In 2015, Flipkart decided to aggressively move from an inventory-based model to a marketplace model where it would allow third-party sellers to sell directly to consumers without Flipkart having to warehouse any inventory. The company founders, Sachin and Binny Bansal, took inspiration from Alibaba, Uber, and Airbnb, who demonstrated the efficacy of this asset-light model.[5] Uber does not own any cars, Airbnb does not own any hotels, and Alibaba started without owning any products. This lowers the fixed costs and capital investment of these companies and improves their return on assets, and by extension the return on equity. Low capital requirement also allows a company to rapidly scale.

However, not all companies have followed a similar model. Zappos, an online shoe company acquired by Amazon, started as a marketplace in 1999 but by the mid-2000s it had turned into a pure reseller by stocking its inventory and taking full control of transactions. Amazon uses a hybrid model in which third-party sellers account for about half of its revenues. The remaining half comes from the sale of inventory managed and stocked by Amazon itself.

Why do Zappos and Amazon want to hold inventory if a platform offers scale and growth with limited capital investment? An inventory-based model allows for greater control over product quality, delivery, and availability and over customer service. This in turn leads to better customer experience and enhanced customer loyalty. While a rating system for third-party sellers can help weed out bad sellers, this system is far from perfect. Alibaba started without owning any warehouses and operated as a pure platform relying on third-party providers for logistics. However, in 2013, Alibaba launched its logistics arm, Cainiao, with a planned investment of $16 billion in the following five to eight years.[6]

With this investment, Alibaba wanted to take better control of its logistics, for faster delivery of products, and to avoid the problem of fake and counterfeit products sold by third-party sellers, which had drawn the ire of companies selling branded products.

In summary, a platform offers scale with low capital investment, but it comes with limited control that may lead to poor customer experience. Companies that rely heavily on their platform spend enormous amounts of time and effort managing customer experience.

From Products to Platform

When we think of platforms, we typically think of marketplaces or services like eBay or Uber, which connect buyers and sellers. Can companies that manufacture and sell products become platforms? In January 2014, Google paid $3.2 billion to buy Nest, a smart thermostat that learns what temperature you like and automatically adjusts temperature in your house to save energy. But Google wasn't buying thermostats, instead, it envisioned Nest becoming a platform on which many applications could be developed for the connected home. In an effort to attract developers to its platform, Nest launched the "Works with Nest" program, and within a year the company had over 10,000 developers creating new applications. Nest also attracted large companies that wanted to be a part of the connected home. Nest, the platform, now works with Philips' smart LED bulbs, Whirlpool's washing machines, and Xfinity Home security systems, among other products and services. In the battle to own the home, Amazon created its own device, Echo (a smart speaker that is connected to a voice-controlled personal assistant service called Alexa), and Google responded by launching Google Home. Tesla's car is nothing but software on wheels and could become a platform for entertainment, payment, and much more.

As devices become embedded with sensors, their value is less in the hardware itself and more in the interconnectedness of that hardware. In the connected world, the battle is no longer fought among products.

Instead, competitive advantage comes from building a platform that has an ecosystem around it. However, the journey from product to platform is not always easy or quick, and often a company's business model evolves over time to reach this stage. The digital journey of GE illustrates this transition.

GE's Digital Journey and the Birth of the Predix Platform

Founded in 1892 in Schenectady, New York, GE is an industrial giant that operates in 180 countries, employs over 300,000 people, and generates more than $130 billion in revenue. The company manufactures complex industrial products such as wind turbines, jet engines, and locomotives. For over a hundred years, its strength and competitive advantage had been in its engineering, superior product design, and manufacturing.

In 2010, two facts became clear to Jeff Immelt, GE's CEO at the time. First, industrial productivity was expected to drop to less than 1 percent in the next decade, compared with 4 percent during the last decade.

Second, future improvements in productivity would come from software and analytics instead of physical improvements in products. Bill Ruh, CEO of GE Digital, emphasized this aspect, "Uber and Airbnb own no assets, yet they are valued more than auto manufacturers and hotels. It was clear to us that the future is not about who owns the assets but who makes those assets more productive."[7]

Given this reality, GE was concerned about a new set of competitors. What if IBM, Google, or Amazon used their software and analytics capabilities to make GE assets more valuable to GE customers? Would they become the industrial version of Uber and extract all the value? GE could insert sensors into its jet engines and wind turbines to collect data, but could it be more competitive in software and analytics than IBM or Google?

After much deliberation, GE management came up with the idea of "digital twin," a combination of the physical model of, say, a jet engine that allowed GE's engineers to forecast the failure probabilities of various components over time; and the real-time operational data from the sensors in an engine in use that could complement the theoretical model of the engineers to more accurately predict failure and offer predictive maintenance. This deep knowledge not just of data and analytics but of physics and engineering gave GE capabilities that IBM or Google could not match effectively.

The question then became how digital twin and improved software capabilities should change GE's business model. GE could develop software and give it away for free with the capital equipment sales. This would be consistent with GE's traditional hardware and product focus and would require the least change to its business model. Alternatively, GE could license the software as a separate product to generate additional revenue. A third option would be to deeply integrate GE's software and analytical capabilities with customers' own data in order to offer new outcome-based services. That last option could eventually lead to building a platform, but it would require significant investments and new capabilities.

Jeff Immelt decided to transform GE into an industrial digital company, and in 2011 he created GE Software, located in San Ramon, California, and installed Bill Ruh as its head. As with most digital transformations, this one evolved over time. During the transition, which was marked by three distinct phases, GE Software changed from a center of excellence to a stand-alone business unit, GE Digital, with over 30,000 people.

Phase 1: GE for GE

GE started its digital journey to improve the productivity of its own assets. Having been in business for more than a century, GE had a very large installed base that provided it a unique competitive advantage when launching this initiative. The goal was not simply to collect data for the sake of data but to improve the productivity of assets.

GE's analysis showed that a 1 percent efficiency gain could lead to billions of incremental dollars for its customers. Digital twin and asset-performance-management (APM) tools allowed GE to do predictive maintenance, minimize downtime, and optimize assets, all of which saved billions of dollars for its clients.

Phase 2: GE for Customers

As the company developed in-house software and analytical capabilities to improve the productivity of its assets, it decided to invite outside developers to build apps for its cloud-based system, Predix, and also share these apps with GE customers. Soon the company's relationship with its customers transformed from selling products to selling outcome-based services. One example of this is the GE Renewable Energy Group, which has an installed base of 33,000 wind turbines around the world, almost one-third of all turbines. For customers who bought GE turbines, the company started an outcome-based system called "PowerUp." As GE got data from sensors in the turbines, it could make real-time changes—for example, changing the pitch of a turbine blade if it got icy in cold weather. These changes have led to as much as a 5 percent increase in annual energy production for some of GE's clients, which translates into a 20 percent increase in their profits. This productivity improvement is not limited to optimizing each turbine individually. The location of turbines and the prevailing direction of wind on a farm may warrant a farm-level optimization that is suboptimal for an individual turbine but beneficial for the farm a whole.

A strong relationship with its customers is also helping GE develop new services. For example, wind farms, who are GE's customers, are at nature's mercy for the amount of energy they can generate on a given day or in a given week. However, customers of wind farms—governments, utility companies—expect the farms to deliver a certain amount of energy. If a farm falls short, it has to buy energy in the spot market, which can be very expensive. Using weather forecasts and historical data from its turbines, GE Renewable can now forecast farms' power production seven days ahead, allowing them to better manage their power-generation business.

Phase 3: GE for the World

In the next phase GE decided to open up its Predix platform to non-GE customers. Bill Ruh explained GE's decision to become the platform for industrial products: "There are lots of platforms optimized for consumer Internet applications and consumer devices. There are some aimed at the enterprise world, optimizing the IT environment. We saw nothing in the industrial world."[8] Customers such as Pitney Bowes and Schindler started using Predix and its analytical capabilities for their own clients. Roger Pilc, executive vice president and chief innovation officer of Pitney Bowes, explained his company's decision to use the Predix platform:

> We placed value with GE because they not only built the data and analytics platform, but also because of the journey they've been on for the last several years. They've been using data from their own machines, doing the data analytics and then ultimately evolving their own services organization in the exact same way as us. That was an important element to us. We speak regularly not just about the technology and the applications, but also about this digital-industrial transformation.[9]

In his 2015 letter to shareholders, Jeff Immelt highlighted the impact of GE's digital journey: "This year we will generate $500 million of productivity by applying data and analytics inside GE. The revenue for our analytical applications and software is $5 billion and growing 20% annually . . . We are creating a $15 billion software and digital company inside of GE built on agile practices and new business models."[10]

Can Banks Become Platforms?

In 2016, Goldman Sachs shocked the financial-services industry by opening up its structured-notes business to competitors.[11] Structured notes, designed to help clients create highly customized risk-return products, had been popular in Europe but had seen limited penetration in the United States due to a highly fragmented market of broker-dealers and a lack of education among them. Goldman Sachs entered this market by creating its own product, called Structured Investment Marketplace and Online Network (SIMON), which was built on the company's "Marquee" platform.

The evolution of Goldman Sachs's digital journey followed a pattern remarkably similar to that of GE. In a process championed by Goldman's chief information officer at the time, R. Martin Chavez (who is now the company's CFO), Goldman first embarked on creating internal efficiencies across business units. Next, it opened up its Marquee platform to clients so that they could use Goldman's proprietary database and tools to analyze risk or construct their portfolio. One of the first tools available to clients through application-program-interface (API) integration was SecDB, a powerful database that calculated 23 billion prices across 2.8 million positions daily across 50,000 market scenarios. Giving clients access to SecDB, which had long been considered Goldman's "secret sauce," puzzled the market. However, by making these tools available to clients and by tightly integrating Goldman's systems with those of its clients, Goldman hoped to create stickiness and a unique competitive advantage.

SIMON started as an application on Marquee, and in the beginning Goldman sold only its own products on SIMON. However, the company soon realized the benefit of opening up its platform to competitors. Paul Russo, the global co-chief operating officer of the equities franchise, explained this decision: "We realized that growth of the single dealer model had reached capacity. To continue to grow we need to add more issuers. Clients also like competition. Having multiple issuers allows clients to mix and match credit risk against payoffs effectively."

Opening the platform to competition effectively increased the size of the pie, and Goldman Sachs took a cut from the sale of competitors' products on its platform. By 2016, Goldman's structured-note business had grown to become the second-largest in the United States.

Banks have traditionally been very product focused, and it may be useful for them to rethink their business model. Francisco Gonzalez, the group executive chairman of BBVA, the leading bank of Spain, has argued that banks will have a hard time competing on products as those products become less and less differentiated. Instead, an incumbent bank may want to consider the benefits of creating a platform on which it provides its large customer base access to its own and competitors' products. In the digital age customers are likely to compare products anyway, and by providing a central place for them to do so, the bank would benefit from getting a portion of revenue if a competing product were sold on its platform.

Developing a Platform Business

The GE and Goldman Sachs cases illustrate some of the issues in transforming a product-focused company into a platform-based company. The goal of a product-focused company is to develop the best product and maximize its sales and profits while ensuring competitive advantage through tight control of proprietary knowledge. In contrast, a platform business creates value not simply by selling products or services but by enabling transactions and by creating an entire ecosystem. Therefore, a platform-based business attempts to build a network of third-party players who can develop complementary services; designs its systems through APIs and tools to facilitate transactions; often supports an open and shared system instead of a closed, proprietary one; and develops mechanisms to manage partners who may have conflicting interests. In the next part of this chapter we delve deeper into some of the major challenges a company faces in building a platform-based business.

Building Critical Mass

Platforms enable transactions between multiple parties (e.g., buyers and sellers), and companies often struggle on how to jump-start the process—should they first focus on buyers (demand side of the platform) or the sellers (supply side of the platform)? Here are some guidelines:

- **Develop Compelling Applications or Services Yourself.** To jump-start the process, a firm needs to create a supply of good products and services first—after all, without anything to sell, it will be hard to attract potential buyers to the platform. In the early stages, when third-party sellers may be reluctant to join the platform, the firm has to build its own applications or create its own supply. Companies such as Microsoft and Sony—makers, respectively, of the Xbox and PlayStation gaming consoles—rely on the variety and scale of games produced by third-party developers. However, to attract these third-party developers to their platforms, they first developed a handful of engaging games themselves that attracted users, which in turn encouraged third-party developers to join these platforms. GE developed its own applications for its custom-ers before opening the Predix platform for outside developers and non-GE customers. Apple showed the power of its platform by building iTunes. Soon after acquiring Nest, Google acquired Dropcam, maker of a Wi-Fi enabled security camera that could be connected to Nest. This showed the power of the platform and attracted potential developers. Instead of starting with UberX or UberPOOL, in which users drive their own cars, Uber started its service with black cars driven by professional drivers. To jump-start its service, Airbnb used professional photographers to take pictures of apartments, which encouraged users to follow suit.[12]

- **Start with a Focus.** Since platforms typically have strong network effects leading to winner-take-all markets, it is tempting to scale quickly by getting into multiple applications fast. However, at the early stage it is critical to develop a compelling use case and pow-erful customer experience by focusing on a small market to have a proof of concept. Uber started in January 2010 with a test in New York City and later launched the service in San Francisco in May 2010. In the beginning, as mentioned, Uber used black cars driven by professional drivers. While clearly not scalable in the future, this approach was designed to attract enough users to jump-start the process and to ensure great customer experience, which eventually created strong word of mouth. Travis Kalanick, founder of Uber, relied on users' word of mouth for early growth of the company: "I'm talking old school word of mouth, you know at the water cooler in the office, at a restaurant when you're paying the bill, at a party with friends—'Who's Ubering home?' 95% of all our riders have heard about Uber from other Uber riders."[13] It took Uber almost a year to test and refine its service in San Francisco before going to a new city in California, Palo Alto. In the realm of social media, even though it faced the dominant incumbent MySpace, Facebook started by focusing only on Harvard students, gradually expanding to more US and international students, before ultimately opening up its platform to everyone. Reflecting on the early growth stage of Flipkart, an Indian e-commerce company that started by selling books, cofounder Sachin Bansal noted, "We were sure from the beginning that we would enter more categories. Initially we thought we would launch the next category in a year. It took us three years to move beyond books."[14]

- **Subsidize One Side of the Platform.** When a company sells a product, it needs to charge each buyer in order to make money. In contrast, a platform connects multiple parties, and the company can afford to subsidize one side to stimulate demand while making profits on the other side. Research shows that the best approach is to subsidize the side of the platform that contributes more to demand for the other side.[15] When Adobe introduced Acrobat software, it initially charged $35 to $50 for Acrobat Reader software and $195 for the software to create PDFs. Later, to encourage adoption, it changed its approach and offered the Acrobat Reader for free.[16]

- **Build a Freemium Model.** Platform businesses have strong network effects that can create a virtuous circle. To encourage adoption and create this network effect, many companies are

beginning to adopt a freemium model in which a basic version of
the product is free for customers. Dropbox, Spotify, Pandora, and
The New York Times are examples of companies using such a strategy. A freemium model has several benefits: For digital products,
the marginal cost of an additional customer is close to zero. A free
basic product encourages adoption and creates a large customer
base of users that generates strong network effects. And over time,
the use of a basic product encourages customers to upgrade to
paid premium products. However, designing freemium products and their pricing is a complex issue that requires careful
consideration.[17]

Facilitating Access and Transactions

The primary function of a platform is to enable and facilitate transactions. Recall that a platform business works by aggregating demand
from a fragmented market and by reducing transaction costs. Therefore a platform owner needs to build tools and services to provide
easy access to third-party players on its platform, use algorithms to
match players on multiple sides of the platform, and offer additional
services that make it easy for them to do business. For example,
software platforms offer APIs to help developers build applications.
Facebook helped its users to find friends, which increased Facebook's
value to users. Amazon offers warehousing and shipping services
to its marketplace sellers, which makes it easy for the sellers to do
business.

Choosing between Open and Closed Systems

One of the main challenges for a company building a platform business
is the choice between an open, or shared, system and a closed, or proprietary, system. An open system generally attracts a larger number of
independent players to the platform, which fosters greater innovation
and variety, builds more complementary products, lowers prices due to
competition among players, and creates a larger market. In contrast,
a company has more control with a closed system, which allows the

company to create better integration and coordination across various products and services offered on its platform, which in turn creates a superior customer experience. A closed system also allows the platform host to capture a larger share of the pie.

Google's Android is an open system, whereas Apple tightly controls its iOS and carefully screens apps before approving them for its system. As a result of these choices, Android enjoys a larger market share while Apple provides a superior customer experience. In the second quarter of 2017, Android had 87.7 percent of global market share compared with 12.1 percent for Apple's iOS.[18] In the credit- and debit-card market, Mastercard and Visa have open systems in which they partner with banks that ultimately issue cards to customers and acquire merchants. In contrast, American Express manages a closed system in which it acts as an issuing and acquiring bank as well as a processor of transactions. In 2015, Visa accounted for 56 percent of all global card transactions, followed by Mastercard, with its share of 26 percent. American Express had a mere 3.2 percent share of all such transactions.[19]

For its in-car software, BMW opted to build an open system. Dr. Michael Wuertenberger, the managing director of BMW's Car IT, explained:

> We definitely would like to have an open system. It will not be simply an Apple or a Google system inside the car. BMW has to work with both of them. Two years ago, we launched the first open-source in-car "infotainment" system that is Linux-based and can integrate with both Apple's and Google's software. We would like to share that system with other car makers to place into their vehicles. Openness is good.[20]

The choice of an open or a closed system is not usually black and white, as there are various parts of the platform that can be kept open or proprietary.[21] However, in general, an open system creates a larger market and a closed system creates a better customer experience. So the choice of an open or a closed platform depends on the goal and strategy of the company. For example, Google, Apple, and Samsung

FIGURE 3-1

Starbucks's mobile transactions as a percentage of total transactions, 2013–2018

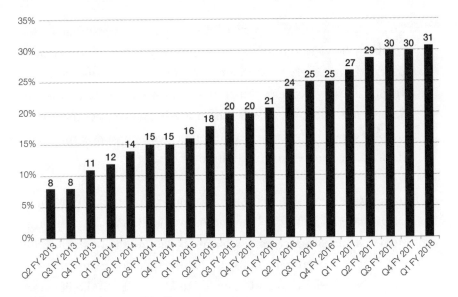

Source: Company reports and BI Intelligence.
Note: Q4 FY 2016 excludes week 53. Starbucks's fiscal year ends on the Sunday closest to September 30.

are creating open mobile-payment systems to build a large market. However, Starbucks created a very successful closed system for mobile payment that works only at Starbucks stores. Part of its success stems from enhancing customer experience by providing a compelling value proposition to its frequent visitors, who can order and pay ahead for their coffee, before they walk into a Starbucks store. (Figure 3-1 shows the growth of transactions on the Starbucks mobile-payment platform.)

Managing Partners in the Ecosystem

Platforms develop an ecosystem of partners who provide complementary products and services. The word *ecosystem* was first coined in 1930 by British botanist Roy Clapham, and later popularized by ecologist Arthur Tansley to describe a community of organisms who, in conjunction with their environment, interact as a system.[22] These organisms share resources, compete and collaborate, and co-evolve. This idea was adapted for business by the writer James Moore in a 1993 *Harvard Business Review* article:

> To extend a systematic approach to strategy, I suggest that a
> company be viewed not as a member of a single industry but as
> part of a *business ecosystem* that crosses a variety of industries.
> In a business ecosystem, companies co-evolve capabilities around
> a new innovation; they work cooperatively and competitively to
> support new products, satisfy customer needs, and eventually
> incorporate the next round of innovations.[23]

Today, business ecosystems have become even more important as technologies are increasingly blurring industry boundaries. "A vibrant ecosystem can enable activities, assets, and capabilities to be flexible and constantly reconfigured in response to the unexpected," argue the writers Peter James Williamson and Arnoud De Meyer. "Both the demands of consumers and the technologies available to satisfy them have changed dramatically. Today's world requires the capacity to deliver complex solutions to customers, built by bringing together specialized capabilities scattered in diverse organizations around the world."[24] While the nineteenth and twentieth centuries focused on efficiency and economies of scale, the current era requires coordination across a wide variety of firms to provide complex and dynamic solutions to customers.

Deloitte, a consulting firm, defines business ecosystems as "dynamic and co-evolving communities of diverse actors who create and capture new value through both collaboration and competition."[25] It is this unique aspect of collaboration *and* competition among firms that makes ecosystems unique and complex to manage.

Firms have varying degrees of control in this environment. For example, Apple largely controls its iOS. Individual developers have limited power. In contrast, Apple had significantly less power when it introduced Apple Pay in partnership with banks and merchants and had to carefully manage its relationship with these partners. In this complex

environment, a company must understand the motivations of its partners in order to manage the ecosystem effectively. The launch of Apple
Pay illustrates this complexity.

In September 2014, Tim Cook, Apple's CEO, announced the launch
of Apple Pay and said, "Our vision is to replace this [wallet], and we are
going to start with payments."[26] Apple did not blow up the existing payment system. Instead, it decided to work within the current payments
ecosystem. Jennifer Bailey, vice president of Apple Pay, explained this
decision:

> We want to support what people already use and love. Consum-
> ers are already comfortable using their credit and debit cards
> that are supported by the majority of merchants and banks.
> Banks are good at what they do: they are good at credit, brand-
> ing, customer service and conducting payments. Apple's role was
> simply to bring together the hardware, software and services to
> create the experience on the phone.[27]

This choice led Apple to work with its partners: the banks, the
merchants, and the payment networks (Mastercard, Visa, American
Express). While each of these partners collaborated with Apple, they
were also considering launching their own mobile-payment systems.
Soon after the launch of Apple Pay, some of the largest US merchants
launched Merchant Customer Exchange (MCX), Chase created its
own mobile-payment system called Chase Pay, Mastercard started
Masterpass, and Visa introduced Visa Checkout as its online and
mobile-payment system. In this collaboration the key battle is for the
control of customers. Banks don't want Apple to own the user interface
and effectively become a utility in the background, yet they can't ignore
Apple either, because of Apple's strong affinity among consumers.

A similar battle for the customer is brewing in the automotive ecosys-
tem, and the participants include incumbent auto manufacturers like
GM, Ford, and BMW; new players like Tesla; technology companies like
Apple and Google, which are developing in-car technologies such as

FIGURE 3-2

New ecosystem of automotive industry

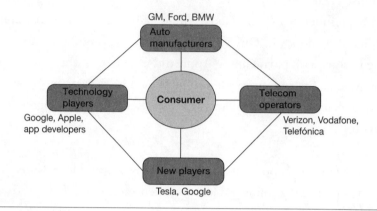

CarPlay; and telecommunication companies like Verizon, Vodaphone, and Telefónica, which are vying for a position in the era of connected cars (see figure 3-2).

Reflecting on Mercedes-Benz's strategy, Wilko Stark, vice president of Daimler's group strategy, product strategy, and product planning, noted:

> The company that has access to the customer interface is the one who possesses the opportunity to do one-to-one marketing and personalized services for each customer through the data that is collected. We already know a lot about each of our customers, where they drive, what is their location—we want to offer them personalized services as well.[28]

There is no easy solution for managing these complex partnerships. Players need to understand the motivations of their partners and carefully balance their own interests with those geared to the success of the overall ecosystem. For instance, even though Apple and Google launched competing mobile-payment systems, they have very different motivations. Apple's business is largely driven by hardware, so its motivation is primarily to create complementary services for the iPhone, while Google's business depends on advertising and data. Not surprisingly, in launching Apple Pay, Apple decided that banks and merchants, not Apple, would own the data. In contrast, Google needs mobile-payment data to close the loop from search to purchase to show the effectiveness of its advertising.

Governance

In 2016, Facebook was blamed for influencing the US presidential election by not identifying fake news stories on its site, many of which went viral. Mark Zuckerberg, Facebook's founder and CEO, described these allegations as crazy. After all, Facebook is an open social platform where people are free to express their opinions without any effort by Facebook to tilt the conversations one way or the other. In a November 12, 2016, Facebook post, Zuckerberg said,

> Of all the content on Facebook, more than 99% of what people see is authentic. Only a very small amount is fake news and hoaxes. The hoaxes that do exist are not limited to one partisan view, or even to politics. Overall, this makes it extremely unlikely hoaxes changed the outcome of this election in one direction or the other.[29]

However, this did not satisfy the critics, who argued that Facebook has a large influence on social conversations and therefore has a responsibility, like a media company, to separate the truth from hoaxes. Using technology and users' input, Facebook is now trying to identify and curb fake news. In early 2018, Facebook again faced strong criticism for failing to protect consumer data as the news broke that a UK-based company, Cambridge Analytica, used consumers' Facebook data to target political ads to influence the 2016 US presidential elections.

To avoid market failures, platform owners need a governance system to create rules by which various players operate within its ecosystem— whether it is to limit fake news and pornography on Facebook while still encouraging free and open conversations or to delist sellers with bad customer service on Amazon's marketplace while still trying to increase the number of sellers. Insights from diverse corners—such as corporate governance in finance and accounting, laws governing interactions among nation-states, and research on the proper function of the kidney exchange—can provide guidance on how to govern and manage a platform business.

Based on his research on the medical labor market and the kidney exchange, Alvin Roth, winner of the 2012 Nobel Prize in economics, said, "Traditional economics views markets as simply the confluence of supply and demand. A new field of economics, known as 'market design,' recognizes that well-functioning markets depend on detailed rules."[30] He went on to explain three things that are needed for markets to function properly: Markets or platforms need to provide *thickness*, which brings large numbers of buyers and sellers together. They need to make it *safe* for participants to reveal and act on confidential information they may hold. And they need to manage *congestion*, or competition and complexity, that arises from thickness.

In conclusion, platforms provide a new way of conducting business that warrants an outside-in perspective, meaning that firms need to open up their systems in order to collaborate and partner with many players, some of whom may even be their competitors. And this requires new skills and capabilities to manage and govern a platform.

PART TWO

Reevaluate Your Value Chain

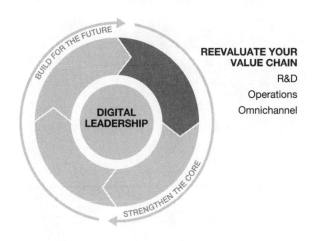

REEVALUATE YOUR
VALUE CHAIN
R&D
Operations
Omnichannel

DIGITAL
LEADERSHIP

BUILD FOR THE FUTURE

STRENGTHEN THE CORE

Chapter 4

Rethinking R&D and Innovation

No matter who you are, most of the smartest people work for someone else.

—Bill Joy, cofounder of Sun Microsystems

The National Aeronautics and Space Administration (NASA) employs some of best scientists in the world, so it may have seemed strange when in 2013 NASA announced a public contest to solve a problem for the International Space Station (ISS). This is how NASA described the challenge for its contest:

> The ISS is powered by the sun and the sun's energy is captured by the Station solar panels. Ensuring the Station harvests as much energy as possible is obviously a complicated matter. The long thin rods that hold the solar panels to the Station are called Longerons. Any time an odd number of Longerons are in full sunlight with others in shadow, they bend and would eventually break. So ISS Program engineers position the station in orbit

to limit shadowing. And simply put, this positioning reduces the amount of overall power that can be collected. More power means more science on orbit and would certainly enhance ISS operations. The goal of the Longeron challenge is to develop a complex algorithm that would allow NASA to position the solar collectors on the ISS to generate as much power as possible during the most difficult orbital positions.[1]

The contest, run in partnership with Harvard University, was open to anyone in the world for an initial prize of $30,000.[2] Did NASA really believe that ordinary people could find a better solution to the problem than its own rocket scientists? Not surprisingly, there were plenty of skeptics within NASA's own group of scientists, who considered this approach as looking for a needle in the haystack.

When the competition closed, on February 6, 2013, 459 competitors from a wide range of backgrounds had submitted 2,185 solutions. As one competitor noted on his blog, "Two weeks ago, while waiting for my flight to San Francisco at an airport in Paris I stumbled on a coding challenge by NASA to optimize the solar arrays of the International Space Station ... Being very interested in Optimization for my soon-to-be-unveiled new startup, I was quite excited and promptly downloaded all the required material to spend my 10-hour flight hacking ;-)."[3]

How did these submissions perform compared with what NASA's own scientists had come up with? Based on only a few months' worth of work and only a tiny fraction (if that) of a typical NASA budget, almost half of the 2,185 submitted entries performed better than NASA's internal solution. Of those whose entries were in the top ten, five were from China, and one each from Russia, Poland, Romania, Canada, and Italy. (In October 2016, NASA announced a new contest, called "Space Poop Challenge," seeking solutions for in-suit waste management to be used in the crew's launch and entry suits over a continuous duration of up to 144 hours.[4])

Is this an anomaly? Let's take another example, this time in the field of genomics. Like NASA, Harvard Medical School (HMS) recruits some of the best scientists in the world. A few years ago, HMS decided to run a contest inviting the general public to solve a complex computational genomics problem. Scientists at HMS and the National Institutes of Health (NIH) had been working on this problem for years, spending millions of dollars in research. In contrast, this contest ran for just two weeks, with a prize of only $6,000. Nonetheless, 122 people from eighty-nine countries submitted 650 entries. Of these, 30 exceeded NIH and internal Harvard benchmarks, and the best of them advanced the state of the art by a factor of a thousand.[5]

These are not isolated examples. Leveraging the expertise and insights of both users and experts outside the company, often called *open innovation* or *crowdsourcing*, has been on the rise in recent years. Companies have used this approach for innovation in a wide range of applications. For many years, Doritos ran a "Crash the Super Bowl" advertising contest, with prizes ranging from $400,000 to $1 million, in which the company invited its fans to create ads that—if selected— would air during the Super Bowl broadcast. When Procter & Gamble (P&G) wanted to launch a new line of Pringles potato chips with pictures and words printed on each chip, it used an open-innovation approach and found a solution from a small bakery in Bologna, Italy, run by a university professor who had invented an inkjet method of printing images on cookies and cakes. Reporting this development for Pringles, two executives from P&G concluded that the world had moved from R&D (research and development) to C&D (connect and develop). They reported that more than 35 percent of P&G's innovations, and billions of dollars in revenue, were being generated by open innovation.[6] Since the launch of the General Mills Worldwide Innovation Network (G-Win), General Mills has worked with a wide variety of external partners to develop new products. Successful products include Nature Valley Protein bars and Nut Clusters, Fiber-One 90 Calorie Brownies, and Chex Chips. Now, companies such as GE, Samsung, Coca-Cola, and Eli Lilly are adopting open innovation to tap the knowledge of outside experts, suppliers, and lead users as well as that of their own internal networks.

The Rise of Open Innovation

Companies spend billions of dollars on R&D with the hope of creating innovative products that will give them a sustainable competitive advantage. Most business managers assume this producer- or company-led model to be the dominant mode of innovation. However, as Adam Smith noted almost three centuries ago in *The Wealth of Nations*, "a great part of the machines made use of in those manufactures in which labor is most subdivided, were originally the invention of common workmen, who, being each of them employed in some very simple operation, naturally turned their thoughts towards finding out easier and easier methods of performing it."

In the 1970s, Eric von Hippel, one of the pioneers of user-led innovation, showed evidence of Adam Smith's idea about the important role played by users in developing and modifying products.[7] Other scholars built on his research, and in the next four decades hundreds of research studies showed the power of user-led innovation. National surveys in six countries—the United States, the United Kingdom, Canada, Finland, South Korea, and Japan—found that from 1.5 percent to 6.1 percent of the consumer population over the age of eighteen engaged in developing products in these countries. These developments cut across a wide range of categories, including sports, gardening, medicine, food, clothing, autos, home, and child-related products.[8] Users and communities were also found to play an important role in innovation in B2B industries such as oil refining, chemical production processes, scientific instruments, and software.[9]

Early research found that most users engage in product development out of personal need to adapt and modify existing products for their own specific use. Recognizing this, companies started sponsoring contests to explicitly leverage these user communities for product innovations. Over time contests expanded the pool beyond users by engaging people from completely different fields and skill sets, people who were simply drawn to the challenge posed by these competitions. Contests have also had a significant role in historical technological innovation, including the design of the dome at the famous Florence cathedral, determining the longitude at sea, the invention of food canning, and innovations in agriculture and aviation.[10]

As product lifecycles become shorter and R&D costs continue to increase, internal innovation alone is no longer enough to support companies' growth expectations. To remain competitive and hit topline growth goals, and to extend the reach of their innovation pipeline and leverage their limited resources, many companies have found open innovation to be a necessity.

Technology has also played a significant role by making design, development, and collaboration tools affordable and accessible, which in turn has made innovation possible for small businesses, communities, and individuals. As discussed earlier, firm boundaries become less rigid as transaction costs go down, which makes it easier for outside players to provide input to a company without being its employees. Technology has also enabled like-minded people to gather in large virtual communities where they share information and brainstorm ideas. You can find a community for almost any group. Vocalpoint is a community of several hundred thousand moms who provide feedback for product improvements. Topcoder is one of the largest communities of software coders who are actively engaged in contests. There are hundreds of communities dealing with sunless tanning. And there are even dozens of chainsaw forums with thousands of members.

Low investment and quick solutions obtained through open innovation make this approach financially attractive. A 2014 study of 489 projects at a large European manufacturer found that projects with open innovation partnerships had better financial returns than traditional projects.[11] General Mills also highlighted open innovation as a key determinant to the financial success of its products. Of the sixty new products it launched in a year's time, those that had incorporated open innovation outperformed those that hadn't by 100 percent.[12]

Why Does Open Innovation Work?

Why are users and contest participants able to outperform companies' internal high-caliber scientific teams for some of the most complex problems? Research suggests the following reasons:

Diverse Approaches

Internal company teams often view a problem with a single lens and attempt to find a solution using a handful of approaches. In contrast, open innovation casts a wide net and attracts large numbers of participants with various areas of expertise who employ a range of methods and perspectives to solve a problem. For example, the Harvard Medical School contest received entries in which contestants had used a total of eighty-nine different approaches to solve the complex computational genomics problem.[13]

Why does diversity of methods matter? In a seminal paper published in 1969, two economists showed that combining forecasts from different models produces better results than does a forecast from a single complex model.[14] Later studies by several scholars confirmed this idea, showing that even taking a simple average of forecasts from several different models produces a far superior result than any single method can generate.[15]

One of the best examples of why diversity of methods matters is illustrated by the 2006 Netflix competition where the company offered a $1 million prize to anyone who could improve its algorithm for movie recommendations. During its awards ceremony in 2009, Netflix's chief product officer described the key lesson learned from this competition: "At first, a whole lot of teams got in—and they got 6-percent improvement, 7-percent improvement, 8-percent improvement, and then it started slowing down … Then there was a great insight among some of the teams—that if they combined their approaches, they actually got better."[16]

People who participate in open innovations are usually part of a large community such as Topcoder. While they are highly competitive during a contest, they often share their winning entries with others, which provides a strong learning platform for other contestants to improve upon in the future.

Extreme Values

Companies aim to hire the best people, so *on average* their scientists and engineers are smarter than the outsiders and therefore likely to produce better ideas. However, we are usually not interested in averages but—rather—in one or two winning ideas that can lead to a successful innovation. The sheer diversity of contest participants ensures that even if, on average, they are not as good as the inside experts of a company, they are more likely to generate the rare but valuable idea. In other words, a company is interested in the *extreme values* of a probability distribution instead of its mean.

Better Customer Insight

In one of his early studies, Eric von Hippel found that 77 percent of the most important innovations in scientific instruments over four decades were developed by scientists using these instruments, and not by the scientific instrument companies.[17] Using data from a wide range of inventions made in more than twenty countries, Dietmar Harhoff confirmed von Hippel's claim that users are the most important source of knowledge for innovations across all major technologies.[18] User innovators are by definition close to their market, as they are in essence innovating for themselves. This reduces the need for and cost of consumer research and allows for quick and inexpensive in-market product testing. It also avoids the potential mistake a firm may make in trying to identify the true customer needs. These users are often working to meet their own needs before firms even identify the opportunity. By default, this puts user innovators ahead of firms on the innovation timeline.

Self-Selection

When a company embarks on an innovation project, its employees have no choice but to work on the assigned task regardless of their conviction or passion. In contrast, contestants in an open innovation are self-selecting, working on the problem they are most passionate about. Self-selection leads to a good match between the task and the innovator, and it also solves the incentive problem because individuals are self-motivated.

Why Do People Participate in Open Innovations?

Several intrinsic and extrinsic motivations drive people to participate in open-innovation contests. A *Wall Street Journal* article captures the intrinsic motivation of many user-led innovations:

> Jason Adams, a business-development executive by day and a molecular biologist by training, had never considered himself a hacker. That changed when he discovered an off-label way to monitor his 8-year-old daughter's blood-sugar levels from afar.
>
> His daughter Ella has Type 1 diabetes and wears a glucose monitor made by Dexcom Inc. The device measures her blood sugar every five minutes and displays it on a nearby receiver the size of a pager, a huge advantage in helping monitor her blood sugar for spikes and potentially fatal drops. But it can't transmit the data to the Internet, which meant Mr. Adams never sent Ella to sleepovers for fear she could slip into a coma during the night.
>
> Then Mr. Adams found NightScout, a system cobbled together by a constellation of software engineers, many with diabetic children, who were frustrated by the limitations of current technology. The open-source system they developed essentially hacks the Dexcom device and uploads its data to the Internet, which lets Mr. Adams see Ella's blood-sugar levels on his Pebble smartwatch wherever she is. It isn't perfect. It drains cellphone batteries, can cut out at times and hasn't been approved by the Food and Drug Administration. But for many, it has filled a gap.[19]

Focusing on such user-led innovations, von Hippel and his colleagues conducted a study in Finland and found four factors that influenced user participation in open innovation: personal need, fun and learning, desire to help others, and the monetary reward. While a small number of people were motivated primarily by money, almost 80 percent of the users participated because of personal need or to have fun and learn.[20] For contestants who are not users of a product, additional motivations include developing and showcasing their skills, which can often help them secure a job, and improving their stature among their peers.

How to Do Open Innovation in Your Firm

To successfully leverage the power of open innovation, firms should consider the following issues.

Defining the Problem

Open innovation is best suited for well-defined problems. You won't get very useful insights by organizing a challenge around a broad and vague question such as "What is the future of banks?" Kevin Boudreau and Karim Lakhani, who have done extensive research on open innovation, have found that the solutions improve when the problem is broken down into manageable pieces and generalized to make it understandable to innovators across multiple industries and areas of expertise.

Commenting on the importance of defining a problem, Jon Fredrickson, vice president and chief innovation officer of InnoCentive, a firm that helps companies with their open-innovation projects, said, "One of the most difficult challenges we face with clients is clearly defining the problem. They can tell us what they want, but we often have to go back to the first principles to find out what is preventing them for achieving what they want."[21]

To highlight this difference, Fredrickson described the challenge InnoCentive ran for the Oil Spill Recovery Institute, which was established by the US Congress in response to the 1989 *Exxon Valdez* oil spill in Alaska:

> During cleanup, the oil-water mixture they extract from the ocean and put on barges becomes very thick and viscous in subarctic temperatures. When the barges try to unload this oil-water mixture at the shore, the process becomes very difficult and slow. As one of the engineers described, "[We] could pump the oil if we could get it to the pump, but we could not get the oil to flow within the barge." So what the client wanted was to speed up the process of offloading oil from its barges. After discussions with the client we changed the question to, "How do you break shear in a viscous fluid."

The winning solution came from John Davis, who used his experience from the cement industry. This is how he described it:

> I have some experience pouring concrete, and when we pour concrete that would begin to set up we will use these concrete vibrators. What that would do is they would actually restore flow to the concrete and allow it to flow as a liquid. And that's kind of what inspired me in my solution to the problem. Solution was to use pneumatic concrete vibrators to keep oil-water slush as a fluid.[22]

"The solution was so simple and intuitive that people in Alaska could not believe that they hadn't thought of it," Fredrickson remarked. But it all came from both defining the problem in clear and concise terms and taking it out of the specific context of the oil industry to get the benefit of diverse approaches.

Creating a Clear Metric for Evaluation

Participants in an open-innovation contest want to win, so the company should have a very clear sense of how it is going to evaluate the contest entries. Karim Lakhani, who leads the Harvard–NASA Tournament

Lab at Harvard University, and who oversaw NASA's ISS Longeron Challenge, explained the importance of clearly defining the problem and the evaluation criteria:

> When NASA came to us to create a contest for ISS, they wanted the space station to be optimally positioned to generate maximum power. Our first task was to convert what NASA wanted into a clear problem. We had several meetings with their scientists to understand what prevents ISS to generate power, and after many conversations we finally came to the conclusion that when [an] odd number of Longerons are in sunlight they break, which leads to loss of power.
>
> Before we ran this contest, we had another set of meetings with NASA scientists to discuss how they would evaluate the solutions from contestants. NASA had to build new models that would predict how a particular positioning of the space station would lead to power generated by ISS. These models did not exist before, and only after we were convinced that this is the right way to evaluate the entries, we launched the contest.[23]

A clear and crisp problem helps in creating unambiguous evaluation criteria. If, on the other hand, the problem is broad and vague, open innovation turns into brainstorming rather than problem-solving. While there is nothing wrong in using crowdsourcing for generating ideas, and many companies do just that, the purpose and expectations should be clear to both the company executives and the contestants.

Designing the Challenge

Several things need to be considered in designing a challenge, such as the prize money, the length of the contest, ownership of the intellectual property, protections for the confidential data of the sponsoring firm, the criteria and process for selecting the winners, etc. Each choice involves a tradeoff. For example, offering a large prize would attract the best talent but might limit the diversity of ideas, as it discourages people who may consider their odds of winning low.

The contest can also be designed to run in different stages, where each stage draws on the expertise of a different set of people. This process follows the diverge-converge-diverge-converge sequence, where the first stage may generate lot of ideas from which a few are selected, and then in the second stage these selected ideas are used to generate a new set of implementation solutions.

Tongal, an open innovation platform for creative content and videos for advertisers, uses a three-stage process. In the first stage Tongal posts a client's brief and invites people to submit ideas for an ad based on the brand's objective. These ideas are typically submitted in short form, 140 to 400 characters, just like a Twitter post. Tongal's internal team and client review these submissions and narrow them down to three or four promising ideas. In the second stage, Tongal reaches out to the community of directors and production companies to bring these winning ideas to life in the form of pitches. The internal team and client again review these pitches to select the best production. In the final stage, the winning team of producers and directors is provided the necessary funding and related resources to create the final video or ad.

While Tongal uses its internal team for evaluating the contest entries, certain situations may call for using the crowd to select the winners. Threadless invites consumers to submit ideas for T-shirts and then asks them to pick the winners as well. By inviting consumers to pick the winning ideas, Threadless is effectively doing market research and ensuring the success of the items that it finally produces. *American Idol*, a reality TV talent show, also invites viewers to vote, which ensures that the winner has a large preestablished fan base that would ensure the success of the winner's first music album.

Organizational Challenges

In spite of the tremendous potential of open innovation, its use in companies is still limited. Even the companies that are using this approach are allocating only a small fraction of their budget and time for it. Jon Fredrickson of InnoCentive described two major organizational challenges in the adoption of this radical approach to innovation:

> The first challenge is the organizational culture of "not invented here" syndrome. Firms are designed and organized to function in the traditional way of doing R&D. Often a senior leader gets excited about open innovation, the firm tries it as an experiment, but later it becomes unclear who owns the solution. The second challenge is personal—open innovation threatens the job and role of the scientists who are hired by the firm to tackle those problems. Many view this as a personal failure, which creates huge barriers to adoption of this approach.

Open innovation also requires firms to give up control and broaden their lens. Often ideas come from a very different field, and it is tempting to reject them out of hand. Many of these ideas may not be as polished or refined as those the firm receives from its R&D engineers or ad agencies. Finally, open innovation creates anxiety about intellectual property and competitive intelligence.

Limits of Open Innovation

Open innovation does not work in all situations. As mentioned earlier, it is less effective for very broad and conceptual questions such as "What is the future of banking?" Such a question would invoke many opinions, and it would be hard to separate the wheat from the chaff. Many skeptics also suggest that crowdsourcing can't create breakthrough innovations. For instance, could you have invented the iPhone or driverless cars through crowdsourcing?

Part of this criticism is true. But there are three interrelated issues here. First, for the situation to be suitable for open innovation the problem—say, how to create driverless cars—needs to be broken down into smaller components, such as how to use sensors to detect pedestrians. Second, even if the problem is well defined and modularized, in many cases the potential investment in hardware or the infrastructure needed to solve this problem is huge and therefore beyond the scope of an individual or a small team of independent solvers. Third, in some cases the potential commercial value of a solution is in billions of dollars, and small prize money is not enough of an incentive for people to solve it without retaining the intellectual property. For example, even if someone could find a solution to wirelessly charge a smartphone, it is unlikely that this solution would be found through crowdsourcing in exchange for a few thousand dollars' worth of prize money.

Leaders in organizations also worry what would happen to their competitive advantage if everyone started leveraging the crowd for their innovation. The competitive advantage in the future would come from defining the problem, breaking it down into components, and integrating the solutions to these modular, smaller problems. No two companies view market trends and customer needs in the same way, and how one company or another framed its future direction would determine its success. In other words, in a crowdsourcing future, it will be the questions companies ask, not the solutions they know, that will determine their success.

Chapter 5

Operational Excellence

On August 2, 2016, Samsung unveiled its latest smartphone, the Galaxy Note 7, almost a month ahead of the launch of the new iPhone later that fall. The introduction of the Note 7 was an important event for Samsung, as the company was getting into a close contest with Apple to become the leading smartphone company in the world. Two weeks later, the company started selling the Note 7 in ten markets, including South Korea and the United States. The device received rave reviews from critics and fans, and initial demand was so high that it broke preorder records in South Korea and created supply shortages in some markets. However, within a week there were dozens of reports of Note 7 phones catching fire and exploding.

Samsung urged hundreds of its employees to quickly diagnose the problem, but none of them was able to get the phone to explode. After a frantic effort, Samsung engineers concluded that the defect was most likely caused by a battery that had come from one of its suppliers, and according to Samsung officials, "the problematic battery" had been installed in "less than 0.1 percent of the entire volume sold."[1]

As news of the exploding phones continued to surface, the company—on September 2, 2016—suspended sales of the device and recalled almost 2.5 million Note 7 phones from the market. Samsung promised that within two weeks customers would receive replacement phones that would have batteries from a different supplier. However, the problem persisted, even with replacement phones, and most airlines banned consumers from carrying Note 7 phones onto the planes. Recognizing the severity of the problem and the potential impact on its reputation, Samsung, on October 11, 2016, decided to kill the Note 7 altogether. This news led to an 8 percent drop in Samsung's share price, wiping almost $17 billion from its market value.[2]

While Samsung's case is a cautionary tale for all firms, Siemens, in Amberg, Germany, would probably never face this problem. Using state-of-the-art technology, Siemens is ushering in the era of industry 4.0 and smart manufacturing.

Industry 4.0

In 2011 the German government conceived Industry 4.0, or the fourth industrial revolution, and since then the concept and the ideas behind it have caught the attention of many companies around the world. The first industrial revolution, during the eighteenth century, was powered by steam, which led to the mechanization of equipment and revolutionized a variety of industries, from transportation to textiles. The invention of electric-power generation and transmission in the late nineteenth century and the use of electricity in the early twentieth century in assembly-line processes ushered in the second industrial revolution, which saw the mass production and increasing affordability of everything from automobiles to household appliances. In the mid-twentieth century, electronics and computer technology led the third industrial revolution, which had a major impact on manufacturing through computer-aided design (CAD), computer-aided manufacturing (CAM), and automation through robots. Today, digital technology is leading the fourth industrial revolution, which allows the convergence of digital and physical products.

According to Germany Trade & Invest, an economic-development agency within the German government, Industry 4.0 represents a paradigm shift from centralized to decentralized production, where a machine no longer simply processes a product but where the product communicates with the machine to tell it exactly what to do.[3] Through machine-to-machine communication, problems can be diagnosed and autonomous decisions can be taken without human intervention. The German conglomerate Siemens has set up a factory that, as a model of smart manufacturing, highlights the potential of Industry 4.0.

Smart Factory

In Amberg, a small town in Bavaria, Siemen's has built a factory of the future that produces programmable logic controllers (PLCs), devices used for automating industrial equipment and processes. Almost 75 percent of the operations in this factory are digitized and automated. Each component has its own marker—a bar code or an embedded chip—that communicates with a machine. This interaction then determines the precise action that needs to be taken by that machine. Data flows in real time between components and machines, and any changes—due to a new component, a new supplier, a new machine, or a new assembly process—can quickly be programmed to optimize the production process. At the end of production and for every product, Siemens has complete information on each component and each stage along the assembly process.

To understand the importance of digitization, it is helpful to distinguish it from automation. Eckard Eberle, CEO of process automation in the Siemens Process Industries and Drives Division, describes the classic automation process:

> In manufacturing and process industries, people are running their plants deterministically. By this I mean they have a complete understanding . . . [of] process . . . so everything operates under the assumption that the complete system is described. This is something that is very static, but also stable. It has the advantage that it is very robust.[4]

Stable and robust automation, as used by automobile companies, eliminates defects and speeds up operations. But it comes at the cost of limited flexibility. This is one of the reasons that it typically takes several years for car manufacturers to introduce a new car model. A digital factory, by comparison, provides all the advantages of automation in terms of speed and efficiency but also allows for flexibility and tracking. For many products, such as PLCs for Siemens or smartphones for Samsung, frequent innovations in electronic components and product design make classic factory automation less practical. Siemens has 99.99885 percent defect-free production even though its factory produces twelve million units per year, or almost one unit per second. Digitization of operations allows a company to quickly change any component, machine, or process. And this flexibility, again, has not come at the cost of speed and productivity. Through digitization, Siemens has increased its output 8.5 times without adding space or people.

As manufacturing gets complex, with potentially hundreds of components from scores of suppliers going into a product that is assembled in dozens of factories around the world, keeping track of changes and potential defects becomes increasingly important. This is how Siemens describes its Amberg smart factory and the future of Industry 4.0:

> Here, products control their own manufacturing processes. In other words, their product codes tell production machines what requirements they have and which production steps must be taken next. This system marks the first step toward the creation of Industry 4.0. In this vision of a fourth industrial revolution, the real and the virtual manufacturing worlds will merge. Factories will then be largely able to control and optimize themselves, because their products will communicate with one another and with production systems in order to optimize manufacturing processes. Products and machines will determine among themselves which items on which production lines should be completed first in order to meet delivery deadlines. Independently operating computer programs known as software agents will

monitor each step and ensure that production regulations are complied with. The Industry 4.0 vision also foresees factories that will be able to manufacture one-of-a-kind product without being unprofitable, as they will produce items quickly, inexpensively, and in top quality.[5]

Siemens's digital factory provides a glimpse of the future of manufacturing, which will usher in a new era of improved productivity in a wide variety of industries.

Industrial Internet and Predictive Maintenance

The early growth of the internet was fueled by communications and consumer commerce. With the rise of connected devices, which are estimated to reach fifty billion in number by 2020, data can now flow among machines. Falling costs to connect, store, and process machine data are driving the growth of the industrial internet. By adding sensors into machines ranging from jet engines to wind turbines, GE is able to collect data on the performance of its assets, which allows it to do predictive maintenance and reduce down time. This increased efficiency of equipment can translate into huge savings for its clients. GE estimates that if predictive maintenance could improve efficiency for its clients by even 1 percent from reduced downtime and increased asset utilization, it could save the oil and gas industry $90 billion over fifteen years. Savings in other sectors, while not as great, are still impressively large (see figure 5-1).

To realize this potential, GE developed Predix, a cloud-based operating system for industrial applications. It did so out of the recognition that the industrial internet differs from the consumer internet in several important ways. First, mistakes are costly in the industrial world. If Amazon makes a mistake in recommending you a book, the error is not very costly for you or Amazon. However, an error in a software algorithm for the industrial world could lead to the failure of a gas turbine, resulting in millions of dollars' worth of damage. Second, security for industrial equipment, such as a power plant, is far more critical. Third,

FIGURE 5-1

The power of 1%

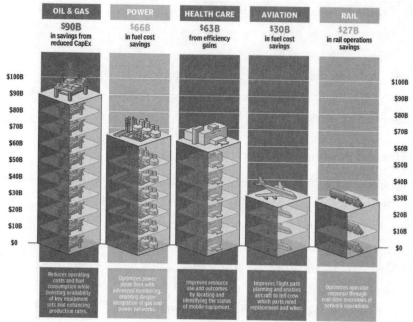

OIL & GAS	POWER	HEALTH CARE	AVIATION	RAIL
$90B in savings from reduced CapEx	$66B in fuel cost savings	$63B from efficiency gains	$30B in fuel cost savings	$27B in rail operations savings

Reduces operating costs and fuel consumption while boosting availability of key equipment sets and enhancing production rates.

Optimizes power plant fleet with advanced monitoring, enabling deeper integration of gas and power networks.

Improves resource use and outcomes by locating and identifying the status of mobile equipment.

Improves flight path planning and enables aircraft to tell crew which parts need replacement and when.

Optimizes operator response through real-time overviews of network operations.

INDUSTRIAL INTERNET BENEFITS

Source: Karim R. Lakhani, Marco Iansiti, and Kerry Herman, "GE and the Industrial Internet," Case 614–032 (Boston: Harvard Business School, 2014).

getting data from machines located in remote places, such as an oil rig in the Gulf of Mexico, is not possible using the consumer internet.

Next, GE built applications on top of its Predix platform. One suite of applications, for asset-performance management (APM), was designed to increase asset reliability and availability while reducing maintenance cost. This gave GE the ability to answer three critical questions: Will an asset fail? When will it fail? And what could GE do to prevent it from failing?

APM had a significant impact on GE's clients, such as Gerdau, a Brazilian steel producer that was looking to cut costs to remain competitive with its Chinese rivals. One area where Gerdau asked for GE's help was to reduce its $300 million annual maintenance costs by 40 percent. By doing an APM trial on fifty assets in one steel plant and monitoring their performance, GE was able to drive down Gerdau's maintenance costs significantly within a year. This successful trial led Gerdau to expand APM to its eleven plants and 600 assets. It also prompted other major steel manufacturers to reach out to GE for predictive maintenance.[6]

Remote monitoring and automated predictive maintenance—some of the common applications of the internet of things—are even more important for industries such as oil and gas, where a majority of assets are located in remote locations such as the arctic, offshore, or in deep waters. Many of these industries have mature assets with declining productivity, and failure is not only costly but has serious consequences for the safety of employees. McKinsey Global Institute estimates that operational efficiencies in factories through the internet of things has the potential to add $1.2 to $3.7 trillion in value annually to the global economy by 2025.[7]

Additive Manufacturing (3-D Printing)

In 2015, MX3D, a robotic 3-D-print-technology company, started building an intricate steel bridge in Amsterdam using its 3-D printing technology.[8] In February 2017, Apis Cor, a startup, used a mobile 3-D printer to build, on-site, a thirty-eight-square-meter (roughly four-hundred-square-foot) house in Russia.[9] In April 2017, MIT researchers were able to 3-D print a domelike structure fifty feet in diameter and twelve feet high, in fourteen hours.[10] Local Motors has built the first 3-D printed electric car, called Strati, which took only two months from initial design to prototype.[11] Using human cells instead of ink in the 3-D printer, Dr. Anthony Atala at Wake Forest Institute for Regenerative Medicine is "printing cells, bones, and even organs on an 800 pound steel machine called 'ITOP', or Integrated Tissue and Organ Printing System."[12]

In the last few years, 3-D printing has transitioned from being a mere curiosity for techies to prototyping for machines and printing large volumes of hearing aids and dental implants. It is now finding its way into the mainstream operations of companies. GE's aviation group started investigating 3-D printing many years ago for fuel nozzles that go into its jet engines. To reduce fuel consumption and emission from its jet engines, GE had developed a fuel nozzle with a complex interior design in which twenty different components had to be welded and brazed together. These parts not only had to come together with a high degree of precision but also had to be able to withstand very high temperatures and extreme weather conditions while the engine was in operation. Traditional manufacturing efforts to build this fuel nozzle had failed several times, which led GE to investigate 3-D technology.

GE partnered with Morris Technologies, a pioneer in 3-D printing. By adding thin layers of metal powder, Morris Technologies was able to successfully create fuel nozzles that not only passed the stringent quality tests of GE but also were less expensive to produce, weighed 25 percent less, and were five times more durable than traditional nozzles. Mohammad Ehteshami, former head of engineering at GE Aviation and current head of GE Additive, recalled his reaction to this experiment: "The technology was incredible. In the design of jet engines, complexity used to be expensive. But additive allows you to get sophisticated and reduce costs at the same time. This is an engineer's dream. I never imagined that this would be possible."[13] This successful attempt led GE to focus on mass production of 3-D–printed nozzles that would go into 12,200 units of its best-selling jet engine, LEAP. To achieve this goal, GE has "spent more than $1 billion to buy controlling stakes in two leading manufacturers of industrial 3D printers."[14]

In his 2016 annual letter to shareholders, Jeff Immelt, GE's CEO at the time, said that "the long-term market potential for additive manufacturing [is] huge at about $75 billion. We plan to build a business with $1 billion in revenue in additive equipment and service by 2020, from $300 million today."[15]

Implications of 3-D Printing

Additive manufacturing provides many benefits and has several implications that go beyond manufacturing:

- **Ability to Produce More Complex and Better Products**. As the GE case illustrates, in many cases traditional manufacturing processes are unable to produce a complex product that needs to combine or fuse several components. In addition, this technology has the potential to produce better and cheaper products. Airbus found that using 3-D printing for its brackets reduced material waste by 25 percent, carbon emissions by 40 percent, and airplane weight by ten kilograms.[16]

- **Customization**. In the fall of 2017, Mattel introduced Thing-Maker, a $300 3-D printer that allows kids to print their own toy parts that they could assemble through ball-and-socket joints to create a large number of Lego-like toys.[17] It is easy to imagine Mattel updating the software of this device to continuously introduce new toy components and new designs without shipping any physical product through retailers. Adidas is testing a service that would allow consumers to use their smartphones to scan their feet, upload that information onto the Adidas site, and customize the design and color of their shoes. As the technology advances, it is conceivable that Adidas could bring this technology into its stores, where consumers could get their personalized 3-D printed shoes made on the premises while they wait. In health care, customization through 3-D printing is already being used for prosthetics and surgical implants. According to Gartner, a research and advisory company, by 2019 "3D printing will be used in over 35% of all surgical procedures requiring prosthetic and implant devices . . . and up to 10% of the people in the developed world will be living with 3D-printed items on or in their bodies."[18]

- **On-Demand Production**. 3-D printing can also decentralize manufacturing so that actual production is done on-demand and closer to the consumer. As the cost of 3-D printing comes down, this will reduce the scale advantage of having large factories in a single location. On-demand, on-site production can be especially useful when the product is needed in hard-to-reach places such as disaster-relief sites, oil rigs, navy ships, or the space station. When doctors in an earthquake-stricken area of Nepal had trouble getting basic medical equipment, Field Ready, a nonprofit organization that uses 3-D–printing technology to transform logistics for humanitarian organizations, came to the rescue.[19] According to a DHL report "in 2014 the US Navy installed 3D printers on the USS *Essex* to train sailors to print needed parts and weapon components, reducing lead time and enabling access to critical parts in remote situations."[20] NASA is also working with a company called Made in Space, which is using 3-D printing to build necessary tools at the International Space Station.

- **Reduced Cost of Inventory and Logistics**. On-demand production dramatically reduces inventory, warehousing, and logistics costs. For companies, like Amazon, with very high fulfillment and logistics costs, this provides an attractive opportunity. Not surprisingly, Amazon has filed a patent that would allow a mobile truck to do on-demand printing of customer orders closer to their homes. An MIT study shows that on-demand printing of products has the potential to reduce supply chain costs by anywhere from 50 percent to 90 percent due to major cost reductions coming from transportation and inventory costs.[21]

- **Design Platforms**. As technology automates production and allows for customization at a reasonable cost, the competitive advantage may shift to design. This also has the potential to open up competition from independent designers and small companies, which in turn would lead to the emergence of platforms and marketplaces. Shapeways, a spin-off of the Dutch conglomerate Philips, is one such marketplace, selling digital designs online for products ranging from bracelets to chairs. 3DShoes.com has created a digital shoe marketplace for designers and fashionistas.

- **Intellectual Property**. In 2015, global sales of licensed retail merchandise topped $250 billion, 45 percent of which was due to entertainment characters from movies such as *Star Wars*.[22] By reducing inventory, transportation, and even manufacturing costs, 3-D printing could help companies like Disney reduce the cost of selling these items, allowing the companies instead simply to sell digital designs to consumers. However, as digital designs get pirated, there is the potential risk of counterfeit products inundating the market. The music industry faced a similar dilemma as it shifted to digital production and distribution. Companies would need to think carefully about how to protect their intellectual property.

- **Impact on Workforce.** Decentralized manufacturing enabled by 3-D printing is likely to bring manufacturing back from emerging markets to developed economies. This would have a significant impact on the economies of countries like Vietnam and Bangladesh, which—after China—have become global centers of manufacturing due to their cheap labor. On-demand production would also reduce the need to store products, which would dramatically affect the retail, transportation, and warehousing industries.

According to McKinsey Global Institute, the worldwide economic impact of 3-D printing from all the activities mentioned above could range from $180 billion to as high as $490 billion by 2025.[23] However, some critics see this as hype and wonder if 3-D printing will ever be as economical as traditional manufacturing for mass production. Perhaps this explains why a 2016 report from Ernst & Young found that more than 76 percent of the nine hundred companies in its global survey have no experience with 3-D printing.[24] While high-volume, standardized production for some products, such as automobiles, is unlikely to be replaced by 3-D printing in the near future, increasing numbers of other products will come to be manufactured in such a fashion, as the cost of 3-D printing comes down and the quality of the technology dramatically improves.

Developments in additive manufacturing are already moving beyond 3-D printing. In its self-assembly lab, MIT is experimenting with 4-D printing, in which an object can transform itself in a preprogrammed way in response to a stimulus such as a change in temperature or contact with water.[25] With this technology, water pipes would be able to expand and contract in different temperatures to maintain water flow, and car tires would be able to change their tread according to changes in road conditions. In 4-D printing, the program is embedded in the material itself, allowing the material to transform its shape. Given the pace of technological change, it would be short-sighted for any product company not to investigate this exciting new area.

Augmented and Virtual Reality

Virtual reality (VR), which immerses you in a virtual world, and augmented reality (AR), which overlays virtual elements on a physical product, have improved dramatically in recent years. In the past, many applications of these technologies have been in the consumer domain: Gaming industries have used VR for immersive games. The tourism industry has given potential visitors a real taste of, say, Venice or Paris without the would-be travelers having to leave their homes. Automobile companies are using the technology for virtual test-driving. And real-estate companies are allowing potential buyers to virtually walk through several homes in a short period of time.

These technologies are now being increasingly used for design, assembly, and training in industrial settings.

- **Design**. Whether you are an architect or a manufacturer of airplanes or appliances, creating a prototype of your design has been the standard practice for years. The advent of CAD/CAM technology made this task easier, and now 3-D printing is making it even easier, faster, and less costly. The next revolution in product design is VR that allows designers to virtually interact with their creation and modify it. Lockheed Martin engineers are using VR to visualize their designs before building a spacecraft for NASA's mission to Mars. Going beyond the limitations of a scaled-down model of a prototype, VR allows engineers to be

virtually inside a real spacecraft, which makes it easier for them
to spot and fix errors, and to do so at a much lower cost than traditional approaches allow. Lockheed Martin has built what it calls
a collaborative human immersive laboratory, which allows it to
"analyze designs and manufacturing processes in virtual worlds
prior to physical manufacturing."[26]

- **Assembly.** Building complex products such as wind turbines or
  commercial aircraft requires hundreds of steps during the assembly process. Augmented reality—delivered via wearable devices
  such as smart glasses—overlays computer-generated instructional
  videos, images, or text, all of which enables engineers to operate efficiently and accurately without having to rely on physical
  manuals. These devices are being used in manufacturing, warehousing, and field operations. GE technicians have used them for
  wiring a wind turbine's control box, which improved technicians'
  performance by 34 percent.[27] Reporting on the productivity
  improvement from AR, one article states, "[A] study conducted
  by Boeing showed that AR improved productivity in wiring harness assembly by 25%. And at GE Healthcare a warehouse worker
  receiving a new picklist order through AR completed the task
  46% faster than when using the standard process, which relies on
  a paper list and items searches on a work station. Additional cases
  from GE and several other firms show an average productivity
  improvement of 32%."[28]

- **Training.** For decades, brain surgeons have been preparing for
  surgery by looking at 2-D images of a brain scan and using their
  experience to imagine what they might encounter during the
  actual surgery. VR allows them to navigate the 3-D image of a
  patient's brain beforehand, which eliminates surprises during
  the operation itself and, as a consequence, significantly improves
  success rates. Touch Surgery, a London-based company, has
  developed two hundred training centers that would allow sur-
  gical training using mobile phones and tablets. In the future,

the company plans to use its technology to provide assistance to doctors in operating rooms.[29] Walmart is planning to use VR instructions in each of its two hundred Walmart Academy centers in the United States to train 150,000 employees each year.[30] More and more companies are beginning to use VR for training purposes. Bosch is using Oculus Rift, a VR system, to train its automotive technicians about direct-injection and braking technology. General Motors is distributing Google glasses to be used in the training of new factory workers. The National Football League is using VR to train and improve the performance of athletes. Lowe's is using Microsoft's HoloLens to develop how-to VR videos for helping consumers with their home-improvement projects.

Goldman Sachs estimates that the market for AR and VR will be between $80 billion and $182 billion by 2025.[31] It also suggests that VR and AR have the potential to become the next big computing platform that will have a major impact on many industries, similar to what we experienced with PCs and smartphones. Not surprisingly, all major digital players—Google, Facebook, Microsoft, Amazon—are investing heavily in these technologies. Once again, it will be wise for companies to understand the potential of these technologies and to take inspiration from the early users to create their own unique advantage.

Digital Supply Chains

Technology is transforming not just design and manufacturing. It is revolutionizing the entire supply chain, including warehousing, inventory management, logistics, and delivery.

Demand-Driven Supply Chain

Consumer-product companies are using sensors on shelves in retail stores to monitor real-time shifts in demand. Using computer vision (i.e., acquiring and processing images), sensors, and deep learning,

Amazon can detect when a customer picks up a product from the shelf in its Amazon Go store. By using data analytics and monitoring real-time shifts in demand, Kimberly-Clark Corp., a consumer-goods company, has built a demand-driven supply chain that helps reduce the company's forecasting error by as much as 35 percent for a one-week planning horizon and its finished goods inventory by 19 percent over eighteen months.[32]

Procter & Gamble, designated as one of the supply chain "masters" by Gartner in its 2017 report, links daily demand flows from point of sales to distribution centers and plants and even to its suppliers.[33] Amazon, whose clothing and apparel sales were expected to grow to $28 billion by the end of 2017, has obtained a patent for on-demand apparel manufacturing that would dramatically cut down its inventory cost and enable it to avoid deep discounting of unsold products.[34] Zara, the fast-fashion leader, is putting RFID chips into its merchandise. Each time a garment is sold, the chip sends a message to the stockroom to replace that item in the store. Not only does this free up employees from having to take frequent inventory to avoid stockouts. It also gives Zara an accurate picture of real-time demand and which fashion items are selling. Nestlé is exploring using sensors in vending machines with auto-replenishment capabilities. Demand-driven supply chains have an even greater benefit for high-tech companies that face shorter product life cycles and decreasing component costs over time.

Real-time information and data analytics are key to implementing demand-driven supply chains. Amazon uses these resources to predict the demand for various products near each of its fulfillment centers, to ensure that the correct (and correct number of) items are stocked at each location. This capability enabled Amazon to launch Prime Now and to promise delivery within an hour. In a move that evokes images from *Star Wars*, Amazon has filed a patent for a "flying warehouse," equipped with drones, that will move close to key locations based on their demand patterns.

According to Gartner, demand-driven supply chains are able to reduce inventory by 15 percent, increase order fill rates by 20 percent or more, increase revenues by 2 percent on average, and improve gross margins by 3 percent to 5 percent.[35] If your company does not have these systems in place, you are missing out on a significant opportunity to improve your operations and supply chain.

Warehousing, Logistics, and Fulfillment

Jeff Bezos's mantra of "start with the customer and work backwards" drives everything at Amazon, including its warehousing and fulfillment strategy. In its customer surveys, Amazon found that speed remains the most important aspect of delivery (see figure 5-2).

Delivering individual packages to customers within a day or two (or an hour or two in the case of Amazon Prime Now), with close to 100 percent accuracy, when you have to pick, pack, and ship that package from a warehouse that stocks millions of items, is a nontrivial task. And it isn't cheap. In the second quarter of 2017, Amazon's fulfillment cost of over $5 billion was almost 14 percent of its total operating expenses. Not surprisingly, Amazon relies heavily on technology to increase speed and reduce fulfillment cost. Its acquisition of Kiva Systems for $775 million in 2012 transformed the way Amazon manages its warehouses using robots. One of the largest of Amazon's warehouses—in Etna, Ohio—has

FIGURE 5-2

Amazon customers' most important factors for delivery

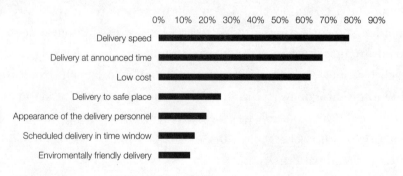

Source: Amazon customer survey, 2017, courtesy of Rohit Sodha, Amazon's country lead for transportation in Middle Europe.

more than a million square feet of space and stocks 50 percent more inventory than standard warehouses, since robots eliminate the need to have wide aisles.[36] Locus Robotics, a startup based in Andover, Massachusetts, has developed the next generation of robots for warehouses. By using its robot, called LocusBot, Quiet Logistics—a third-party logistics company that does fulfillment for Gilt, Bonobos, and Zara—was able to increase its productivity by eight times.[37]

In addition to using robots, tagging individual items with RFID chips enables better and more accurate management of inventory. American Woodmark, a manufacturer of cabinets and vanities, is using nine million RFID tags to track material in its factories and warehouses, which has "reduced the labor for cycle counting—a regular inventory process—by 66% and improved accuracy from roughly 80% to 100%."[38] RFID tags on its merchandise has enabled Macy's to inventory items in its stores every month instead of once or twice annually, and this has increased the accuracy of its inventory to 95 percent.[39] Airlines are using RFID tags for tracking luggage so that a customer can be told about lost baggage ahead of time instead of waiting at the baggage area in frustration.

With the rise of e-commerce, delivery has become more critical than ever before. The last mile of delivery is perhaps the most complicated and expensive part of any delivery operation. With more than 100,000 trucks, cars, and vans, UPS delivers 19.1 million packages every day around the globe.[40] Running this large fleet of vehicles is complex and expensive. Reduction of every single mile driven by its fleet can improve the company's profitability by $50 million. Which route a driver takes can significantly affect his efficiency and fuel consumption of his truck. To design an optimal route to maximize efficiency and minimize fuel consumption, known as the "traveling salesman" problem in operations research, is a complex problem. The 120 stops that a driver makes on a typical day can be routed in trillions of ways. To solve this problem, UPS installed chips in its trucks to monitor their real-time movement. Knowing the location of a driver and the real-time traffic information, route-optimization software called ORION (on-road integrated optimization and navigation) directs the driver to take the optimal route. In the four years since its roll out, ORION has eliminated 1.6 million hours of truck idling time, and has produced an annual savings of 85 million miles in driving and 8.5 million gallons in fuel consumption.[41] The company expects to save from $300 million to $400 million a year after the program is fully implemented (which it was scheduled to be by the end of 2017).[42] With autonomous driving on the horizon, ORION can potentially maneuver a truck automatically, without any human intervention. DHL is also testing this idea with its SmartTrucks, which use RFID chips and route-planning software to ensure—respectively—that the right products are loaded onto the right trucks and that those trucks avoid city traffic jams during delivery.

Operational Excellence in Service Industries

Using technology to improve operational efficiency is not limited to product companies. Real-time data flow and automation are radically transforming service industries as well. For several years banks have been using online and mobile banking to reduce their transaction costs and the overall number of their bank branches as well as to enhance customer experience. In the health-care industry, the use of electronic medical records is enabling hospitals and doctors to have a complete view of a patient across hospitals and physicians.

Goldman Sachs is in the process of automating its IPO process. The company broke down a typical deal into 127 steps and then went on to identify that about half of these steps could be handled by algorithms. According to Bloomberg, "a computer interface called Deal Link has replaced informal checklists that were once tended and passed down between generations of rainmakers. It now arranges and tracks legal and compliance reviews, fills in forms and generates reports."[43] Goldman is now expanding this idea to other areas, such as mergers and acquisitions and bond sales. This change in Goldman's strategy is reflected in a shift in the composition of its workforce. Approximately nine thousand of its employees, or one-fourth of Goldman's current staff, are engineers.[44]

Auditing companies like Deloitte are using artificial intelligence and machine learning to identify high-risk accounting areas and to spot patterns in financial transactions. Like Goldman, Deloitte and other auditing companies can automate a large portion of their tasks. Such automation can reduce costs and increase reach to small businesses that currently can't afford the services of Deloitte or PwC. Instead of waiting for quarterly statements, clients can receive automated, real-time information, which can be very helpful for managing their businesses. Effectively, auditing could shift from being a tool for reporting what happened in the past to being a valuable asset for helping clients figure out how to run their businesses in the future.

Technology is also making a significant impact in the legal industry. Companies like Rocket Lawyer in the United States and LawCanvas in Singapore and Malaysia are offering consumers and small businesses legal templates at affordable rates.[45] Online marketplaces for legal services, such as Asia Law Network, are emerging to match demand and supply. A new service called LawGeex allows users to upload documents related to legal cases and to compare those against a database of documents from similar cases, eliminating hundreds of hours spent by junior associates in a law firm.[46] IBM Watson has developed an application, ROSS, that allows lawyers to ask questions in plain English. LexisNexis developed Lexis Advance MedMal Navigator that allows malpractice attorneys to determine within twenty minutes whether a case is worth pursuing. Lex Machina has created a database for intellectual-property litigation that uses historical information to calculate the odds of winning a case.[47]

In conclusion, technology is making inroads in the operations of both product and service companies. Factories, warehouses, supply chains, and internal processes are poised for a significant transformation in the near future. Companies that position themselves to leverage these emerging technologies are likely to have a significant competitive advantage.

Chapter 6

Omnichannel Strategy

Soon after his appointment as chairman and CEO of the French hotel chain AccorHotels in August 2013, Sébastien Bazin confronted a major challenge. Online travel agencies (OTAs), such as Travelocity, were gaining a greater share of hotel bookings. He realized that OTAs were both a blessing and a curse—they were an important source of business for his hotels, yet their increasing power was a threat to Accor's long-run profitability. In India, meanwhile, an insurance company was facing a similar challenge. It had built its business almost entirely through insurance brokers, but as digital technology evolved and consumer behavior changed, the company faced the dilemma of how to develop the online channel without jeopardizing its broker business. Back in the United States, many retailers have been facing internal competition from their own e-commerce ventures and continue to grapple with the question of how to craft a unified strategy for their physical and digital stores.

As the world moves from bricks to clicks, companies are struggling to develop an effective omnichannel strategy. By now everyone recognizes that the choice is not whether to have physical stores or digital channels but how to manage both at the same time. How do you avoid channel conflict? How should you link digital and physical channels?

Should physical stores be redesigned as digital channels evolve? In this chapter we will explore some of these questions.

Are Channels Substitutes?

Inherent in the discussion of channel conflict is the assumption that different channels compete with each other as substitutes. The insurance company believes that the online channel would take away business from brokers and that this would create conflict. Financial services firms are concerned about the reaction of their brokers as robo-advising gains traction. Banks feel that online banking would replace branch banking. Retailers see online shopping coming at the expense of sales in their stores.

To some extent these beliefs are true, and in the long run online transactions may indeed replace a large fraction of physical transactions. However, the challenge is how to manage the transition. How do you build the online channel without jeopardizing the large and often profitable business from the offline channel? The key to managing this transition is to think of different channels as complements, not as substitutes. Each channel is best suited for certain products, for a specific group of customers, or for a certain part of a consumer's decision journey. The trick is to identify these complementarities and build around them.

Complementarity Across Products

Consider the case of the Indian insurance company. In my conversation with the company's CEO, he described the situation as follows:

> With the large mobile penetration in India and changing
> consumer behavior, I am convinced that the future of our
> company lies in a well-developed digital channel. This channel
> will not only be more convenient for our consumers, but it will
> also be significantly cheaper and it will allow us to collect valuable
> consumer data to target them effectively with personalized offers.
> The old way of selling insurance through independent brokers

is likely to become a thing of the past in five to ten years. But brokers see any investment in the digital channel as a threat to their very survival and are threatening to take their business away to our competitors.

How do you manage this conflict? A solution that is often considered in these situations is to offer the same commission to brokers even if customers do transactions online. However, as the online channel gains traction, this option becomes increasingly costly and unsupportable, as brokers benefit without putting in the requisite effort.

After much discussion and debate, the senior management team realized that given current consumer behavior, the online channel was perhaps best suited for selling simple products. With its extensive reach and low cost of marketing, this channel could become an effective and efficient customer acquisition tool. And once customers were acquired through the online channel, they could be handed over to existing brokers, who could cross-sell more expensive and complex products to them. This approach appealed to brokers, too, since it reduced their burden of customer acquisition, leaving them to focus on selling complex, higher-margin products that required their expertise. Now, as the company gains experience in building its online channel and as customers become more comfortable in navigating through a complex array of products on this channel, the company expects to see an increasing migration of customers and of revenues from its physical distribution system to its digital channel.

Let's consider another case—this time for one of the largest luggage companies in India, VIP Industries. The company manufactured the first VIP suitcase in 1971, and since then it has sold over sixty million pieces of luggage worldwide. It has 8,000 retail outlets in India and a network of 1,300 retailers across twenty-seven countries. In one of my visits to India, I met Radhika Piramal, the managing director of VIP Industries and an alumnus of Harvard Business School, who mentioned a difficulty similar to that of the insurance company—how to build VIP Industries' digital channel without alienating its independent retailers and distributors? At that time VIP Industries generated almost all its business from the offline retailers, but it believed that future growth would come from the online channel.

Once again it helps to think about the role each channel might play for different products. In the case of VIP Industries, retailers carry only a limited set of products, usually the best-selling variety. The online channel can offer more variety and customize products for consumers by, say, engraving their names on the luggage or even producing luggage in unique colors. Such offerings would not cannibalize retail sales. Instead, they would provide different and complementary products to a subset of customers who desire distinct, customized choices. And even though it is cheaper to serve customers through digital channels, the company could charge a premium for these offers, further reducing cannibalization and potential conflict with its retailers. Over time the digital channel would grow as the company gains more experience and as customer behavior evolves.

Complementarity Across Customers

If you were to ask any bank about its digital strategy, you would probably hear that it is closing retail branches and migrating customers to its digital and mobile channels. This was true for most of the banks in Turkey— except for one, QNB Finansbank, the fifth-largest private bank in Turkey.[1]

Founded in 1987 by Hüsnü Özyeğin, Finansbank initially focused on wholesale commercial banking, serving the needs of Turkish corporations that local banks did not cater to. A decade later, as retail banking flourished in Turkey, Finansbank entered that market with a focus on mass segment through credit cards and consumer loans. In 2010, Ömer Aras, the chairman and one of the founding members of Finansbank, noted a big gap in its customer base. "We were quite strong on the retail end of the mass market," Aras said, "and we had a pretty good presence on the private banking side. The in-between area, which was the fast-growing middle-income segment, was essentially ignored."

Aras and Temel Güzeloğlu, the company's CEO, considered offering the existing services of the bank to this new consumer segment, but they had a hard time coming up with a unique value proposition that would distinguish Finansbank from its competitors. By 2010, the Turkish banking industry had strong and sophisticated banks, such as Garanti Bank and Akbank, which dominated every segment of the market. To create differentiation and to serve this tech-savvy mass segment, Finansbank created a completely new brand, called Enpara, a purely digital bank with no branches and high interest rates, offering ease of use and a strong focus on the customer experience. Within a year of its launch, Enpara acquired 110,000 customers and three billion Turkish lire in deposit. Three years after its launch, Enpara became profitable and boasted an enviable customer satisfaction rate of 99.4 percent.

Complementarity Across Customer Lifecycle

Different channels may serve customers at different stages of their decision journey, as illustrated by the L'Oréal case. In 2011, Carol Hamilton, the president of the Luxe Division of L'Oréal USA, was contemplating the role of different channels for Kiehl's, one of the beauty brands that L'Oréal had acquired in 2000. The Luxe portfolio consisted of eight brands, including Lancôme, Giorgio Armani, Ralph Lauren, Yves St. Laurent, and Viktor & Rolf.

"Kiehl's Since 1851," as the company is officially known, was founded in 1851 in New York City by John Kiehl.[2] Since its inception, the company has avoided advertising and has instead focused on extensive personal consultation with its customers to offer them the right products. Kiehl's started with a single store and over time came to include fifty-two company-owned retail locations around the country. In 1975, the company's distribution strategy changed and Kiehl's started offering its products in department stores such as Neiman Marcus and Bloomingdale's. Later Kiehl's started its own e-commerce channel to offer the company's products to consumers on the web. By 2010, Kiehl's was generating $121 million in sales by three different channels (see table 6-1).

Throughout its evolution Kiehl's stayed true to its "no advertising" policy to keep its exclusive appeal. However, this strategy came at the cost of underexposure. A March 2009 study of beauty brands showed

TABLE 6-1

Kiehl's sales and profitability by channel

Channel	% of sales	Operating profit as % of sales
Company stores	48%	17.9%
Department stores	42%	17.6%
Kiehls.com	10%	40.0%

Source: Adapted from Robert J. Dolan and Leslie K. John, "Kiehl's Since 1851: Pathway to Profitable Growth," Case 514-044 (Boston: Harvard Business School, 2013, revised 2015).

that awareness of Kiehl's among women eighteen years old and older was only 12 percent, compared with 73 percent for Lancôme and 88 percent for Estée Lauder. Hamilton's challenge was to grow brand sales by 15 percent per year for the next five years while being consistent with the original heritage of the brand. She elaborated:

> How do we best manage "going to market" in so many different ways with Kiehl's? We want to accommodate the way a Kiehl's buyer wants to shop. Lots of companies are now dealing with "bricks and clicks" integration. We have to harmoniously manage two sets of "bricks and clicks"—our own and our retail partners'.[3]

Looking at table 6-1 it may be tempting to conclude that Kiehl's should retrench from its expensive brick-and-mortar stores and instead grow its e-commerce business, which accounted for only 10 percent of the company's sales but which also generated a significantly higher margin. However, after rigorous consumer research and careful analysis, Hamilton and her team concluded that each channel serves a unique purpose at different stages of its customers' decision journey.

Company-owned stores, with their engaging window displays, serve as expensive billboards to intrigue passersby and entice new customers. Once a customer walks into a store, a trained salesperson can communicate the Kiehl's value proposition to her and identify the best products that might suit her. In effect, these stores are a great vehicle for customer *acquisition*. Department stores and other retail partners generate lots of foot traffic and also help in extending the reach of the Kiehl's brand. Given the brand's low awareness, the company's e-commerce site is used mostly by existing Kiehl's customers looking to find new products or to order supplies of their favorite product. In other words, the online channel serves best for customer *retention*.

Recognizing this role of the online channel, Brigitte King, the senior vice president of digital strategy, e-commerce, and CRM for the Luxe Division, launched several successful retention programs. An example of this was the "four touch" program for buyers of the company's Midnight Recovery Concentrate, a product that was offered in a one-ounce bottle for $46 and would typically be consumed in twelve weeks. Seven days after purchase, the company sent its customers a "thank you" email along with information on what results they should expect at this time. Fourteen days after purchase, the customers received recommendations for complementary products (which they could buy on Kiehls.com) along with results to be expected after fourteen days of use. After twenty-one days, customers received testimonials from "customers like you" and results expected after three weeks of product usage. And twelve weeks from purchase, customers received a message with the headline "Are You Down to Your Last Drop?" along with a link to "Shop Now" at Kiehls.com.

Managing Channel Conflict and Gaining Channel Power

Sometimes offline and online channels do create significant conflict for a company. Sébastien Bazin, the chairman and CEO of Accor hotels, saw this conflict grow out of the rising power of online travel agencies (OTAs).[4] By aggregating demand for multiple hotel properties, OTAs managed a 23 percent penetration in the European hotel market in 2014, compared with only 9 percent by hotels' own websites. In 2015, Priceline and its online platform, Booking.com, offered rooms from 600,000 hotels that attracted over 234 million unique monthly visitors and generated $50 billion in gross bookings. In contrast, even with its global footprint, Accor had only about 4,000 hotels and 2014 gross revenue of €12 billion.

Accor is not alone in facing this pain. Almost all hotels and airlines are facing similar pressure from OTAs. These channel partners are both friends and enemies at the same time—friends because they bring additional business in an industry (hotels) with high fixed costs and an average occupancy rate that doesn't reach 70 percent, but also enemies because they divert a large portion of traffic from a hotel's own website and because bookings made through OTAs cost hotel owners as much as 25 percent in commission. Summing up the ongoing battle between hotels and OTAs, technology consultant Robert Cole said, "So the burning question is what is more powerful—brand or distribution?"[5]

In the United States, airlines have been handling a similar challenge with a variety of different approaches. Southwest Airlines refuses to make its inventory available to OTAs—perhaps as a result of its unique position in the industry as a low-cost carrier and its loyal customer base. In an attempt to regain control, American Airlines, in December 2010, decided to make its own inventory unavailable to OTAs. However, recognizing consumers' desire to compare prices across various airlines, in June 2011 an Illinois court ordered American Airlines to make its flights available through OTAs. Even without the court order, American Airlines' strategy was not sustainable in the long run since the OTAs control a large portion of demand in the airline industry.

Bazin was keenly aware of how channel conflict was playing out in the airline industry. He was also intrigued by a new initiative, Room Key, started by a consortium of six major hotels (Choice, Hilton, Hyatt, IHG, Marriott, and Wyndham). By creating Room Key, the hotels hoped to offer consumers an alternative to OTAs. In addition to some financial investment in Room Key, each hotel partner decided to redirect to Room Key 10 percent of the customer traffic that exited its own proprietary website without booking. Since only 5 percent of customers that visit a hotel website actually make a booking there, this represented a large pool of customers who could be directed to Room Key and from there potentially to one of the other five hotel partners.

For Bazin it was a difficult decision whether or not to join Room Key. While it provided a counter to the growing power of OTAs, Room Key did not have the resources to build a brand and generate awareness among consumers. Trivago and Expedia spent over $100 million each to build their brands. Priceline's global ad-search budget with Google was estimated to be over $1 billion in 2012. And even with six hotel partners, Room Key would have only 75,000 hotels on its site compared with 435,000 on Expedia and 600,000 on Priceline. Was Room Key the answer to Accor's problems?

The Enemy of My Enemy Is My Friend

As OTAs continued to wield more power, new players were emerging in this field. Two in particular caught Bazin's attention—Google launched instant booking, which allowed consumers to book hotel rooms directly on Google without navigating through hotel or OTA sites, and TripAdvisor, which until recently had been a lead generator for OTAs, decided to offer hotel booking on its own site. In order to gain traction in a market dominated by Priceline and Expedia, these new aggregators were charging almost half the commission rate of traditional OTAs. So instead of joining Room Key, Accor decided to partner with Google and TripAdvisor, hoping to reduce the power of Priceline and other OTAs.

In a further attempt to create a balance of power, Accor—in 2015—became an OTA itself. The company changed its name to AccorHotels and started offering independent hotels the opportunity to make their rooms available on its booking site, at commission rates lower than those charged by traditional OTAs. Explaining this move, Bazin said, "Transforming our distribution platform into an open marketplace is a major initiative for the Group . . . We are becoming a trustworthy, selective and transparent third party . . ."[6] However, two years later it abandoned this strategy as it had difficulty attracting other hotels to its site.

Is Channel Conflict the Real Problem?

For Accor, perhaps an even more important matter to consider is whether channel conflict is its real problem. After all, OTAs bring in new customers to Accor properties—customers who otherwise might not have found Accor. Is Accor doing enough to ensure that these customers keep coming back to its properties? In 2014, the company's loyalty program, *Le Club Accorhotels*, had eighteen million members but only 24 percent of them booked directly with Accor. Why are Accor's loyal customers not booking directly on its site? If Accor offers a superior value to its customers, we would expect a much higher booking rate on its site. Amazon's customers are far less likely to comparison shop on the web than Accor customers seem to be doing, even though Amazon sells standard products that are available at many other retailers.

Physical and Digital Fusion

Talk to any retailer and you would hear of the importance of embedding technology, such as beacons, in stores. Beacons would capture data about consumer traffic patterns, data that would enhance retailers' ability to serve their customers—at least that is the theory. Yet there is hardly a retailer who has been able to leverage such data effectively. Starting with technology is rarely productive. Instead, ask yourself what consumer problems you are trying to solve and how technology might enable you to solve those problems.

In a retail environment there are at least four consumer pain points that warrant attention:

- **Finding Things.** How many times have you gone to a hardware store, a bookstore, or a department store and been unable to find the exact item that you were looking for? And how difficult was it to find a sales associate who was willing and knowledgeable enough to assist you? You don't need to do market research to know that this is a common pain point for consumers. It has an easy solution, too: Retailers can install kiosks or iPads in strategic locations in the stores, and customers can use these to search for items. If it turns out the items are unavailable in the store, customers can use the same devices to order them online. Yet retailers who are willing to invest millions in sophisticated technology have given little thought to this simple solution that addresses a major pain point of consumers.

Hointer, a retail-technology consulting firm based in Seattle, prototyped a new store to solve this consumer problem. When customers walk into a Hointer store, they see over 150 styles of jeans, shirts, and tops hanging from steel cables. Not all sizes and colors are visible, but if a customer likes a particular style, he or she can scan a barcode on the selected item, indicating the desired size, and walk to a nearby dressing room. Within thirty seconds, micro-robots dispatch the products to the dressing room from the back of the store via chutes. Customers can try on the items, discard the ones they don't want in a chute, and pay for the selected items in the same dressing room by swiping their credit cards. Since products are stored in the back of the store rather than displayed on shelves, Hointer stores have one-fifth the floor space and half the number of staff of a typical retail store. Apart from lowering costs and making shopping easier and faster, this approach has increased sales, as customers end up trying on—and buying—many more products. Hointer found its shoppers, on average, try on twelve items instead of the usual three to five, which has in turn increased sales by 30 percent to 50 percent.

- **Trying Things.** Most consumers want to try multiple items before selecting the one they'll buy. Recognizing this desire, companies that were once purely digital players, such as Bonobos, Warby Parker, and Rent the Runway, have started opening physical stores. Sephora, the French chain that sells over three hundred cosmetic and beauty brands, including makeup, lotions, fragrances, nail polish, and hair-care products, always knew the importance of offering free samples of products in its stores for consumers to try. However, the company recognized that consumers are informed and influenced by online content offered not only by the company itself but also by several independent "beauty gurus" who have large followings on YouTube. Sephora already had a strong digital presence, but as a next step, its mobile app now allows customers to scan physical displays in stores in order to view online content such as customer reviews and tutorials on YouTube on how to use specific products. And in March 2017, Sephora launched the Sephora virtual-assistant app, which allows customers to scan their faces and virtually apply different lip colors, eye shadows, and eye lashes.

teamLab, a Japanese company of creative professionals and engineers who call themselves ultra-technologists, designed an interactive hanger for clothes. When a consumer picks up a dress from one of these hangers, the wall in front of the consumer turns into a giant digital display showing several models wearing that particular dress. It is not hard to imagine extending this technology to show the consumer, instead of models, on the display screen with that dress.

- **Paying for Things.** Perhaps the worst part of a shopping experience is when you've found the ideal product but have to wait in a long line to pay for it. And there is always someone in front of you who needs to return some item—which will take a very long time. Why can't retailers make the payment process easier and more efficient for consumers?

  Starbucks's mobile app has been a huge success because it solved exactly this problem for consumers. You can now order and pay ahead using your Starbucks app, and by the time you reach the store, your steaming hot cappuccino will be waiting for you. Panera Bread has also started offering its customers the option to pay within its app, using Apple Pay, so that they won't have to wait in line to pay when they come to pick up their order. Amazon surprised everyone by testing a new store concept, Amazon Go, which allows its prime members to walk into its store, pick up any item or items, and simply walk out—no need to stand in line to pay for anything, since Amazon already has your credit card if you are a prime member and the technology in the store recognizes you.

- **Returning Things.** According to the National Retail Federation, over 10 percent of the holiday gifts purchased in 2015 were returned. Return rates for online purchases are even higher, estimated to range from 15 percent to 30 percent. While returns are costly for retailers, allowing them has to be weighed against the potential benefit of making it easier for consumers to buy without worrying about the difficulty of returning the items. Often, returning the items is a very painful experience for consumers—they have to stand in a separate line that has limited staff and a long wait. For some retailers, this is part of a deliberate strategy to dissuade consumers from returning products. However, making the shopping experience difficult and painful for consumers is usually not very productive in the long run.

   Recently some retailers have been trying to improve consumers' experience with returning items. In early 2017, the Nordstrom Rack in New York's Union Square was testing a "Drop & Go" service that allowed customers to scan an item and drop it off without standing in line for a cashier. Happy Returns, a Santa Monica–based startup, is opening "return bars" for e-commerce companies that do not have any physical presence.[7]

As Jeff Bezos, the founder and CEO of Amazon, has often said, the goal of a company should be to remove friction for consumers, and technology should be used to do exactly that.

Disney's MagicBand

For decades, Disney's Magic Kingdom in Orlando, Florida, has been delighting young children and their families with their favorite characters and amazing rides. However, the rising popularity of the theme park created long lines and unbearable wait times at premier attractions such as Space Mountain. To solve this problem, Disney started a program called FastPass, which guaranteed a ride time for popular attractions. Passes were issued at the rides and stamped with a designated return time. Although the idea was to reduce the frustration of families waiting for hours in line for their favorite ride, the way in which passes were issued had an unintended consequence. Families would wait anxiously outside the theme park, and as soon as it opened they would rush to get these passes. Many families would devise elaborate plans to split into different teams so as to get as many passes as possible—hardly a magical experience for consumers.

To solve this consumer problem, Disney introduced the FastPass+ online system, where consumers could reserve up to three rides in advance. It also created MagicBand, a stylish rubber wristband with a built-in RFID chip. Now, when you book your ticket online and pick your favorite rides, Disney's computers analyze your preferences and create a personalized itinerary, which—along with your FastPass+ reservations—are loaded onto your MagicBand. When you arrive at the park, you don't need any tickets or credit cards—you just tap your MagicBand at the gate, at rides, or at restaurants.

Disney has also installed thousands of sensors throughout the park, which communicate with the MagicBands and convert the park into a giant computer system. If you make a reservation and order your food in advance at its restaurant called Be Our Guest, sensors near the restaurant alert the employees of your arrival and the kitchen starts preparing your food, which magically appears soon after you sit at a table.[8] If the sensors detect too many visitors approaching a ride, Disney can, in real-time, start a parade around the corner to entertain guests without them experiencing the pain of waiting for their ride. The technology also allows Disney employees to optimize their time. Instead of handling tickets and payments they can now spend more time with guests and help create magical memories. By blending the digital and physical worlds, Disney is creating a truly magical experience for its guests.

Amazon's Omnichannel Experiment

In recent years Amazon shocked the retail industry by opening a handful of physical stores. Why would a highly successful e-commerce player open physical stores when it had gained a unique competitive advantage by eliminating the fixed costs associated with brick-and-mortar stores? There are at least four reasons for Amazon to test this omnichannel strategy.

1. **New Product Categories.** Retail stores continue to dominate several product categories, such as groceries, furniture, and large appliances. For such categories, consumers still prefer to shop in person. Amazon has struggled to make a dent in the (estimated) $770 billion grocery category. And even for consumers who *are* comfortable buying groceries online, fresh produce is still difficult and expensive to deliver, which is why Amazon charges $15 a month for its AmazonFresh service on top of its $99 annual Prime membership.

2. **Amazon Devices.** In recent years Amazon has become a major player in devices, with such offerings as Echo, Dash Buttons, and Kindle. Most of these products are designed as complements (they are the razors) that help Amazon sell things such as books and other merchandise (which are the blades). Amazon has sold these devices through retailers such as Best Buy, and in recent years it has also started opening pop-up stores to increase their visibility. Its own stores are the next step in this direction and may further enhance the sale of its devices.

3. **Prime Membership.** As mentioned in chapter 1, Amazon has roughly 75 million Prime members globally, and they not only provide a substantial income through their annual membership fees but also on average spend twice as much on Amazon as non-Prime buyers do. Since online commerce in the United States accounts for only about 15 percent of all retail sales, the offline market represents a huge untapped area for Amazon. Physical

stores can potentially become a customer acquisition channel for Amazon's Prime membership and online commerce.

4. **Reinventing Retail.** Testing physical stores also allows Amazon to reinvent the retail industry. It has already done so, to a degree, with Amazon Go. Further, it is using customer data and customer reviews to select and display books for its bookstores. In the future, it is conceivable that Amazon will sell retail-technology services to other retailers—just as it built Amazon Web Service (AWS) first for its own e-commerce business and later offered it to other companies.

Disney's use of technology in its park and Amazon's foray into the offline market demonstrate that companies need to reimagine the synergies between physical and digital channels for creating a powerful omnichannel experience for their customers.

PART THREE

Reconnect with Your Customers

DIGITAL
LEADERSHIP

BUILD FOR THE FUTURE

STRENGTHEN THE CORE

**RECONNECT
WITH YOUR
CUSTOMERS**

Acquiring

Engaging

Measuring

Chapter 7

Acquiring Customers

Growth is a key priority for every business, and acquiring new customers is a major driver of growth. Digital- and social-marketing tools provide new and innovative ways to spur this growth. However, acquisition costs and profitability vary widely across customers and channels, so in this chapter we will focus on two fundamental questions: Which customers should you acquire, and how should you go about acquiring them?

Which Customers to Acquire

In 2016, Chase introduced its new Sapphire Reserve Card with a very attractive offer: a signing bonus of 100,000 points, $300 in travel credit, triple points earned on all travel and dining expenses, and a value of 1.5 times applied to points redeemed on travel. In spite of its hefty $450 annual fee, this offer generated so much enthusiasm among consumers that within a month of the card's introduction Chase ran out of the metal from which the card was made. Chase management said that the company exceeded its annual target of customers in less than two weeks.[1]

A great success? Perhaps. This generous offer was expensive for the bank. In December 2016, Jamie Dimon, CEO of JP Morgan Chase, said that the new Sapphire Reserve Card would reduce the bank's fourth-quarter profits by as much as $300 million. According to Sanford C. Bernstein & Co., it would take the bank five and a half years to break even on its promotional investment in the card.[2]

With the card's high annual fee, Chase was clearly aiming for the affluent customers who have historically been the prime target of the American Express Platinum card. Yet surprisingly, the majority of people who signed up for the Sapphire card were millennials. Chase management justified the acquisition of these customers: "That is significant because millennials make up the majority of our new deposit accounts today, and their wealth is expected to grow at the fastest rate of all generations over the next 15 years." However, whether or not acquiring these customers was the right decision for Chase depends on how many of these new customers will stay with Chase after the first year, especially when competing firms are also making attractive offers to them. In a note to their clients, Bernstein analysts said, "Lucrative sign-up bonuses give an issuer an opportunity to acquire a large number of customers in a short period of time, though we question whether the type of consumer this attracts leads to a less profitable card product in the long run."[3]

To address analysts' concern, in February 2018, Chase management provided an update on the new Sapphire Reserve customers. It stated that the average income of new cardholders is $180,000; their annual spend on the card is $39,000; and their retention rate is over 90 percent. Chase is also running a pilot in 2018 to convert many of its Sapphire card customers into Chase Private Client and mortgage customers.[4]

Customer Lifetime Value (CLV)

The Chase example illustrates that the number of acquired customers or their acquisition cost do not provide sufficient information to evaluate a customer acquisition strategy. It is critical to know customer spend and their retention rate to estimate their long-term value. Yet most companies track a host of short-term metrics to assess their marketing campaigns—impressions, number of clicks, click-through rate (CTR), conversion rate (from clicks to purchase), and customer acquisition cost (CAC). Of all these, CAC often becomes the key metric for managers when evaluating the effectiveness of their marketing efforts and when allocating budgets. A media channel that is less expensive in acquiring new customers is often preferred over an expensive channel. However, CAC ignores how much customers spend with the firm and their retention rate, both of which determine the long-term profitability of customers, also called customer lifetime value (CLV).

Gaming companies lose a majority of their customers after the first day of app installation. On average, 80 percent of mobile app users either uninstall or stop using an app within ninety days of downloading it.[5] Put differently, firms have a leaky bucket—they keep adding new customers at the top but lose 80 percent of them every three months. Retention rates also vary by media channel, so a cheaper way to acquire customers may not necessarily be the most profitable in the medium to long run. In June 2017, Blue Apron, a meal-kit maker, stumbled in its initial public offering as analysts recognized that almost 60 percent of its customers left the service after six months.[6]

The 200–20 Rule

All animals are equal, but some animals are more equal than others.

—*Animal Farm*, by George Orwell

According to the familiar 80–20 rule, 20 percent of the customers provide 80 percent of the revenue. However, research shows that if we focus on profitability instead of revenues, the rule would be 200–20, where 20 percent of the customers provide almost 200 percent of the profit! How is that possible? Because the remaining 80 percent of customers actually destroy profitability. In other words, a company's profits would soar if it were to jettison the bottom 80 percent of its customers. Of course, some of these unprofitable customers may be important for other, strategic reasons, but this analysis forces management to articulate the reasons for retaining these unprofitable customers.

Figure 7-1 shows the customers of Kanthal, a Swedish manufacturer of industrial heating technology, ranked according to their profitability. Only the top 80 customers out of 200 are profitable for the firm. Figure 7-2 shows Kanthal's profit as we add customers starting with the most profitable to the most unprofitable. The most profitable 5

FIGURE 7-1

Profitability of Kanthal's customers ranked from most to least profitable

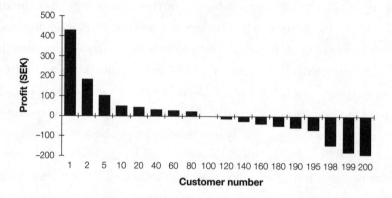

Source: Robert S. Kaplan, "Kanthal (A)," Case 190-002 (Boston: Harvard Business School, 1989, revised 2001).

FIGURE 7-2

Cumulative profitability of Kanthal's customers

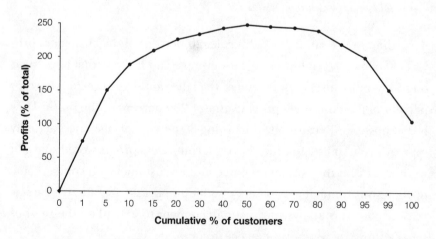

Source: Robert S. Kaplan, "Kanthal (A)," Case 190-002 (Boston: Harvard Business School, 1989, revised 2001).

percent of Kanthal's customers generated 150 percent of the profits. Only 40 percent of its customers were profitable at all, and that group, taken together, created 250 percent of the firm's profits. This figure also shows that the bottom 10 percent of the customers lost about 120 percent of the profits.

The graph in figure 7-2 is often called the "whale curve" because of its whale-like shape, and it shows that 20 percent of Kanthal's customers account for more than 200 percent of its profits. This is a common finding among many companies and illustrates the 200–20 rule of customer profitability. In 2008, Elkay Plumbing, a US manufacturer of sinks, faucets, and fountains for residential and commercial customers, found a similar pattern—the top 1 percent of its customers accounted for 100 percent of its profits, and the most profitable 20 percent of its customers generated 175 percent of its profits.[7]

These findings underscore the importance of acquiring and retaining the right customers, those who are likely to be profitable in the long run. It also suggests that simple metrics like total number of customers or overall market share—metrics used by a majority of companies as measures of success—may be misleading. A company with a large market share may be saddled with a significant proportion of unprofitable customers.

Implementation Challenges

Even if a firm recognizes that it should acquire customers based on their expected long-term profitability, it faces several challenges in implementing this idea. First, most companies are organized by product or business units that mask huge variation in the profitability of customers within that product or business unit. Second, to measure customer profitability a firm needs to adopt activity-based costing to allocate costs to each customer or customer segment. While this task may seem tedious, advances in cost accounting, data analytics, and technology-based solutions are making it easier to achieve this objective. Third, firms need to keep track of cohorts of customers—for example, those acquired from different channels—to understand their long-term profitability and to allocate resources accordingly. Aggregating customers in a single database regardless of where they came from makes it difficult to assess the effectiveness of customer-acquisition programs.

In 2010 BBVA Compass bank, a US subsidiary of the BBVA Group of Spain, was facing a similar challenge. BBVA Compass spent almost 20 percent of its 2010 marketing budget on acquiring customers online. Management believed that the retention rate of customers who were acquired online was significantly lower than the retention rate of those acquired through branches. However, once the customers were acquired the bank kept a single customer database regardless of the channel by which customer had been acquired, which made it difficult to allocate the budget based on customer profitability.[8]

How to Acquire Customers

The customer-acquisition process must begin with a deep understanding of a customer's decision journey or path to purchase. Figure 7-3 shows four key stages of the consumer journey. In 2005, A. G. Lafley, CEO of Procter & Gamble (P&G), described what he called two moments

FIGURE 7-3

Moments of truth

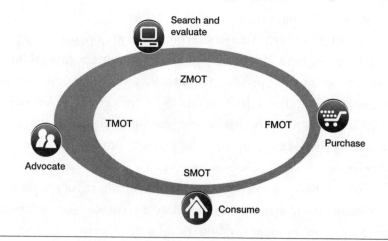

of truth: "The best brands consistently win two moments of truth. The first moment occurs at the store shelf, when a consumer decides whether to buy one brand or another. The second occurs at home, when she uses the brand—and is delighted, or isn't."[9] Introduction of electronic scanners in stores in the 1980s and the rise of e-commerce in the last two decades have made it possible for firms to know the first moment of truth (FMOT) by tracking the sales of their products.

Although P&G could measure sales, Lafley was concerned that the firm had no visibility into how people actually consumed and experienced products—the second moment of truth (SMOT). Recent developments in technology are making it possible to track product consumption. For example, Nestlé could introduce chips into Nespresso machines to know consumers' coffee-consumption behavior and automatically order Nespresso capsules when consumers' supplies got below a certain threshold. A medication event–monitoring system offers bottles with microelectronic chips that record the date and time of every bottle opening to ensure that patients adhere to their medication regime.

The battle for consumers begins long before they buy or experience a product. It starts when they open their laptops or tap on their mobile phones to search for a product. In 2011, Google coined the term "zero moment of truth" (ZMOT) to reflect the importance of this period of online searching before consumers show up in a store or make an online purchase. In a Google study 84 percent of shoppers claimed that ZMOT shaped their decisions of which brand to buy.[10] Using consumers search data, Google created heat maps to visualize how and when consumers actively searched for a product. For example, a consumer's search for a new automobile is typically most active two or three months before the actual purchase.

In addition to doing Google searches, consumers read product reviews on Amazon, hotel reviews on TripAdvisor, restaurant reviews on Yelp, and movie reviews on Rotten Tomatoes before making any decision to buy a product. The rise of social media and the increasing use of reviews by consumers have made the third moment of truth (TMOT) a critical factor. This is when loyal fans of a product become passionate advocates for it on social media and consumer-review sites.

A vital part of any successful customer-acquisition strategy is understanding these moments of truth and ensuring that a brand is well represented at each stage.

From Search to Purchase

The consumer journey from ZMOT to FMOT typically involves four stages: awareness, consideration, evaluation, and purchase. For a long time this process was believed to be linear: A consumer may be aware of eight brands of smartphones. She may consider three brands seriously, brands whose various product features and prices she evaluates more thoroughly, leading ultimately to her decision to buy a specific brand.

Recent studies by McKinsey and others have shown that consumers' search processes may not be linear. A consumer looking to buy a car may start with only BMW and Mercedes but in the course of searching may come to include other brands in the deliberations. McKinsey has found that for automobiles consumers have, on average, 3.8 brands in their initial consideration set, but they add 2.2 additional brands during their search.[11] Therefore, brands have an opportunity to influence consumers' decisions during the search process.

A firm can provide information and influence consumers in three ways: through paid media, which would involve search engine marketing (SEM) and ads on TV, radio, newspapers and magazines; through owned media, which would include the company's website leveraged with search engine optimization (SEO) to ensure that the site ranks high in organic online searches; and through earned media, whereby consumers learn about a product from the reviews and opinions of other consumers in social media.

In the last few years a lot has been written about the best ways to do SEM, SEO, and social media. Google and Facebook provide tools, case studies, and best practices on their sites. Instead of rehashing these suggestions (e.g., how to buy a keyword or how much to bid on it), I would focus on some of the novel research findings that may make you pause and rethink your digital marketing program.

Personalization and Retargeting

Digital technology and rich data allow firms to personalize ads to consumers based on consumers' interests, web-browsing behavior, past purchases, and/or the context of the site they are visiting. A novel study by MIT went one step further by morphing banner ads to match consumers' cognitive styles. For example, some consumers like to read text while others are more visual. If an advertiser can define which style any particular internet user possesses, it can enhance the potential effectiveness of an ad by matching the ad to a given consumer's cognitive style. The MIT team surveyed a sample of consumers to learn their cognitive style and then tracked their web-browsing behavior to link the two. In practice, one can observe only consumers' web-browsing behavior, not their cognitive styles. But by using Bayesian models and estimates from the sample consumers, the MIT team could infer consumers' respective cognitive styles and serve personalized ads in real time. The MIT researchers tested this approach in a large-scale field experiment in which more than 100,000 consumers viewed over 450,000 banner ads on CNET.com. Morphing doubled the click-through rates of the ads. In a follow-up experiment for automobiles, the researchers further demonstrated not only that ad click-through rates improved with morphing but that brand consideration and purchase intentions also jumped significantly.[12] In another follow-up study they developed an algorithm to morph the entire website in real time.[13]

Another commonly used approach to improve ad effectiveness is called retargeting, by which ads are shown to consumers who previously visited a firm's site but did not buy. Several studies have shown the effectiveness of retargeting, including a recent large-scale field experiment for an online sports company. Using Google's Display Network of two million websites, the experiment showed that retargeting increased website visits by 17 percent, transactions by 12 percent, and sales by 11 percent.[14] But how specific should retargeting be? A specific or dynamic retargeting shows consumers an ad for the exact product that they searched for previously (e.g., Nike Men's Roshe One running shoes), whereas a generic retargeting may simply show an ad for running shoes. A field experiment for an online travel company, in which almost 80,000 consumers participated, revealed that specific or dynamic retargeting surprisingly does worse that generic retargeting. The authors of the study suggest that many consumers do not have well-formed preferences, especially early in their purchase process, which makes specific targeting less effective.[15]

Social Media and Virality

Social media has gained a lot of attention from marketers since it allows a message to be amplified without additional cost to a firm. Experts also think that social media is more effective than traditional ads since consumers believe the opinions of other consumers.

In a 2010 interview with *Fast Company*, Jason Harris, the president of Mekanism, a San Francisco–based social media company, claimed, "We can engineer virality. We guarantee we can create an online campaign and make it go viral."[16] The idea of viral campaigns is seductive. Without spending much money, you create an ad or a video that is shared and viewed by millions of consumers. Marketers are quick to quantify the value of this earned media in terms of the dollars saved that would otherwise have been required to reach the same number of consumers through paid media campaigns.

But can you really engineer virality? The average YouTube video generates fewer than 10,000 views, and only a tiny fraction of YouTube videos have more than one million views.[17] The notion of virality comes from epidemiology and involves a single person infected with a communicable disease spreading it to a large population. For a disease to reach epidemic proportions it needs a "reproduction rate" of greater than one, so that each person who gets the disease will, on average, spread it to more than one person. Otherwise the disease dies down quickly. A 2012 study examined the spread of millions of messages on Twitter and Yahoo and found that more than 90 percent of the messages did not diffuse at all. About 4 percent of the messages were shared only once, and less than 1 percent were shared more than seven times.[18]

To address the challenge of creating virality, Duncan Watts, a social scientist, and Jonah Peretti, the founder of BuzzFeed, have proposed the idea of "big seed" marketing. Unlike the typical virality campaign, which relies on seeding a message with a small number of influencers in the hope that they will spread the message like a disease, Watts and Peretti suggest seeding the message with a large number of people in the hope of *amplifying* it to a large audience even if the reproduction or sharing rate is less than one.[19]

Recognizing the difference between virality and amplification, Peretti founded BuzzFeed in 2006 with the aim of amplifying messages through native advertising. BuzzFeed learned that amplification depends not just on creating intriguing stories with humor and catchy titles but also on the medium and the authenticity of the message. Commenting on this, Peretti said,

> Because our audience shares content on social networks, Buzz-Feed editors have to understand how social media is used. For example, on Twitter, things happen very quickly. If Twitter is the one-hour network, Facebook is one day, and Pinterest is one week. Slow content—a recipe, for example—will work best on Pinterest. Content that is fast and newsy will do better on Twitter . . . But content that does well on Pinterest never gets tweeted, and posts that do well on Twitter find no audience on Pinterest.[20]

Melissa Rosenthal, formerly BuzzFeed's director of creative services, had this advice for brand marketers: "You can trick people into clicking, but you can't trick them into sharing. Everything that performs well is based on a real insight, something that's actually true [about the brand]."[21] David Droga, the CEO of the innovative ad agency Droga5, agrees. "It's crude," says Droga, "but the essence, whether we're talking to a billion-dollar client or a startup, is: Why would anyone give a shit about what we're making? Not, Do we think it's cool or clever or funny or worthy? It's, Why is this relevant?"[22]

Who should you seed the information with? Most marketing executives believe that social media influencers are the best bet for seeding information. However, in reality it is hard to find reliable influencers. Even using people with a large following on social media does not guarantee success. In 2009, a year before the launch of its new Fiesta, Ford recruited a hundred influential social media personalities to promote the car through blogs, videos, and photos. The list included Judson Laipply, an internet celebrity whose earlier video "The Evolution of Dance" was among YouTube's all-time most-viewed videos, with 115 million views at that time. However, Laipply turned out to be one of the least effective agents for Ford.[23]

In a 2013 article in *Harvard Business Review*, Sinan Aral, a social network expert at MIT, elaborated on the role of influencers in social media:

> In 2009 [Ashton Kutcher] became the first user to acquire 10 million followers; by early 2013 the total was 13.7 million. Kutcher would seem the very definition of a social media "influencer." But . . . how many have ever done something because Kutcher suggested it? . . . If Kutcher is the quintessential influencer but no one does what he suggests, in what way is he influential?[24]

By tracking 74 million events among 1.6 million Twitter users, Eytan Bakshy, a senior scientist at Facebook, and his colleagues found that "although under some circumstances, the most influential users are also the most cost-effective, under a wide range of plausible assumptions the most cost-effective performance can be realized using 'ordinary influencers'—individuals who exert average or even less-than-average influence."[25] Jonah Peretti of BuzzFeed agrees: "Editors can dispense with the probably fruitless exercise of predicting how, or through whom, contagious ideas will spread."[26]

Collectively, these studies suggest that trying to create virality by seeding a message with a handful of social media influencers is unlikely to be successful and cost effective. Instead, it is better to seed the content with a large number of ordinary users. In fact, many social media campaigns gain traction only after they are picked up by the mainstream media.

Acquisition Through Offers

Companies in almost every industry, be it newspapers, telecom, cable, or credit cards, typically offer significant discounts to attract new customers. In the short term these offers may be effective, but what are their consequences in the long run? In a past collaboration with other researchers, I showed that while price promotions have a positive impact on brand share in the short term, they have a negative long-term impact.[27] Another study quantified this negative long-term effect for newspaper subscriptions and showed that acquiring customers through a 35 percent price discount resulted in a long-term value that was about half that of non-promotionally acquired customers.[28]

How do these offer-based acquisition methods compare with acquisition through word of mouth or through referral programs? Two studies provide some insights. Using data from a web-hosting company, one study found that while marketing-induced customers add more short-term value, customers acquired through word of mouth add nearly twice as much long-term value to the firm.[29] Another study tracked ten thousand accounts in a large German bank over a three-year period and found that customers acquired through referral programs were 18 percent more likely than others to stay with the bank, and that they generated 16 percent more in profits.[30] In summary, although short-term discounts may provide a quick win in acquiring new customers, word-of-mouth and referral programs are more effective in the long run.

In practice, a company faces customers with varying price sensitivities. Some customers are more price driven and won't buy unless they are offered discounts. To separate the price-sensitive customers from others, brick-and-mortar retailers have long followed the practice of creating search friction—placing the discounted items in the back of the store or in a separate outlet store. In contrast, online retailers try to reduce search friction and improve user experience for every customer.

This results in either offering lower prices to everyone or charging relatively higher prices at the risk of losing price-sensitive consumers. In a recent study, two of my Harvard Business School colleagues wondered if an e-commerce player should deliberately create search friction for discounted products that only price-sensitive customers would hunt for. They conducted a large-scale field experiment with an online fashion and apparel retailer in the Philippines. For a group of consumers (test group), they eliminated discount markers and the ability to search products by price discounts that the company was using on its site, while the other group of customers (control group) was able to use these features. Compared with the control group, consumers in the test group bought fewer discounted products and at lower average discounts, without any impact on their conversion rate (i.e., percent of people who bought one or more items), leading to a significant increase in this online retailer's profits. After the experiment, the company eliminated discount markers on its site and disabled product search by which item was on discount.[31]

These research studies show that managers should be careful in using price discounts to acquire new customers—this practice may be effective in the short run but costly in the long run. Recognizing that not all customers are equally price sensitive or equally valuable, firms may want to consider deliberately making it a little harder for consumers to find discounted items.

Beyond the Click

In 2010, BBVA Compass Bank spent a significant proportion of its marketing budget online to entice new customers to open checking and savings accounts with the bank. By tracking data both on the bank's budget allocation for search and display ads and on the number of impressions, clicks, and new applications generated, we can construct an aggregate picture of the consumer journey (see figure 7-4).

The bank offered a $150 incentive for consumers to open a new account. The offer enticed many to click on the link, but when they went to the landing page, read the fine print, and learned of the conditions they had to meet (e.g., the minimum balance), only 10 percent of the

FIGURE 7-4

Consumer journey for BBVA Compass Bank's online customer-acquisition campaign

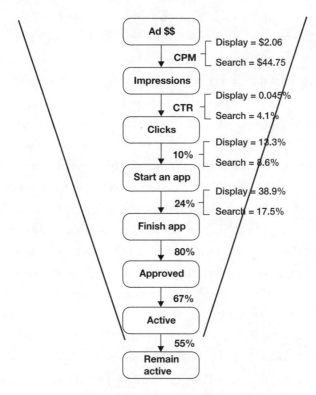

Source: Sunil Gupta and Joseph Davies-Gavin, "BBVA Compass: Marketing Resource Allocation," Case 511-096 (Boston: Harvard Business School, 2011), and Teaching Note 512-051 (Boston: Harvard Business School, 2012).

people who clicked on the ad actually started the application. It is even more intriguing that only 24 percent of the people who started filling out the application for a new account actually completed it. This low rate of completion suggests that the application was either too long and complicated or was asking consumers sensitive information that made them abandon the process.

Of the users who completed the application online, about 80 percent were approved by the bank. In contrast, almost all consumers who came into bank branches were approved for a new account. In other words, the quality of customers that came through the online channel was relatively low. This was further confirmed by the fact that only two-thirds of the approved online customers actually funded the account to make it active. Finally, the retention rate of these online customers was 55 percent, compared with over 65 percent for those acquired offline.

This case highlights several important points. First, most digital marketing programs focus exclusively on improving click-through rates (CTR), even though measuring success by clicks and CTR provides only a partial picture. Second, the effective cost of acquisition should not be measured based on clicks or even completed applications. For BBVA Compass, the cost per completed online application was about $80, but if you add the $150 promotional offer and the drop-off after the click and application, the acquisition cost jumps to about $300. (Of the completed applications, 80 percent are approved and 67 percent of the approved applications are funded, leading to 80 percent times 67 percent, or 54 percent effective success rate. Therefore, the effective acquisition cost of a successful new account is $80/0.54 + $150 promotional offer, or about $300).

Third, the firm should carefully examine the reasons for the drop-offs after the click. Why do only 10 percent of those who click actually start the application? Why do only 24 percent of consumers who start the application complete it? And why do only 67 percent who are approved fund their account?

Online commerce players face a similar problem with cart abandonment at the checkout. Studies show that almost 70 percent of online shopping carts are abandoned at the checkout.[32] The top three reasons include shipping and other fees, requirement to create a new account, and a long or complicated checkout process. Going beyond ad clicks to understand consumer pain points along their decision journey can help companies make their acquisition programs more effective.

Beyond Advertising

For decades marketing textbooks have talked about the four *P*s (or 4Ps): product, price, place (distribution), and promotion (or advertising). Yet most discussions about digital marketing center almost exclusively around digital advertising, even though all 4Ps influence customer acquisition and retention. In the previous chapter, I discussed the importance of place in omnichannel strategies. Here I will briefly highlight how digital technology allows us to think about product and price in new ways.

For digital products with almost zero marginal cost of production and distribution, a powerful strategy is "freemium" (mentioned briefly in chapter 3), in which a basic version of a product is given away for free, and users pay only for upgrading to an advanced version. Those employing a freemium strategy would include producers of gaming apps, Adobe, the *New York Times*, Hulu, Dropbox, LinkedIn, Box, Splunk, Skype, Pandora, and YouTube. Freemium apps account for 95 percent of Apple App Store revenue and 98 percent of Google Play revenue.[33] The freemium strategy has many advantages:

- Firms incur low or no marketing cost to acquire free customers, with the possibility that some free customers will upgrade to become paying customers in the future.

- For products with strong network effects it is a good way to create a virtuous circle in which existing customers become the product's marketing agents. For example, file sharing in Dropbox encourages current users to invite their friends to use Dropbox as well. Many network products result in a winner-take-all market. A freemium strategy allows for quick scaling to gain momentum and become the market leader.

- For experience goods, consumers need to try the product to see its value. Drew Houston, the founder and CEO of Dropbox, elaborated on this by saying, "The fact was that Dropbox was offering a product that people didn't know they needed until they tried."[34]

- Companies gain valuable feedback by observing the way users interact with products. When Adobe changed its strategy from selling a packaged product to a monthly subscription service with a freemium model, it quickly acquired millions of free users.

Monitoring the usage of these consumers allows Adobe to learn what features consumers use more often, where users get stuck, what encourages higher product usage, and so on. This feedback allows Adobe to continuously innovate its product.

- Unlike a limited-time free trial, freemium creates a habit of product usage. The *New York Times* (NYT) decided to give users twenty free articles per month to get them into the habit of coming to the newspaper site frequently.

A critical question in designing a freemium product is how much to give away for free. Give too little and consumers won't be excited to join. Give too much and no one will pay to upgrade. In designing its paywall, NYT arrived at twenty free articles per month in order to balance two revenue sources—from advertising and from digital subscriptions. Giving away too few articles would have created a significant drop in website traffic and therefore digital ad revenue, as the *Times* (of London) experienced. On the other hand, giving away too many articles for free would have limited the potential revenue from digital subscribers. NYT used consumer data and its best judgment to arrive at twenty free articles. It monitored consumers' response to the paywall, and noting a healthy subscription rate for its digital version, it later reduced the number of free articles to five per month.

If you give away your product, how do you make money? Since many of the freemium customers are free, one may be tempted to conclude that their customer lifetime value is zero. However, these free customers bring value to the firm in two indirect ways—through referrals and network effects that reduces a firm's customer-acquisition costs, and (for a small fraction of them) through upgrading to a paid version of the product. In a recent research paper, my colleagues and I showed that for a data-storage company a free user is typically worth 15 percent to 25 percent as much as a premium subscriber.[35] Another study examined the network effects for a European auction house similar to eBay and found that one new seller on the site brings in almost three additional sellers and eleven additional buyers. Given the seller-acquisition cost of between €12 and €60 and the buyer-acquisition cost of between €5 and €25 for this site, the value of customers acquired through network effects is quite significant.[36]

While freemium is a good strategy for digital products because they have almost zero marginal cost of production and distribution, for physical products one must charge a price. In these situations, pricing becomes a decisive consideration for both the consumer and the firm. In the digital era, consumers have the ability to search prices across sites and firms have the ability to do frequent pricing experiments to stay competitive and determine optimal pricing.

Not only third-party sellers on Amazon have a wide variation in price over time. Amazon itself is offering different prices at different times. For many products, Amazon tests several prices on the same day. Temporal price variations are becoming a norm in the digital era, and every executive should consider dynamic pricing for his products, similar to what airlines have done for years.

OYO, India's largest hotel network, boasting more than 6,500 hotel properties in 192 cities across the country, has taken the idea of dynamic pricing to a new level. Ritesh Agarwal, who founded and launched OYO when he was just nineteen years old, initially created a version of Airbnb, but soon realized that India lacked low-to-mid-budget hotels with reliable and standardized services. So he decided to change his business model and started asking existing budget hotels to give him a few rooms and convert them into OYO rooms with such standardized services as Wi-Fi, free breakfast, and clean bathrooms. Hotels with high fixed costs and low occupancy rates were happy to offer OYO some rooms as a way of generating additional income. While OYO's consumer prices varied depending on market conditions and seasonality, the company initially offered hotel owners a "minimum price guarantee" that gave them a fixed monthly fee for the rooms they offered to OYO. Within a year OYO changed this policy to dynamic pricing that works as follows. Twice a day, once in the morning and once in the afternoon, OYO offers each hotel owner a certain price for its rooms. The owner can then decide how many rooms to offer OYO that day. Depending on the supply of the rooms and on market conditions, OYO then determines the price to offer consumers. In effect, OYO's dynamic pricing policy attempts to balance—in real time—both the variability in the supply of hotel rooms and the variability in customer demand.

In conclusion, customer acquisition is critical for the growth of a company, and in this chapter we discussed which customers to acquire and how to acquire them. Engaging customers is a necessary condition for acquiring and retaining them, and this is the topic of our next chapter.

Chapter 8

Engaging Consumers

Advertising people love advertising, but everyone else hates advertising.[1]

—Gerry Graf, former chief creative officer at Saatchi & Saatchi

"The right message, to the right customer, at the right time"—marketing executives around the world are convinced that this goal is now becoming a reality, thanks to their ability to track every single click of a consumer on the web, know her location at any time through her mobile device, and have a deep understanding of her interests and activities through social media and Facebook. Sophisticated approaches such as programmatic media buying, real-time marketing, data mining, geotargeting, and retargeting have given marketing experts new confidence in their ability to achieve this goal.

Yet most consumers, by far, find ads annoying. A 2016 survey found that 90 percent of consumers skip preroll video ads—the ads that sites like YouTube force you to see before you can watch what you want. And if preroll isn't annoying enough, Facebook is now testing a "midroll" video ad format in which an ad plays in the middle of your favorite video! Almost 84 percent of millennials, the prime target segment of most advertisers, admit to skipping or blocking ads all or some of the time.[2] Another survey claimed that 69 percent of consumers skip ads on Snapchat.[3] In December 2016, over 600 million devices were running ad-blocking software globally, a 30 percent increase over the year before.[4] More than 28 percent of mobile devices in India and 58 percent in Indonesia were blocking ads as of December 2016.[5] The advertising industry has come up with innovative metrics for ad exposure: Facebook considers it a view when a video plays for three seconds on its site. Snapchat counts it as a view if the video is rendered on the screen, even if it plays for half a second. In 2016, after months of deliberation, the Media Rating Council, an industry organization that sets standards for ad measurement, reported its ruling that a mobile-video ad impression is delivered if 50 percent of ad pixels are in view for two consecutive seconds. No matter what study you believe in, is a 1 percent click-through rate for online ads a huge success? Put differently, when was the last time you declared a victory when 99 percent of the time you failed to achieve your goal?

In spite of all the developments in technology and the rhetoric about engaging consumers, we have failed to take consumers' perspective. Every brand in the world wants to engage with the consumer, but have the brand managers paused to ask why a consumer would want to engage with a bar of soap, a can of soda, or a bottle of beer?

Advertising was never meant to force people to watch things they did not want to see. The role of advertising is to provide value to consumers by offering them relevant information that helps them make better decisions. Google has been able to achieve this very effectively with search advertising by showing ads that are highly relevant to consumers' search on their desktops and laptops. However, as consumers' attention has moved to mobile devices and as companies have started shifting their ad budgets to mobile, even Google has struggled to make mobile advertising relevant to consumers.

To understand why mobile advertising is so different we need to find out how people really spend time on their smartphones. Unlike on laptops and desktops, where browser search dominates, on mobile devices consumers spend over 90 percent of their time on apps, not browsers.

A study of US consumers by Flurry, a mobile analytics company, shows that the majority of this time is spent on social networks such as Facebook and Snapchat, or using entertainment apps (see figure 8-1). Since there is no compelling reason for a consumer to download an app for, say, Coke or Dove soap, brand marketers spend the vast majority of their mobile budgets on in-app ads. These take the form of banner ads in gaming apps, preroll ads on YouTube videos, or ads in Facebook newsfeeds.

While industry studies are full of success stories that claim amazing return on dollars spent on ads in apps and on Facebook (a topic that we will address in the next chapter), let us pause to consider this from a consumer's point of view. How relevant and useful is a banner ad for, say, BMW or Coke while you are playing Candy Crush or browsing your Facebook newsfeed? Misiek Piskorski, a professor of strategy and innovation at IMD and my former colleague at Harvard Business School, describes an ad in a Facebook newsfeed as being similar to a stranger pulling up a chair next to you when you and your friend are having a private conversation. Put differently, this is the digital version of the 7:00 p.m. sales call

FIGURE 8-1

Time spent by US consumers on their smartphones

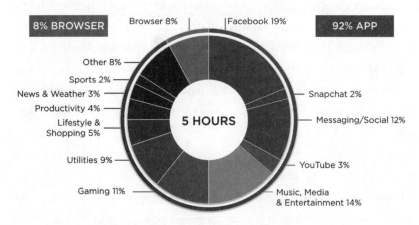

Source: Simon Khalaf and Lali Kesiraju, "U.S. Consumers Time-Spent on Mobile Crosses 5 Hours a Day," March 2, 2017, http://flurrymobile.tumblr.com/post/157921590345/us-consumers-time-spent-on-mobile-crosses-5.

that you used to get when you sat down with your family for dinner. One study found that "to motivate a person to generate as many impressions in the presence of bad ads as they would in the presence of no ads or good ads, we would need to pay them roughly an additional $1 to $1.50 per thousand impressions . . . Publishers are often paid less than 50 cents per thousand impressions to run annoying ads, half as much as the estimated economic damage they incurred in our experiments."[6]

As consumers, we have come to accept annoying ads as the cost of getting free content. But are there better ways to go about this, ways that help both consumers and brands? This critical question is the focus of this chapter.

Providing Value

The goal of marketing is to create value for consumers. Tesco's introduction of virtual stores in South Korea and Unilever's mobile radio station in India provide two excellent case studies of leveraging mobile technology to create win-win strategies for the company and for consumers.

Tesco in South Korea

In 1999, on the heels of Carrefour of France and Walmart of the United States, Tesco entered the South Korean market, one of the most lucrative consumer markets in Asia. As it started opening stores in Korea, under the name Homeplus, it faced a daunting challenge from the largest Korean retailer, Emart. By 2006, both Carrefour and Walmart had decided to pull out of Korea, and Emart acquired Walmart's Korean operation. By 2009, Emart was dominant in the Korean market, with annual sales of $9.4 billion.[7]

How could Tesco attract more consumers and compete with Emart without significant additional investment in opening more retail stores? Most consumers hate going to the grocery store for their weekly shopping, so Tesco decided to bring the store to them. In 2011, the company opened its first virtual store in Seoul's busiest subway station. It plastered the station with a picture of a store shelf that looked identical to an actual shelf in Tesco's grocery store. After downloading the Homeplus app on their smartphones, consumers could scan the QR code of the virtual items while waiting for their morning trains, and the selected items would be delivered to them when they reached home in the evening. It solved a consumer problem, provided consumers significant value, and also drove business for Tesco. Within three months of launching this mobile app, sales of Homeplus increased by 130 percent, and their number of registered users went up by 76 percent.[8] Alas, in 2015 Tesco pulled out of the Korean market, due to its own financial troubles at home and to stronger regulations imposed by the South Korean government. But the company's app nonetheless remains a great example of innovative consumer engagement.

Unilever in India

In 2014, Hindustan Unilever Limited, the market leader of consumer products in India, faced the challenge of reaching the 130 million people in Bihar and Jharkhand. These two regions are among the most media-dark regions of India, where people do not have electricity for eight to ten hours every day. However, at the time, almost 54 million people had a rudimentary mobile phone—a feature phone, not a smartphone. Unilever decided to transform this basic phone into an entertainment conduit and give consumers something they did not have.

The company created an entertainment channel called Kan Khajura Station, which provided fifteen minutes of free, on-demand entertainment that included music, jokes, news, and promotions for certain Unilever brands. To get access to this entertainment channel consumers would call a toll-free number. As soon as the call was received, it was disconnected, to avoid any cost to the consumer, and an automated callback was generated (incoming calls are free in India) to give the consumer the free fifteen minutes of entertainment. Soon after the station's launch, Unilever was receiving as many as 150,000 calls a day, and many consumers were calling several times a day. Within six months Kan Khajura Station had eight million unique subscribers, and awareness for Unilever brands had increased significantly. By converting the mobile phone into an entertainment conduit, Unilever created the largest media channel in Bihar and Jharkhand, at a cost of less than four cents per person.[9] After its initial success, Hindustan Unilever extended Kan Khajura Station to all the remote villages and towns of India, where traditional media are either unavailable or unreliable. By 2015 the station had thirty-five million subscribers, and within two years of its launch these subscribers had listened to 900 million minutes of entertainment programing that included Hindustan Unilever ads forty-five million times. Taking a page out of the platform strategy discussed in chapter 3, Hindustan Unilever has opened up its station for non-Unilever brands that want to reach and engage these subscribers.[10]

Tesco and Unilever have the following things in common:

- Marketing is not just advertising. Neither Tesco nor Unilever created another ad campaign to engage consumers. Instead, they focused on solving consumers' problems and providing consumers significant value.

- As a result, their overtures to consumers weren't annoying. On the contrary, consumers willingly downloaded the Homeplus app and called Unilever to opt in for the entertainment channel. It is ironic that in a world of two-way communication, most advertisers still follow the age-old one-way communication approach in which consumers are passive receivers of banner or preroll ads.

- Both companies took advantage of the unique aspect of mobile devices. Tesco's consumers could not scan the QR code with their laptops, and for Unilever's consumers, radio and TV were not viable options due to frequent and prolonged power outages.

From Storytelling to Story Making

When M. V. Rajamannar (Raja) joined Mastercard in September 2013 as its chief marketing officer (CMO), he inherited a strong brand and the iconic "Priceless" ad campaign.[11] Launched in 1997, this campaign showed vignettes of human interactions that concluded with the lines, "There are some things in life money can't buy. For everything else, there's Mastercard." The campaign was so successful that in the next fifteen years it entered the vernacular in many countries. Yet Raja felt it was time for a change. He explained:

> There were three fundamental reasons for us to rethink how we engage consumers. First, the *Priceless* campaign was designed for end consumers, but Mastercard does not issue cards, our partner banks do that. Any effort in engaging consumers should drive our business by helping our bank and merchant partners—a directive clearly communicated to me by Ajay Banga, our CEO.
>
> Second, our brand was positioned as "the best way to pay" even though payment is the lowest emotional point for a consumer during her purchase. Consumers don't get up in the morning thinking about payments. We needed to look beyond card usage because consumption is only a small part of human life. What happens in the rest of the life directly impacts the consumption of a product or service.
>
> Third, although the *Priceless* campaign is very memorable, it relies on one-way communication while the world has moved to two-way interactions with consumers. In the era of Netflix and ad blocking no one is listening to our story, no matter how compelling it is. We need to shift from storytelling to story making by making consumers an integral part of the story.

To drive this change, Raja and his team decided to position the brand as "Connecting People to Priceless Possibilities." To bring this to life, they created a "digital engine" that leveraged digital and social media (see figure 8-2).

The digital engine is a seven-step process based on insights gleaned from data and real-time optimization.

FIGURE 8-2

Digital engine at Mastercard

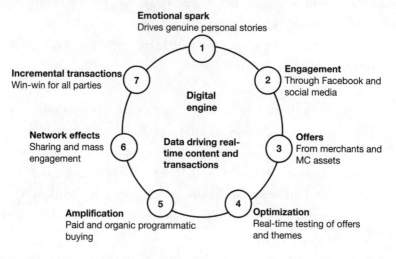

Source: Adapted from company documents.

1. **Emotional Spark.** The first step is to create an emotional spark and a connection with consumers. Using data to understand consumers' key passion points, Mastercard builds videos and creatives to ignite this spark and give consumers a reason to engage. For example, a few weeks before the 2014 New Year's Eve, Mastercard produced a video in which the actor Hugh Jackman announced a promotion encouraging consumers to submit a story about someone who deeply mattered to them ("family, friends, mentors, who influenced us through their passions and wisdom"). The authors of the winning submissions would, on New Year's Eve, be flown "anywhere in the world" to reunite with those both distant and dear. Mastercard envisioned each reunion as a "Priceless Surprise."

2. **Engagement.** By using data to identify the right audience, Mastercard targets that audience with a spark video through Facebook and social media. The goal is to encourage consumers to

share their stories. To continue this excitement, Mastercard often produces a second video—in the Hugh Jackman case, the company showed Jackman surprising his own mentor in New York.

3. **Offers.** With the goal of helping its partner banks and merchants in driving their business, which in turn helps Mastercard's own revenue, the company identifies the best offers to match consumers' interests. In the New Year's Eve campaign, after Mastercard's Asia-Pacific team found that Singapore was a favorite destination for Indian consumers traveling for the holiday, it partnered with Singapore's Resorts World Sentosa with an attractive offer.

4. **Real-Time Optimization.** At any point in time Mastercard may have several offers. Which of these offers should be highlighted and promoted is determined by A/B testing and real-time optimization of offers, themes, and budget allocation.

5. **Amplification.** Real-time testing provides confidence to Mastercard about the potential success of these offers, and it also encourages its bank and merchant partners to co-market and co-fund these campaigns. This process amplifies both Mastercard's budget and the impact of the program.

6. **Network Effects.** A few weeks after consumers have submitted their stories, Mastercard selects winners, produces videos of them surprising their friends and families, and uses these videos in social media to encourage sharing.

7. **Incremental Transactions.** These programs translate into incremental business for banks who issue cards, for merchants where consumers spend money, and for Mastercard, which gets a portion of every transaction.

Figure 8-3 shows data about the business impact of Mastercard's "Priceless Cities" program in the United States.

FIGURE 8-3

Transactional impact of US "Priceless Cities"

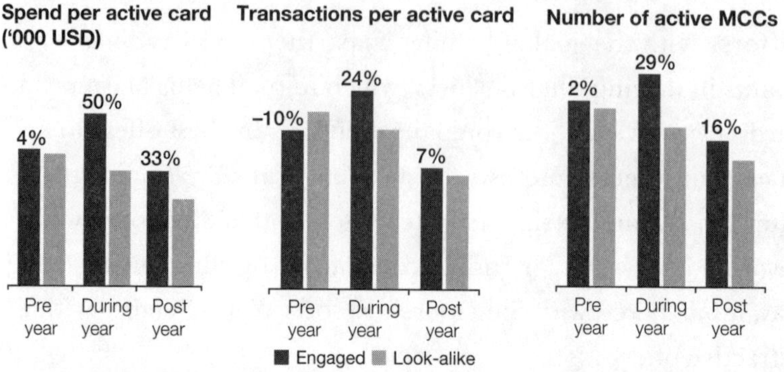

Spend per active card ('000 USD)

Transactions per active card

Number of active MCCs

4% 50% 33%

−10% 24% 7%

2% 29% 16%

Pre year / During year / Post year

Pre year / During year / Post year

Pre year / During year / Post year

■ Engaged ■ Look-alike

Engaged consumers spent 4 percent more in pre-year compared to a matched sample of look-alike consumers in the control group, but they spent 50 percent more during the campaign year and 33 percent more after the campaign year.

Source: Company documents.

Note: *Engaged* denotes cardholders who respond to "Priceless Cities" offers. *Look-alike* is a matched control sample. *MCC* stands for "merchant category code." Pre-year: May 2012–April 2013. During year: May 2013–April 2014. Post-year: May 2014–April 2015.

The Mastercard case highlights important lessons on how to engage consumers:

- **Have a Broad Message.** Brands need to connect with consumers in how they live and spend their time. This means that firms need to go beyond the brand or product message to become more relevant in consumers' lives. As Raja said, "Consumers don't get up in the morning thinking about payments." So even if you are the best form of payment, it does not matter to your consumers. The same is true for a car, a bar of soap, or a can of soda. Dove soap was very successful in creating a conversation among consumers with its "Real Beauty" campaign, which focused not on the brand or even the product category but on how women and society view beauty. More often than not these broader themes connect with consumers in a very emotional way.

- **Shift from Storytelling to Story Making.** Google and Facebook have democratized marketing, making it possible for even a small firm with a limited budget to engage in digital marketing and social media. On top of this, there is huge fragmentation in digital media, with the variety of outlets ranging from Snapchat and Instagram to millions of other websites and blogs. All of this has resulted in a significant increase in the supply of advertising, which in turn has led to clutter and consumers' confusion and annoyance with ads. To break through this clutter, companies need to move from storytelling to story making. As Raja said, "no one is listening to our story, no matter how compelling it is." A broader message that is emotionally engaging allows for a two-way conversation.

- **Be Consistent with the Brand Value.** In search of a broad and emotionally engaging message, brands often lose connection to their core value. Even in the digital world each brand needs to stand for something. Eric Reynolds, the CMO of Clorox, emphasized this aspect: "Nothing ever gets better until you're really clear with yourself about what your brand stands for, why it even exists. At some point, someone has to say, 'Stop. We're doing all of this stuff—why? Why does it matter?' It's a leadership question. It's someone declaring a better future and willing to go back and question some of the fundamentals of the brand."[12] In creating an emotional spark, Mastercard keeps three things in mind: (1) The context should appeal to its target audience. Based on its research, Mastercard identified nine passion points, including music, sports, travel, shopping, and dining. (2) The creative should tap into cultural trends of the time. (3) The content should be relevant and consistent with the image of the brand.

These guidelines are simple and straightforward, yet many companies forget them. Take the example of Pepsi's "Refresh Project," which was launched in 2010. Pepsi announced that it would award $20 million in grants to individuals, businesses, and nonprofits that promote a new idea to make a positive impact on community. A large number of submissions were about social causes that had nothing to do with Pepsi, and some—for example, reducing obesity—were in direct conflict with what Pepsi is trying to sell. In April 2017, Pepsi's attempt to engage its consumers with a Kendall Jenner ad backfired, too, because people saw Pepsi exploiting consumers' sentiment about "Black Lives Matter" without itself having any apparent interest in the cause. Blendtec, a company that sells professional and home blenders, offers the contrasting example of creating an engaging YouTube video series that is consistent with Blendtec's brand. In the series, called *Will It Blend*, Tom Dickson, the company founder, blends a series of unusual objects, such as an iPhone or golf balls. Not only are the videos amusing and popular, garnering millions of views, but they also emphasize the power and features of Blendtec products.

- **Create Engagement that Drives Business**. Advertising needs to achieve two goals: engage and persuade. In the cluttered media environment, we often focus on getting consumers' attention by engaging them with entertaining content. However, the ultimate goal of advertising is to drive business. Research by my colleague Thales Teixeira has shown that too much entertainment in ads may engage consumers but may detract from both communicating the brand message and increasing sales.[13] Simply measuring engagement metrics, such as the number of video views, provides only a partial picture of a program's success. Mastercard built its digital engine with a clear goal to engage consumers in a way that increases transactions. Using its pre and post studies it can monitor the success of its programs. Similarly, *Will It Blend* had a significant impact on the sales of Blendtec products.

Moment-Based Marketing

Advertisers are obsessed with knowing consumers—their demographics and interests, their network of friends, what they post on Instagram or Pinterest, what they write in social media. The more we know the consumer, the more targeted and relevant the ad will be—at least that is the hope. But consumers are complex and multidimensional. I am not only a professor but also a parent and, at different moments, a sports fan, a foodie, a traveler, and so on. My mindset and my receptivity to any message vary greatly depending on the context.

Vineet Mehra, the former president of global marketing services at Johnson & Johnson, noticed such a moment on the company's message board. "At 4:20 a.m.," explained Mehra, "we started seeing a lot of conversations like this: 'Has anyone got any tips for getting a baby to sleep through the night?' 'My ten-month-old had me up six times last night, but can't sleep now.'" Recognizing this moment of opportunity to connect with mothers, Johnson & Johnson created video content to help consumers.[14] The same content would be far less effective in a different context.

Marketing experts have always focused on macromoments such as the Thanksgiving holiday or TV's prime time. However, we now live in the mobile era, when, on average, consumers check their smartphones 150 times a day. More than 87 percent of consumers have their phones by their sides day and night, and 68 percent admit to checking their phones within fifteen minutes of waking up in the morning.[15] Unlike television ads that aired at 8:00 p.m., regardless of whether or not that was the right time for a consumer, we now have the ability to wait for the right moment before sending a message to a consumer's mobile phone. This is the era of *micromoments*, when messages need to arrive at the proper time, in the proper context. In a *Harvard Business Review* article, I explained this idea:

> If you book an Uber ride on Friday evening, ads for restaurants and movies may be relevant at that moment. If you are stuck at an airport because of a delayed flight, you may be more inclined to sign up for Netflix. Driving on a highway at noontime is perhaps the best time for your Google Maps on your car dashboard to show nearby food places.[16]

These examples focus less on consumer demographics, interests, or even past purchases than they do on the moment and the context.

Moment-Based Marketing in Action

The following minicases illustrate how some companies are using moment-based marketing effectively.

- **Sephora.** Shopping in stores can be overwhelming for consumers, as they face a large number of choices. It is not uncommon for consumers in these situations to pull out their smartphones in order to find product ratings and consumer reviews. To Bridget Dolan, Sephora's vice president of interactive media, this provides a great opportunity. She explains, "We think one of the biggest opportunities we have in retail is for our customers to leverage their phones as a shopping assistant when they are standing in the store." To help shoppers in these moments, Sephora created an app that allows them to scan an item in the store and immediately see product ratings and reviews on their phones. "Having access to this information is that perfect new moment for customers to find everything they're looking for and get advice from Sephora," says Dolan.[17]

- **Red Roof Inn.** In the aforementioned *Harvard Business Review* article, I described how Red Roof Inn leveraged technology and consumer insights to send messages at the right moment: "Red Roof Inn realized that flight cancellations in the United States left 90,000 passengers stranded every day. Imagine the emotions of a typical passenger at that moment—it perhaps starts with frustration and anger at the airlines and then turns toward the need to find a place to stay overnight. Recognizing this, the marketing team of Red Roof Inn developed a way to track flight delays in real time that triggered targeted ads for Red Roof Inn near airports. Ads that said, 'Stranded at the airport? Come stay with us!' captured the consumers at the right moment, which resulted in a 60 percent increase in bookings compared to other campaigns."[18]

- **DBS Bank.** As it is for most banks, mortgage lending is an attractive business for DBS, a bank based in Singapore. DBS started by creating a mobile app that allowed consumers to find mortgage rates and calculate monthly payments in order to ascertain the affordability of a house that they were considering. However, this app did not differentiate DBS from any other bank. How could DBS help consumers *and* differentiate itself from others? This question prompted the DBS team to dig deeper into consumers' home-buying processes to understand specific moments where the bank could help consumers. This exercise led to the development of the Home Connect mobile app. If you are visiting a neighborhood to see houses and are curious to know the prices in that area, the app, according to DBS, lets you "simply hold up your phone and scan your surroundings to view the latest transacted prices in the area." Or if your decision depends on schools, or distance to public transportation, the app can also help you with that information: "Can't decide between two options? Check out the amenities and facilities nearby to help you compare. Distance to MRT station or the bus stop? What are the schools nearby? Is there a supermarket in the area?"[19] Recognizing the factors that would help consumers make a better decision, DBS integrated publicly available information from various Singapore neighborhoods in its app. This now gives a compelling reason for consumers to use the DBS app, which has become a lead-generation tool for the bank's mortgage business.

How to Win Micromoments

A 2015 study by Forrester found that only one-third of businesses prioritize a moment-based approach and only 2 percent of firms have all the necessary elements for a moments-ready organization.[20] So how do you create a moment-based program? Here are some guidelines:

- **Map Consumers' Journey to Understand Their Intent and Context.** According to Google a micromoment is an opportunity that arises when a consumer has *intent* for a task in a specific *context* and wants an *immediate* result. Intent requires us to understand what a consumer needs at a specific moment, and

context highlights how that consumer need might change based
on a particular situation—for example, whether a consumer is
in a store or at home. Elaborating on the *intent-context-immediacy*
nature of micromoments, Lisa Gevelber, Google's vice president for
marketing and a pioneer of the micromoments concept, said, "The
advertising game is no longer about reach and frequency. Now
more than ever, intent is more important than identity and demographics, and immediacy is more important than brand loyalty."[21]

To understand consumers' intent and context at a specific
moment, firms need to map the entire consumer journey at every
touchpoint, recognizing two critical things. First, ethnographic
and observational studies are often more insightful for understanding the consumer journey than are surveys or consumers'
digital footprints. It is unlikely that Sephora would have recognized consumers' desire to see product reviews on their smartphones in the store if the company had relied only on surveys
or management judgment. Second, for mapping the consumer
journey, management typically focuses on the firm's product,
not on the broader consumer journey, which often provides better insights. For example, to map the consumer journey for a
mortgage, a bank may consider the following steps: awareness of
the bank → consideration → loan application → loan approval
→ loan origination → monthly payment, etc. If DBS bank had
followed this approach it would have missed the opportunity
to provide unique value to its customers through information
about home prices and neighborhood amenities, information that
was conveyed even before consumers were thinking of applying
for a mortgage.

- **Classify Different Moments into Coherent Groups.** Mapping
  the large number of micromoments among consumers can seem
  daunting and impractical. Therefore it is useful to categorize
  these moments into groups that are relevant for consumers and
  actionable for the firm. Based on its studies, Google has classified

micromoments across four groups: I want to know, I want to go, I want to do, and I want to buy. In the I-want-to-know moment, consumers are looking for information to make a decision but perhaps are not yet ready to buy. In one of its studies, Google found that "1 in 3 smartphone users purchased from a company or brand other than the one they intended to because of the information provided in the moment they needed it."[22] Sephora used its app effectively to provide product reviews to its customers in the store. The I-want-to-go moment reflects consumers' intent to visit a store to check, test, or buy a product that they may have researched online. Knowing the location of the nearby store and the availability of the desired product may be helpful here. I-want-to-do moments are when consumers may need information on such things as how to fix a toilet or how to apply eyeliner. I-want-to-buy moments are when consumers are ready to buy the product. Your business may have similar or different categories of moments. You don't necessarily have to follow Google's classification, but it is useful to group hundreds of micromoments into actionable and meaningful buckets.

- **Provide Useful Information.** As mentioned before, advertising is not about bombarding consumers with messages they don't want. Instead, it is the art of providing valuable information when consumers need it. Technology enables us to identify these micromoments of consumer need, and it is our task to provide useful information at those points in time. In all three examples above—Sephora, Red Roof Inn, and DBS—the companies offered information that was highly valuable to consumers at a particular moment. If you're standing in Home Depot trying to figure out which materials you need to purchase in order to fix your bathtub, won't you find it helpful if Home Depot has how-to videos that show not only what parts may be needed but also how to go about fixing your bathtub? In fact, Home Depot has a large collection of how-to videos, and these videos, taken together, have been viewed more than forty-three million times. These are not intrusive banner ads on consumers' smartphones but useful content that helps the company earn loyalty in the long run.

- **Create Snackable Content.** On average, consumers spend about five minutes per session on the top 100 apps, but for more than one-third of mobile apps engagement lasts for less than a minute.[23] Based on its studies Google concluded that the average time spent per mobile session is only one minute and ten seconds long.[24] Regardless of the precise numbers, all these studies point to the fact that consumers have a very short attention span when they are looking for information on their smartphones. The situation, then, calls for snackable content that addresses a specific intent of the consumer at that moment. BuzzFeed gained a significant following for its news site based on this idea. Recognizing consumers' short attention spans, Facebook designed its newsfeed to include short videos. Safeway produced videos roughly fifteen to twenty seconds long for Facebook, ones that offered consumers culinary tips and cooking advice.

- **Speed Matters.** These days consumers are always in a hurry and very impatient. If a website takes more than a few seconds to load, consumers get frustrated and leave the site. Based on an analysis of 900,000 mobile ads' landing pages across 126 countries, Google found that, on average, it takes twenty-two seconds to fully load a mobile landing page. And 53 percent of mobile-site visitors leave a page that takes longer than three seconds to load.[25] Videos and images make it difficult for many sites to load faster, and often the cliché that "less is more" is applicable in these situations.

The three main topics discussed in this chapter—providing value to customers, shifting from storytelling to story making, and moment-based marketing—all point to a fundamental reality about customer engagement. Even though the tools of reaching consumers have changed in the digital era, we still need to have a deep understanding of consumers and provide value to engage them. Annoying ads are not only ineffective but costly to advertisers and publishers.

Chapter 9

Measuring and Optimizing Marketing Spend

"Half the money I spend on advertising is wasted. The trouble is, I don't know which half." This quote, attributed to John Wanamaker, a department-store magnate in the nineteenth century, highlights a constant challenge for marketing executives. Two new developments—digital advertising, with its ability to track every click, and big data for analyzing and finding patterns—were hailed as potential solutions to this decades-old problem. However, these developments have come with their own challenges. Digital advertising has ushered in an era of new marketing metrics, such as video views, Facebook likes, and click-through rates, even though their link to actual sales and profitability often remains fuzzy. And although big data has allowed executives to easily find patterns and correlations, many of those patterns and correlations are spurious and misleading. In this chapter, we will discuss some of the key challenges in measuring and optimizing one's marketing spend, and the latest research that aims to solve those challenges.

Correlation versus Causality

In 2008, Chris Anderson, the editor of *Wired* magazine, wrote a provocative article titled, "The End of Theory: The Data Deluge Makes the Scientific Method Obsolete," in which he wrote:

> Scientists are trained to recognize that correlation is not causation . . . But faced with massive data, this approach to science—hypothesize, model, test—is becoming obsolete . . . There is now a better way. Petabytes allow us to say: "Correlation is enough." We can stop looking for models . . . Correlation supersedes causation . . . There's no reason to cling to our old ways. It's time to ask: What can science learn from Google?[1]

The same year Google researchers published an article in the journal *Nature* about Google Flu Trends—a model that used hundreds of billions of US consumer searches on Google about influenza to accurately predict the incidence of the flu.[2] Suddenly it seemed that in the era of big data, correlation might really be enough. Why bother understanding how advertising may influence consumers if we can find a strong positive correlation between advertising and sales? With vast amounts of information available in the digital era, we can let the data "speak" for itself.

The problem with this approach is that we often find spurious and misleading patterns in large data. To see this, try correlating two random variables in Google Correlate, a free service provided by Google. There is, for example, an incredibly high correlation between US web searches for losing weight and for townhouses to rent, even though it is hard to believe that the searches are somehow related.

While it is easy to believe that correlation in this example is spurious, in many other instances such misleading results may seem convincing and may prompt wrong decisions. Even Google's study came under criticism in a 2014 article in the journal *Science*, which found that since August 2011, Google Flu Trends overestimated the flu rate for 100 of the 108 weeks of the study, sometimes by more than 100 percent.[3] Assuming without question that correlation bespeaks causality has also led to many incorrect conclusions in measuring marketing effectiveness, as we highlight next.

What Is a Facebook "Like" Worth?

A few years ago, my Harvard Business School colleague John Deighton and I invited a senior digital marketing executive from Coca-Cola to be a guest speaker for a digital marketing course that we were teaching to our MBA students. In his remarks to the class the Coke executive proudly said that Coke had 40 million Facebook fans (today this number is over 105 million)—a key metric that Facebook was promoting. Soon the class started debating about the value of a Facebook "like." Some students argued that the mere fact that 40 million consumers raised their hands to publicly declare their affinity for Coke ought to be highly valuable. Others wondered if Coke "bought" these fans by offering them discounts and free gifts.

Around that time, many research companies were trying to quantify the value of a Facebook fan. A 2011 study by comScore proclaimed that Starbucks fans, and friends of fans, spent 8 percent more and transacted 11 percent more frequently than the average internet user who transacted at Starbucks.[4] A couple of years later, Syncapse, a company that specializes in "social intelligence," created an even bigger splash by declaring that, on average, the value of a Facebook fan was roughly $174. For Coke specifically, a fan was worth a little over $70 (see figure 9-1).

These provocative studies piqued my curiosity, and I wanted to understand how the researchers arrived at these incredible numbers. In addition to brand affinity and media value, a key component of fans' value in these studies came from their increased product spending. To measure it, researchers used a panel of consumers and compared the annual spending on a variety of brands by Facebook fans and by nonfans of those brands. Using this approach Syncapse found, for instance,

FIGURE 9-1

Value of a Facebook fan

Source: Todd Wasserman, "A Facebook Fan Is Worth $174, Researcher Says," *Mashable*, April 17, 2013.

that Coke fans spent $70 more per year on Coke products than nonfans did, which led Syncapse to conclude that the value of a Coke Facebook fan was $70.

But this approach raises a fundamental question: Did "liking" Coke on Facebook encourage users to spend more on Coke, or were loyal and heavy users of Coke more inclined to "like" Coke on Facebook in the first place? This distinction is critical, since these studies were effectively suggesting that Facebook "likes" build loyalty and encourage consumers to spend more on their brands. However, if self-selection was at work, and loyal, heavy users were more likely to become Facebook fans, then using Facebook "likes" as a key metric of success—or, worse, spending marketing dollars to obtain them—would be highly unjustified.

It is hard to control for self-selection when parsing Facebook data, so my colleagues and I decided to undertake a research project where in a series of lab and field studies we randomly assigned consumers to fan and nonfan groups. In one of our experiments we invited consumers in the treatment, or fan, group to like a new brand of cosmetic on

Facebook (most accepted the invitation), while the people in the control, or nonfan, group did not receive this invitation. All participants were then given a coupon for a free sample, and we tracked coupon redemption for both groups. In a second set of experiments we tested whether liking a page influences the behavior of online friends. Across five experiments and two meta-analyses involving over 14,000 consumers, we found that a Facebook "like" has no impact on the attitudes and buying habits of either consumers or their online friends. In other words, the mere act of "liking" a brand on Facebook had no value in our study.[5]

In recent years, Facebook has moved away from touting the value of fans and has instead focused more on demonstrating the actual lift in sales due to advertising on its newsfeed. Yet number of "likes" for a brand continue to be a focus for many marketing executives.

Social Contagion

Social networks, such as Facebook, have the potential to influence friends. In a provocative study, Nicholas Christakis, of Harvard Medical School, and his colleague James Fowler claimed that obesity spreads in social circles like an epidemic.[6] The *Washington Post* reported the findings of this study as follows:

> The study, involving more than 12,000 people tracked over 32 years, found that social networks play a surprisingly powerful role in determining an individual's chances of gaining weight . . . when one spouse became obese, the other was 37 percent more likely to do so in the next two to four years, compared with other couples. If a man became obese, his brother's risk rose by 40 percent.[7]

Soon this study came under a lot of criticism from the scientific community. Using survey data of high school teens and the same approach as used by Christakis and Fowler, one study showed that height, acne, and headaches were also contagious—a highly implausible result according to the authors of this study.[8] Russell Lyons, a mathematician from Indiana University, published a highly critical paper challenging the obesity findings due to "deeply flawed" methods of analysis.[9]

A major critique of studies that attempt to measure the impact of social influence is the confounding effect of what is called "homophily"—the phenomenon that "birds of a feather flock together."[10] Effectively, homophily states that two people, say persons A and B, are likely to be friends if they have similar interests. So, if person A buys a song on iTunes and later person B buys that same song, is it proof of the social influence of A on B or is it attributable to the fact that persons A and B have common interests in music and that this partly informs their friendship in the first place? Again, is this effect causal or purely correlational?

To separate social influence from homophily, Sinan Aral, a social network scholar, and his colleagues used data from 27.4 million users on a global instant-messaging network and examined their adoption of a mobile service application. They found that homophily explained over 50 percent of the perceived contagion and that previous methods had overestimated peer influence in product-adoption decisions by anywhere from 300 percent to 700 percent.[11] This finding is consistent with that of another study, one that examined technology adoption among employees in a firm and found that not controlling for homophily could lead to overestimation of peer effects by 50 percent.[12] It is difficult, though possible, to partially control for homophily from observed data.[13] However, the best way to identify true social-influence effects is through experiments.[14]

Value of a Click

Although it is hard to measure the impact of social influence, measuring the effectiveness of a search ad on Google is considered to be easy and straightforward. You pay based on cost per click (CPC), and knowing the conversion rate from clicks to purchase should give you an estimate of ROI for your search ads. Google provides such analytics to help its clients measure the effectiveness of online ads.

While this may seem deceptively simple, search ads might in fact be dramatically less effective than they appear to be, if—as is certainly possible—some of the users who clicked a search ad would have clicked the organic link of your website anyway. Perhaps one of the most provocative studies to challenge the effectiveness of search ads was done by eBay, which had been buying search ads for over 100 million keywords. Researchers at eBay believed that users who type branded keywords (search terms that contained the name eBay, such as "eBay shoes") were using them with the intent to visit eBay's website. In other words, these users would visit eBay with or without the search ads. In March 2012, eBay decided to test this hypothesis. It stopped advertising for all branded keywords and monitored its traffic in this carefully controlled experiment. It did the same for nonbranded keywords—search terms that did not contain the name "eBay." The study found that branded-keyword ads had no measurable short-term benefit since most of the users who clicked these search ads were frequent visitors to the eBay site anyway. For nonbranded keywords, new and infrequent users were positively influenced by search ads, but frequent users were not affected. The study concluded that since "frequent users whose purchase behavior is not influenced by ads account for most of the advertising expenses, [it results] in average returns that are negative."[15]

In response to this study, a Google spokesperson noted:

> Google's own studies, based on results from hundreds of advertisers, have found that more than 89% of search ad clicks were incremental and that 50% of the search ad clicks were incremental even when there was an organic search result for the advertiser in the top position. Since outcomes differ so much among advertisers and are influenced by many different factors, we encourage advertisers to experiment with their own campaigns.[16]

More recently, one of my colleagues, Michael Luca, conducted a similar test of search ads on Yelp. Using a randomized sample of over 18,000 restaurants, Luca and his coauthor selected 7,210 restaurants that had never advertised on Yelp. For the next three months, they ran free ads for these restaurants (without informing them, to avoid any change in their behavior), and then took the ads down to compare the difference in the restaurants' traffic with and without the ads. This study found that Yelp ads, in fact, led to a significant increase in restaurant page views, requests for directions, and calls.[17]

Why were search ads ineffective for eBay but effective for Yelp restaurants? It seems that branded keywords are ineffective for well-known brands such as eBay or Amazon, but may have a positive impact for lesser-known brands and restaurants. Yet a large proportion of search-ad money is spent on buying the keyword with the company's brand name—type "Hilton hotel" or "Amazon" in Google and you will see an ad for Hilton or Amazon just above the organic link for these companies.

Attribution

A related problem when trying to measure the effectiveness of search ads is attribution, or figuring out who gets the credit for the click or sale. Search is considered a bottom-of-the-funnel activity. In other words, it corresponds to when a consumer is actively looking to buy a product. It is quite possible, however, that in the earlier stages of a consumer's decision journey, she was influenced by the TV, radio, or display ads of a brand, and that this increased the likelihood of her clicking on a search ad at a later point in time. Marketing executives and advertising experts are quite familiar with this problem, although their approaches to solve it are usually less than ideal.

Google provides an overview of various attribution models used in the industry (see figure 9-2). The first five approaches are commonly used, but they are ad hoc. For example, the "last interaction" method gives 100 percent of the credit to the last touchpoint, which usually makes Google search appear more effective than it actually is. The "time decay" approach gives more weight to the later touchpoints and less weight to earlier interactions, though the choice of weights is arbitrary, which can significantly influence both the results and consequent budget allocations. The last two approaches, "model-based" and "experiment-based," are more rigorous. Model-based methods use ad-exposure and consumer-response data to deduce the effect of each ad along the consumer journey. Experiments, often considered the gold standard, show ads of a target brand in the test group but not in the control group. The difference in the response or conversion for the two groups can then be attributed to the ads.

Proper attribution is critical for optimal budget allocation. In 2010, BBVA Compass bank and its advertising agency faced this problem when deciding how to allocate the bank's online budget across several search engines and display-ad networks for acquiring customers. After monitoring the click-through and conversion rates of various channels, BBVA decided to spend about 45 percent of the budget on search and 55 percent on display ads. Past data showed that cost per acquisition for search was $73, whereas it was $88, or 20 percent higher, for display ads. Why spend more on display when it was 20 percent more costly than search? When I posed this question to Sharon Bernstein, the director of insights for BBVA's ad agency, she shared with me the results of an experiment. During January and February 2010, the ad agency randomly divided a subset of users into two groups. Both groups continued to see the search ads, but for one group the agency stopped display ads. It then compared this group's conversion rate through search ads (from search clicks to completing an application for a bank account) with that of the other group, which was also exposed to display ads. The results showed that those who were not exposed to display ads had a conversion rate of 1.26 percent and those who saw the ads had a conversion rate of 1.48 percent. Based on these results, the agency concluded that display ads were responsible for a 20 percent higher conversion rate than search ads alone and that therefore a 20 percent higher cost of acquisition for them was justified.[18] Recently several studies have begun to address the attribution problem in a more rigorous and sophisticated fashion than the mostly simple and incomplete approaches shown in figure 9-2.[19]

FIGURE 9-2

Attribution models

Attribution model	Description	Comments
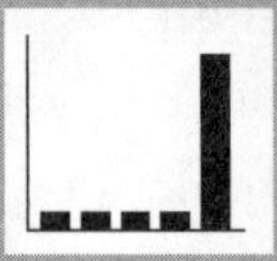 Last interaction	Last ad or click accounts for 100% of the sale	Ignores long-term effects of ads earlier in the funnel Overweighs ads that appear frequently
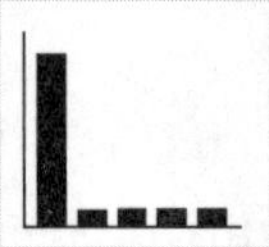 First interaction	First ad or click accounts for 100% of sale	Ignores ads later in the funnel that convert customer Overweighs ads that appear frequently
 Linear	All ads or clicks get a uniform weight	Ad hoc allocation Overweighs ads that appear frequently
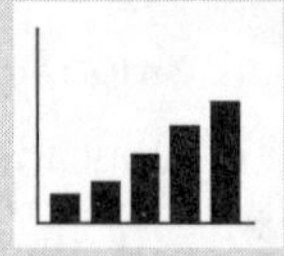 Time decay	All ads or clicks get some attribution; more recent ads get higher weight	Ad hoc weights (How much decay?) Overweighs ads that appear frequently Unclear why ads later in the funnel should have higher weight
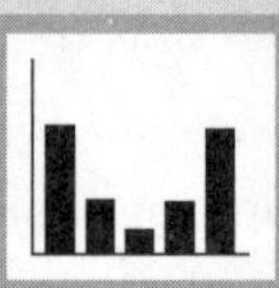 Position-based	Ads get attribution based on position in the path	Ad hoc weights
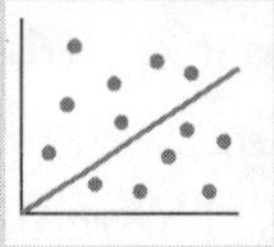 Regression- or model-based	Attributes weight based on regression- or other model-based approaches	Scientific way to allocate weights to ads along consumer journey path Ignores that some ads are viewed simply because they are on the relevant site (e.g., contextual ads) even if the ads themselves have no impact
 Experiment-based	Attribution based on A/B testing	Most accurate way to determine ad effectiveness but difficult to manage across many different ad networks and consumers Difficult or expensive to conduct

Source: Sunil Gupta and Joseph Davin, "Digital Marketing," Core Curriculum: Readings in Marketing, Harvard Business Publishing, and adapted from Google Analytics Help, "Attribution Modeling Overview," https://support.google.com/analytics/answer/1662518?hl=en.

Dynamics

If you see a search or display ad, you may not click on it at that very moment but it may still influence your behavior at a later point in time. This is true not only for brand-building ads that you see on television but also for digital ads designed to elicit immediate response. Ignoring this fact would underestimate the effect of ads and would lead to underallocation of the advertising budget. This effect is especially significant for products such as automobiles, which consumers consider over weeks or months before buying. In its study of the "zero moment of truth" (see chapter 7), using consumers' search data, Google created heat maps to visualize how long before the actual purchase consumers engaged in a search for various products. Figure 9-3 shows

FIGURE 9-3

Intensity of consumer search for automobiles

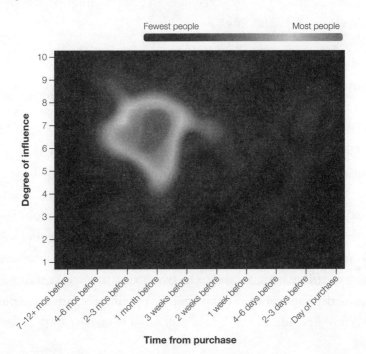

Source: Jim Lecinski, *Winning the Zero Moment of Truth* (Palo Alto: Think with Google, 2011), 25.

the "heat map" for automobile purchases, which highlights that the most intense search for cars occurs about one or two months before the actual purchase.[20]

Consumers' search behavior over time made me reflect on my discussion with BBVA bank and its ad agency. In its experiment to identify the attribution effect of display ads, the agency tracked the impact of these ads for two weeks (an arbitrary choice) after consumers were exposed to the ads. But what if the effect of the ads lasted for more than two weeks? To investigate this, my coauthors Pavel Kireyev and Koen Pauwels and I obtained data from the company and built time-series models to isolate both the short-term and the long-term effects of search and display ads on the completion of new applications. Consistent with the company's experiment, we found that conversion rate of search ads was higher when display ads preceded them, but surprisingly we also found that search ads had a significant long-term impact beyond two weeks. Taking into account the long-term effects of search ads, we concluded that the company should increase its search-ad budget by 36 percent, even after accounting for the attribution effect of display ads.[21]

Online–Offline Interaction

Even though some of the largest advertisers, such as General Motors and Unilever, now spend a large portion of their advertising budget online, the majority of their sales still happen in offline channels. In 2016, digital had a 38 percent share of total US ad spending, and this was expected to rise to over 50 percent by 2020.[22] However, by the first quarter of 2017, e-commerce accounted for only 8.5 percent of total US retail sales.[23] Clearly marketing executives believe that online advertising drives offline sales. While it is relatively easy to track a consumer who is exposed to an online ad and then buys online, connecting the dots between online ads and offline sales has not been easy until recently.

Tracking the link between online ads and offline sales is possible through field experiments. Even Facebook, which in the past relied on its own metrics, such as the number of "likes" or fans, is shifting to this approach to show sales lift from its ads. Facebook has introduced a new platform, Lift, which randomly splits the target audience on Facebook into two groups—one group sees the ads in its newsfeed and the other does not. By comparing the conversion rate, Facebook is able to measure the effect of its online ads on offline sales. Using this approach, Facebook showed that offline sales of data plans for GM's OnStar system increased by 2.3 percent because of ads on Facebook newsfeeds.[24]

While clients may not be comfortable trusting Facebook to prove the effectiveness of its own ads, several academic studies have also used field experiments to show strong cross-channel effects of online ads. Using data from a Dutch company that sells office furniture to businesses, one study found that 73 percent of the profit impact of Google's AdWords was from offline sales, and 20 percent of the profit impact of direct mail was from online sales.[25] Another study for a major US clothing retailer found that over 80 percent of the ROI from online ads came from offline sales.[26] Ignoring these cross-channel effects would lead to suboptimal budget allocation.

Not only do online ads influence offline sales, but there is also strong synergy between online and offline advertising itself. For example, a television ad may amplify its message through Twitter or Facebook. Using data from a major German car company and taking into account these cross-media synergies, one study concluded that the optimal advertising budget for online media should be double that of the company's current allocation.[27]

In conclusion, the ability to conduct field experiments quickly and cheaply and the possibility of building rigorous models using large amounts of advertising and purchase data are enabling firms to better measure and optimize their marketing budgets. However, managers must be vigilant against the false metrics and spurious analyses that still seem to permeate the industry.

PART FOUR

Rebuild Your Organization

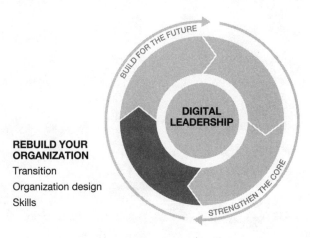

REBUILD YOUR ORGANIZATION
Transition
Organization design
Skills

DIGITAL LEADERSHIP

BUILD FOR THE FUTURE

STRENGTHEN THE CORE

Chapter 10

Managing Digital Transition

Driving change in a large, established organization is never easy, but it is even harder in the face of rapidly evolving technology and emerging business models that create huge uncertainties for the future. Unlike startups, legacy companies have assets they can't ignore and shareholders who demand profits. Incumbents have to strengthen their core and build for the future at the same time—a much harder task than starting from scratch. In this chapter we will discuss key elements that are necessary for a successful digital transition.

Creating a Vision and a Road Map for the Future

It is almost a cliché to say that a CEO must have a vision to drive change. But a vision and a sense of direction for the future are even more important when a company faces unprecedented challenges due to technology disruption and when employees and shareholders are uncertain about what the future holds for the company.

Sometimes the future direction becomes clear when conditions limit options for current business practices, as the *New York Times*

(NYT) realized. Faced with a significant decline in revenue from classified advertising, revenue the newspaper could not make up for with online advertising due to low online ad rates and the dominance of Google and Facebook in online ads, NYT realized that its century-old business model of relying heavily on advertising revenue was not tenable anymore. Cost cutting could help it survive in the short run, but it needed a vision and a path for the future. So the company decided to focus on its other source of revenue, subscriptions, and plunged headlong into creating a paywall, whereby readers had to pay for online news—something that no general-purpose newspaper had successfully implemented at the time and something that all experts claimed was doomed to fail since "information wants to be free" in the digital era. But NYT persisted in its vision and proved the naysayers wrong. In the fourth quarter of 2017, NYT added 157,000 net new digital subscribers, a 41.8 percent increase compared with the end of the fourth quarter of 2016, ending the year 2017 with over 2.6 million digital subscribers. The company's total subscription revenue (print and digital) was almost double its advertising revenue—a significant shift in its business model that historically relied heavily on advertising.[1]

The future path also becomes clear if you broaden your lens, as Shantanu Narayen, CEO of Adobe, did to steer his company from a tough situation in 2008 to a dominant position in 2017. Narayen's appointment as CEO in November 2007 was quickly followed by a time of great challenges for Adobe. The company was hit hard by the 2008 financial crisis, and its video-editing software, Flash, long the standard for making both web and desktop videos, came under fire from Steve Jobs, who refused to make it available on the iPhone. In 2009, Adobe's revenue dropped by 20 percent, its income by 50 percent, and its stock price by 60 percent.[2] Most leaders would perhaps start playing defensively at such a time, but Narayen decided to make the bold move of acquiring Omniture, a digital-marketing company, for $1.8 billion. Adobe's share fell 4 percent in after-hours trading on the day the Omniture acquisition was announced, and a *Wall Street Journal* article titled "Adobe Buys Omniture: What Were They Thinking?" captured the market sentiment.[3]

To understand what Adobe was thinking, I talked to Narayen, and this is how he explained his decision-making process:

> If you believe that growth is a fundamental imperative, and
> if your business is not growing, and you are the market leader in
> a lot of spaces, you need to broaden the lens by which you look at
> opportunities—more extensions and adjacencies become obvious.[4]

Three observations guided Narayen to broaden his lens. First, he noted that in the digital era content was exploding as people were creating more content than ever before, yet Adobe, the market leader in content creation, was not growing. Narayen believed that this was due to the fact that Adobe was not mission critical to a client's business. Second, Narayen recognized that data was becoming important, so it was critical for Adobe to play a role in that space. Third, marketing provided a unique opportunity for Adobe. IBM and Oracle were the go-to companies for CIOs, and Salesforce had cornered the market for sales executives, but there was a white space for CMOs. Adobe's acquisition of Omniture turned out to be a remarkable success, and by the end of FY2016, the company had generated almost $1.7 billion from digital marketing, which represented about 30 percent of the company's total revenue.

A good understanding of consumers' pain points and of shifts in their behavior is also helpful for setting the future direction of a company. Amazon has been a master of this strategy. Jeff Bezos's customer-centric philosophy led Amazon to get into video streaming, ebooks, and ebook readers as consumers shifted from buying books and DVDs to consuming media on their devices. While retailers are struggling to find a way to compete with Amazon, Bezos is teaching them a lesson with his experimental store concept, Amazon Go, where customers walk in, pick up an item, and leave the store without ever stopping to pay a cashier. Instead of installing beacons and focusing on technology to try to define customer movement and current behavior, retailers may be better off focusing on solving consumers' pain points in the store.

Often there is a tendency to get seduced by the latest technology or the new business model of a hot startup. While incumbents should always learn from others, they should stay true to their core DNA and leverage the assets they have. Jeff Immelt realized that the large installed base of GE machines provided the company a huge advantage in creating a platform for the internet of things, something that a startup would have a hard time mimicking. Walmart cannot become Amazon, because it has thousands of stores that add to its fixed costs. But it is exactly these thousands of stores that can be extremely valuable for reducing Walmart's shipping costs for its online customers. In April 2017, Walmart announced a "pickup discount" for online customers who came and picked up online orders in stores.

Creating a road map for the future does not mean that the CEO has all the answers or knows exactly how the future will unfold. Instead, the goal is to provide broad direction, recognizing that the journey will never be linear and that the company will have to continuously evolve and shape its strategy within the broad guidelines of its vision.

Navigating a Turbulent Transition Period

Digital transition involves managing existing business and building for the future at the same time. It is like changing the engine of a plane while in flight. The plane is going to go down first before it goes up again—and that is a scary and uncertain time, when everyone in the organization starts questioning the company's strategy. Even though existing businesses may be under threat and in need of change, they are usually still profitable in the short run, and it is hard to give up all those profits for an uncertain future.

To understand this challenge and how to navigate through it, let's revisit NYT and Adobe. As mentioned earlier, NYT had no choice but to transition to a digital newspaper and tilt its model toward subscription even though, at the time, print subscriptions and advertising still generated far more revenue than their digital counterparts. Imagine a scenario where in the long run NYT transforms itself from a print company to a fully digital company with no print version. Given declining print circulation and the high cost of printing and distribution, this is not a purely hypothetical scenario—in recent years several publications have decided to shift entirely to digital: *Newsweek* in 2012, *Information-Week* in 2013, and *Computerworld* in 2014.

If NYT moves to an all-digital future, its digital subscription and advertising revenues may be less than its current print subscription and ad revenues, due to the higher prices of the latter. However, going all digital would also significantly reduce its production and distribution costs, which typically account for almost 50 percent of the total cost of a newspaper. In the end, the overall profit for NYT could be comparable to its current profit. But what would happen during the transition, which could take several years? Figure 10-1 shows a potential path of the newspaper's profitability during this period. While the future, all-digital profitability may be good due to lower costs of production and distribution, during the transition period the newspaper would be operating both the print *and* the digital businesses, which would increase rather than reduce its costs. In other words, the plane would go down before going back up.

Adobe faced this situation during its digital transition. In addition to acquiring Omniture to get into digital marketing, Shantanu Narayen decided, in 2013, that instead of selling Adobe's software, Creative Suite, as a package or perpetual license for $2,500, it would move to a software-as-a-service model, with a subscription plan that would cost users as low as $50 per month. The goal was to shift from a one-time sale to a recurring source of revenue that would be more stable and predictable and that would attract new users because of its lower entry price. However, this shift had a major impact on Adobe's revenue and income in the next few years, as consumers paid $50 per month over time instead of $2,500 up front. Adobe hoped that as new subscribers joined, the recurring revenue, over the long run, would surpass the revenue it would have generated under the old model, but the short-term hit on revenue and income was certain. Figure 10-2 shows the fall and rise of Adobe's net income during this period of transition.

FIGURE 10-1

Potential profit path of NYT during its digital transformation

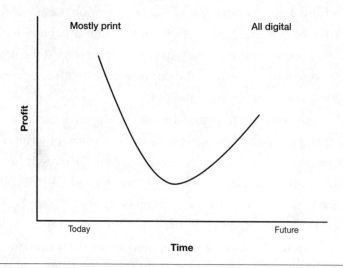

FIGURE 10-2

Fall and rise of Adobe's net income during its digital transition

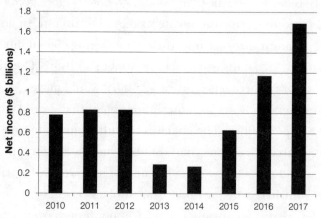

Source: Compiled from Adobe's financial statements.

In spite of a steep decline in income during 2013 and 2014, and levels that remained below those of the pretransition period through 2015, Adobe's stock price climbed steadily. How did Narayen manage this change successfully? He described a process of managing change both internally and externally:

> Internally we used as a galvanizing function the fact that revenue was not growing as fast as we needed to. We were not attracting new customers to the platform, because the up-front cost may have been too expensive, and piracy continued to be an issue. You have to find some internally galvanizing functions to show why change is needed. Externally, the challenge was to convince people that if they stuck with us through this transition, there would be benefits that would accrue—growth would increase dramatically, revenue predictability would increase, and we would get more recurring revenue. What was needed was our ability to paint [a] picture [of] how this transition would happen in the next three years so the financial community could make a good assessment. We were very transparent with the analysts.[5]

To support his vision and to drive this change, Narayen and his senior management team communicated to the entire company that there was no Plan B. When I visited Adobe to write a case about its digital reinvention, the phrase that kept coming up in conversation was "burn the boats," so people don't have the urge to go back to the old way of doing business. Courage, conviction, and clear communication, combined with a clear path for the future, led to a dramatic turnaround for Adobe. From May 8, 2013, when Adobe announced this transition, to April 1, 2018, Adobe's stock increased by 400 percent, more than Apple's or Google's during the same period.

Speed of Transition

Given the uncertainty about the future and the U-curve of profits during the transition period, how fast should this shift be? When I ask this question to a roomful of executives I typically get two extreme responses. Some argue that it should be quick, since there is no reason to prolong the pain. These executives also point out that the longer the transition period, the greater the cumulative loss or decline in profits over time (i.e., the wider the low part of the U-curve). Those who favor slow transition argue that the future is uncertain, and it would be foolish to jump in quickly. It may be better to pilot and test things before committing resources to a new direction. If the current business model is more profitable than the future business model might be (as shown, for example, in figure 10-1), they wonder why one would want to rush to a lower profit point instead of delaying the process and milking the current model.

There are reasonable arguments on both sides of this discussion. In the end, the speed of transition depends on three key factors:

- **Consumers.** The first and most critical factor is the trend in consumers' behavior. It is clear that media-consumption habits are shifting dramatically. Newspapers and cable companies cannot afford to ignore this trend. In many cases, a company may want to encourage consumers to change their behavior even if consumers are reluctant to do so at first. When Adobe moved its creative software to the cloud and shifted to a subscription service, many consumers complained that they were being forced to "rent" the software, an arrangement that could cost them more in the long run and that came with the risk that they might lose their work if their subscriptions lapsed. Within a few days of Adobe's announcement of its new subscription model, more than a thousand consumers filed a petition against Adobe on Change.org. However, Adobe executives decided that instead of reversing course, the company would move ahead and address the concerns of these unhappy consumers.

- **Competitors.** Newspapers have long been dabbling with the idea of online paywalls, but the concept picked up steam after NYT successfully launched its version. Soon, every newspaper was building its own paywall. While a change by a competitor may indicate a shift in the market, two factors should be carefully considered when thinking about competitors. First, what may work for NYT may not work, for example, for the *Boston Globe*. In other words, blindly following another player in the industry without recognizing your specific strengths and market position is likely to result in failure. Second, as discussed in chapter 1, industry boundaries are getting blurred, and it would be myopic to define your competitors narrowly. Consumers tend to use benchmarks from a wide variety of players across industries to judge the quality of your product or service. Whether you are a bank, a retailer, or a brand, consumers expect your web page to load as quickly as Google's, your delivery to be as fast as Amazon's, your products to be as flawless as Apple's, and your service to be as smooth as Uber's.

- **Company.** Perhaps the most significant bottleneck in any digital transition is the company itself—its skills, capabilities, and organizational structure. GE prides itself on making the best and most-sophisticated machines, such things as jet engines and gas turbines. Not surprisingly the company has some of the best engineers. However, as part of its transition to becoming a digital player with a strong emphasis on the internet of things, GE had to build digital capabilities. By 2017, GE Digital had more than thirty thousand employees who were experts in software, data analytics, and cloud computing. The movement toward autonomous cars has all the automobile companies scrambling to hire engineers with skills in software and artificial intelligence. Hiring new talent and developing new skills, and integrating them both into the old system, can be tricky and time consuming, and it is this aspect that often determines the speed of transition.

During my research, I also noted that many companies go through digital transition in three stages. The first stage usually involves using technology to reduce cost and improve efficiency in existing business operations. This requires breaking silos across different business units—a nontrivial task. As discussed in chapter 3, GE's digital journey started with the goal of making the company's own machines more efficient, by doing predictive maintenance. After the 2008 financial crisis, Goldman Sachs also decided to leverage technology to improve internal efficiency and reduce costs. Ezra Nahum, the global head of Goldman's FICC (fixed income, currency, and commodity) strategies in the securities division, explained this:

> FICC is comprised of seven different businesses—interest rates, foreign exchange, emerging markets, mortgages, flow credit, structured credit, and commodities. We used to operate in silos, where each of those businesses was run as a unit. We began to ask ourselves "Is there a common denominator that's reasonably large and can benefit all seven businesses?" We still need product experts in each business, but maybe they can work from a common technological platform. So instead of having seven separate and distinct teams, we have seven smaller teams focused on what is unique to each business and one bigger team underneath.[6]

Focusing on internal efficiencies in the first stage provides a tangible benefit for digital transition and may be more palatable within the organization. It also allows a firm to learn before opening up to a broader marketplace.

In the second stage, companies open up their technology platform to clients. Both GE and Goldman Sachs gave their customers access to their technology platforms. R. Martin Chavez, chief financial officer and former chief information officer of Goldman Sachs, built Goldman's technology platform with the explicit intent that it would be used for both internal business units and external clients. The firm developed a suite of applications that clients could use to do risk analysis or build and analyze a custom investment strategy.

In the third stage, companies tend to move toward a platform strategy by opening up their system to third-party players, sometimes even competitors. Amazon became a marketplace by inviting third parties to sell on its platform. GE encouraged developers to build on its Predix platform. Goldman Sachs created a platform for structured notes where it initially sold only its own products, but the company later invited third-party sellers to join, including competitors such as Wells Fargo, TD Bank, and CIBC. Spanish bank BBVA made its application programming interface commercially available to third parties, which could use BBVA's own customer data to build new products of their own.

Impact on Internal Operations

Digitization often leads to significant changes in the internal operations of a company, and every company should be ready for those changes to ensure a successful transition. Goldman Sachs's, for instance, saw a dramatic shift in the number and type of personnel on its US cash-equity desk. In the year 2000, the desk was staffed with 600 traders, but by 2017 it was staffed with two traders and hundreds of computer engineers. As NYT developed its digital strategy, it also had to struggle with the issue of managing its print version. Who should get the privilege of breaking news—print or digital? If the digital group publishes the breaking stories, what should the print group publish the next day?

Shifting from selling packaged software to selling a subscription-based service changed almost every function within Adobe (see figure 10-3).

- **Product Development.** Adobe used to release a new version of its software every eighteen to twenty-four months, and its R&D team had to anticipate customers' needs two years ahead of time to start building new features. However, with the subscription model, the team can continuously innovate and test new features to get quick customer feedback. Instead of relying on their intuition about the future needs of customers, engineers

FIGURE 10-3

Impact of new business model on Adobe's operations

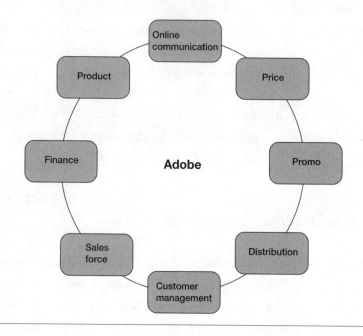

can now get ideas for product innovation from how consumers are actually using the product. Adobe can also allow consumers to create customized products, thereby reducing the company's development costs.

- **Distribution and Sales Force.** In the past Adobe had a large sales force that would call on retailers like Best Buy to sell its software. Moving to the cloud made this task redundant, and Adobe had to manage this shift with its sales force and retail partners.

- **Promotion and Communication.** The promotion of packaged software used to involve large marketing budgets and big events announcing the release of a new version. Adobe now relies on digital marketing tools to acquire and retain customers.

- **Customer Management.** Adobe did not have any visibility into its end users in the past. With the subscription service, it has detailed data on customers' usage and retention, and this allows the company to target consumers with the right products and offers.

- **Pricing.** Instead of charging a single price to all users, Adobe can potentially charge consumers based on their usage behavior. Heavy users get more value out of the product and are therefore potentially willing to pay more for its use.

- **Online Communities.** Adobe now has the ability to create an online community of its users. It could even become a platform on which, say, an amateur photographer who needs help with his son's graduation photos could connect with a Photoshop professional willing to provide that help for a fee.

- **Managing Wall Street.** As discussed earlier, moving from selling a $2,500 software package to a $50-per-month subscription service changes how revenue is recognized. This changed Adobe's accounting and its financials and had a dramatic impact on its revenues and income in the short run. To ensure that this did not affect its stock adversely, Mark Garrett, Adobe's CFO, had the challenging task of educating financial analysts on how they should value Adobe as it shifted to this new model.

What may seem like a small shift—from selling packages to selling a subscription service—created a cascade of changes that affected almost every part of Adobe's operations. Adobe had to execute flawlessly on these internal changes to ensure a successful transition. Of course, all such changes should be supported by an appropriate organizational structure that leverages the assets and synergies of the firm instead of creating conflict between the old and the new—a topic for our next chapter.

Chapter 11

Designing an Organization for Innovation

In this book's introduction we highlighted how starting an independent unit to spur innovation in a legacy company is like launching a speedboat to turn around a large ship—often the speedboat takes off but does little to change the course of the ship. This was the experience of Turkey's Finansbank, which in 2012 launched Enpara, a digital-only bank.

Finansbank's Speedboat

In 1987, during a period of liberalization in the Turkish banking industry, Hüsnü Özyeğin founded Finansbank.[1] A few domestic banks dominated the market at the time, so Özyeğin decided to focus on wholesale commercial banking. Later, when retail banking in Turkey began to flourish, Finansbank entered this area, focusing on the mass consumer segment with credit cards and consumer loans. In 2010, Özyeğin left the bank and Ömer Aras took over as its chairman. Recognizing the potential digital disruption of the banking industry, Aras and Temel Güzeloğlu, Finansbank's CEO, decided to launch Enpara, a digital-only bank that would focus on the fast-growing middle-income segment where Finansbank did not have any presence. By targeting a different segment, Enpara would avoid any cannibalization of Finansbank's own online and mobile banking operations.

Güzeloğlu hired Elsa Pekmez Atan, a senior McKinsey consultant, to head Enpara and gave her complete independence to run this unit with no immediate pressure to generate profits. Güzeloğlu hoped that in addition to attracting middle-income customers, Enpara would allow the parent company to learn about digital banking. Taking a page out of Amazon's book, Atan built Enpara with a relentless focus on customer service, simplicity of operations, and low transaction costs (no branches), which allowed it to offer high interest rates to its consumers. Within a month of its launch, Enpara had 20,000 customers and deposits worth almost $390 million. By the end of the first year, Enpara exceeded its goal, with 110,000 customers and $1.5 billion in deposits. Competing banks tried to mimic this strategy by launching their own digital-only versions, but cannibalization concerns forced them to fold their operations after a few years.

By the end of 2016, Enpara was a clear success for Finansbank. The digital bank had 630,000 customers, $5.5 billion in deposits, and a very low ratio of nonperforming or bad loans compared with industry averages and those of its parent company. In an industry where consumers hated banks, Enpara was loved by its customers. Atan noted, "We have near-perfect customer satisfaction (99.4%) and [an] exceptional net promoter score (NPS) of 75%, compared to 25% for the Turkish banking industry."[2]

Even though this speedboat was taking off, the mother ship was undergoing some pain. The retail operation of the parent company was unhappy that many of its projects were put on hold as IT resources were directed to Enpara. Running Enpara as an independent company was creating cost redundancies. Enpara was now large and beginning to face profit pressure from the company. Also, Ömer Aras wondered why the parent company's online-banking operations could not do for its customers what Enpara was doing for its own. Finansbank's acquisition by Qatar National Bank in late 2015 put further pressure on Aras and top management. To bring Enpara's learning back to Finansbank, Aras gave Atan the additional role of managing customer relations for the parent bank. However, even after a year in this new role, Atan was finding it hard to change the culture and behavior of Finansbank employees. Derya Düner, who managed Enpara's customer relations and was part of Atan's team in charge of transforming Finansbank, explained:

> At Enpara, we started from scratch and hired people for
> their attitude to serve customers. But that was not the case at
> Finansbank. The culture at the parent company is about quick
> wins and profits, not service. The hardest part has been to
> convince Finansbank people that this is not a temporary project.[3]

In early 2017, Enpara was at a crossroads, and Finansbank's management was wondering what to do with its digital bank. Merging the two operations was going to be difficult, and they were wondering if they should simply spin off Enpara as a separate company. The speedboat had taken off, but it did not do much for the mothership.

Creating a Landing Dock

Ajay Banga, the president and CEO of Mastercard, has taken a different approach to fostering innovation. He describes his philosophy as follows:

> Given the nature of our industry, most startups need large
> companies to get to scale. So we can do things together and
> benefit from the innovation of these startups. I am not interested in launching a speedboat that takes off as though it's in
> a different ocean. The best thing large companies can do is to
> make their ship accessible to startups and innovators. We need
> to create a landing dock as a way for them to enter the ship.

My rule for both internal innovation teams and external startups who work with us is simple—you should use my infrastructure, the engine of my ship, to power your venture and build something new. Don't go around in a little speedboat and leave the big ship behind.[4]

To create a landing dock, Banga first ensures that everyone in the organization is completely aligned with the vision and strategy of the company and its operating rules. This is how he describes them:

We provide the rails on which the cars of commerce travel. To strengthen these rails and build the rails of the future, we focus on three broad categories: our core business, which consists of prepaid, debit, credit, and commercial payments; diversification across new geographies and new customers; and developing new businesses (e.g., data analytics and services) for the future. This strategic focus must be guided by three operating principles: we are a B2B2C company, since we don't issue cards or accounts and don't interact directly with consumers— our merchant and bank partners do; governments are our critical stakeholders, since any change in policy can have a significant impact on our business; and cybersecurity is crucial for us, since our business is built on trust. We also believe that innovation has to be somewhat aligned with the company's strategic priorities—otherwise you run the risk that innovation is rejected by the organization.

With his broad vision and operating principles, Banga has focused on the following five things to accelerate innovation.

1. **Mastercard Labs.** After Mastercard acquired Orbiscom, an Irish payment-technology company, in 2009, Banga created Mastercard Labs and made Orbiscom's CEO, Garry Lyons, Mastercard's

chief innovation officer and the head of Mastercard Labs. Banga described his initial conversation with Garry:

> I gave Garry a budget and told him that you don't have to justify to me how you spend it—no spreadsheets that rationalize assumptions to get to [an] ROI. But if your team doesn't produce quantifiable and commercially viable innovations in two years, we will disband the group. The Labs is standalone on budget, but not standalone in using our base infrastructure. This ensures that any innovations coming out of the Labs are connected to what we do.

2. **Tapping into External Ecosystem.** Recognizing that no company can create every innovation by itself, Banga wanted to build a system that allowed him to tap into the exciting technological developments in Silicon Valley and elsewhere. For this, his team created three things.

First, they built "incubators" and "accelerators" in different locations around the world. These provide small amounts of funding, and access to Mastercard's infrastructure, to startups for developing their own ventures. In return, Mastercard gets a first look into the new technologies and the new thinking coming out of these ventures, and it can decide whether to invest in or strike commercial deals with the startups themselves.

Second, Mastercard invests money with a handful of venture-capital firms that invest in early-stage companies working within the payment-technology space. "VCs are better than Mastercard in identifying promising startups," argues Banga. "It's their bread and butter, and they allow me a visibility in this space with a small amount of investment."

Third, Mastercard allocates some money for larger investment firms that invest in late-stage startups. "This way I cover the spectrum, from a guy in a garage, to a startup with five or six employees, to a twenty-five-to-three-hundred-person pre-IPO company," Banga notes. "It serves two critical roles for us. First, it provides us visibility into the future technology that might threaten our business or that we could leverage. Second, it creates a level of osmosis within our company when our employees see all these exciting developments happening in the outside world and start asking the question, How can we connect them to what we do?"

3. **Direct Investment and Joint Ventures.** "We also do joint ventures with a number of companies," says Banga. "Although a large percentage of innovations don't succeed, because it is hard to know which ones will succeed until you invest in many and encounter the failures. But it is a small cost for us to see technology of the future and inspire our people."

4. **Building a Pipeline of Deals for Acquisition or Commercial Partnership.** Banga emphasizes that not all innovations happen in Silicon Valley. He notes, "To tap into technological developments all around the world, it is important that our country managers understand our innovation agenda and find local talent and local innovation. This way we are creating many more entry points and tentacles in our ecosystem." One example of this was the 2016 acquisition of a UK-based company, VocaLink, for £700 million. VocaLink is a leading company that has built the technology for fast ACH, which allows bank-to-bank payment in real time across several countries. This enables payments via mobile, internet, or phone without wire transfer.

5. **Internal Competitions and Hackathons.** To spur excitement and innovation within the company, Mastercard encourages its employees to develop innovative ideas related to its payment, data, or services business. Favored ideas gradually move up by getting increasing amounts of funding, and the ultimate winner gets a substantial budget to develop, launch, and run his or her business as its effective CEO.

"In the end, the goal is to create a landing dock for people to link their venture to our ship and help us navigate it in the future, and at the same time benefit from our resources and infrastructure for their startup," summarizes Banga.

Building a New Company from Within

Can you morph an old company into a new one by transforming it from within? Although many people believe that it may not be possible, since the white blood cells of the old organization would gobble up the new ideas of innovation, recent evidence suggests that this may not be entirely true. Even human cells, on average, renew themselves every seven to ten years.[5]

At Mastercard, Ajay Banga is trying to "build a new company from inside an established one." When he became CEO of Mastercard, in 2010, services (e.g., data, advisory, safety, and security) accounted for only 7 percent of the company's revenues. Today it is in excess of 25 percent. Even if technological developments, such as mobile payments via fast ACH, could present a threat for Mastercard, Banga is preparing the company for this future by building other businesses, and in the process is slowly morphing the company into one that may look quite different ten to fifteen years from now.

Digital Journey of Goldman Sachs

Inspired by Lou Gerstner's transformation of IBM from a hardware to a services company, Goldman Sachs embarked on a journey to create a new firm from within by leveraging technology.[6] While technology always played an important role at Goldman, the 2008 financial crisis and the new regulations that followed accelerated the pace of change. The Dodd–Frank Act and Volcker rule prohibited financial-services firms from engaging in proprietary trading and required them to hold higher levels of capital to weather a downturn. These regulations had a significant impact on Goldman's business—revenues and pretax earnings in 2011 were down 37 percent and 65 percent, respectively, compared with those of 2007. In addition, every financial institution, including Goldman, was facing a threat from financial-technology, or fintech, companies.

To weather this storm, Lloyd Blankfein, Goldman's CEO, and R. Martin Chavez, Goldman's chief information officer at the time (now its CFO), led the company on a journey that had three broad phases. First, they built a technology platform for the entire firm by centralizing core components of work, removing duplication and breaking divisional silos. This was a nontrivial task in a company where business units were responsible for their profitability and prized their independence. Next, in order to strengthen the core, Goldman opened up its platform to its clients. Chavez explained this shift using an analogy to Google:

> Imagine if Google were closed and proprietary. You would call Google to do a search, it would come back with results, and then you would call it back to refine or redo the search. This is how our business was done—we would go back and forth with our clients on the phone until they were satisfied with the product we developed for them. Why not give them direct access to our platform and our tools?

To position itself for the future, Goldman also started building new businesses. Two examples of this are SIMON, its platform for structured notes, which even Goldman's competitors are invited to join, and Marcus, its online consumer-lending unit.

To implement this strategy, Goldman formed two internal groups: Principal Strategic Investment (PSI) and the Digital Strategies Group (DSG). PSI, led by Global Head Darren Cohen, had the dual goal of leveraging new technology to shape and strengthen the core businesses of Goldman, and also managing the firm's $1 billion strategic-investment portfolio by identifying promising technology startups, similar to what Banga was doing at Mastercard. PSI worked closely with Goldman's business-unit heads to identify potential technology-investment opportunities that could strengthen and enhance their current business practices. For example, many functions of the trading and IPO processes have been automated, reducing costs and improving speed. In its strategic-investment-management role, PSI acts as part VC and part private-equity player, with the idea of investing in technology startups that could help improve the performance and potentially change the direction of the mothership.

In 2016, Goldman created the DSG, a complementary executive committee with representation from heads of several business units, to ensure coordination and implementation of these initiatives. A June 2016 internal memo introduced the DSG: "As our digital initiatives expand, the DSG will enable us to make globally coordinated, cross-product, timely decisions on the strategy, resourcing, implementation, and marketing of our digital offering."

More and more companies are beginning to realize that while it sounds intriguing and trendy to create stand-alone, independent units full of energetic young entrepreneurs charged with out-of-the-box thinking, these efforts often do not help in transforming a large legacy company. Creating a speedboat that is not tied, even with a long rope, to the mothership does not help change the direction of the ship. And investing in startups without a clear idea of how they will end up on the landing dock of your ship is nothing more than playing a VC game, not transforming your core business.

Chapter 12

Skills, Capability, and Talent Management

For centuries, agriculture remained unchanged—farmers plowed their fields with the help of farm animals and irrigated them using water from nearby rivers. In many emerging countries, such as India, small farmers still use these centuries-old methods, which require limited skills. Innovations in agriculture started in the eighteenth century, with crop rotation, and continued in the twentieth century with mechanization, synthetic fertilizers, pesticides, and high-yield seeds.

Today, farming has become a high-tech operation. GPS in autonomous tractors ensures that they do not cover the same ground twice or miss any spots, thus reducing fuel consumption and improving the utilization of fertilizers. Technology has also led to "precision farming." John Deere's equipment can plant individual seeds accurately within an inch, and a sensor on its equipment can measure the amount of nutrients in the soil and adjust the amount of fertilizer in real time. The University of Sydney has developed a solar-powered device that can identify individual weeds and zap them.[1]

An article in *The Economist* compared farming to matrix algebra: "A farmer must constantly juggle a set of variables, such as the weather, his soil's moisture levels and nutrient content, competition to his crop from weeds, threats to their health from pests and diseases, and the cost of taking action to deal with these things."[2] Using past and real-time data on these variables from sensors and other sources, companies like John Deere are developing software algorithms to help farmers optimize yield and maximize profits.

These developments in software and data analytics are not limited to any one industry. From farming to financial services, companies are hiring hundreds or even thousands of software engineers with computer-science and data-analytic skills. In 2017, over nine thousand employees, or about one-quarter of Goldman Sachs's staff, had engineering backgrounds, and 37 percent of its 2016 analyst class had STEM (science, technology, engineering, or math) degrees.[3] Data is the new oil, and companies need people with the skills to refine and extract value from this important resource.

Data Analytics, Machine Learning, and Artificial Intelligence

According to an IBM report, we create 2.5 quintillion bytes of data every day. Put differently, 90 percent of the data in the world today has been created in the last two years.[4] This data comes from consumer activities such as web browsing, social media posts, and mobile usage—and increasingly from sensors built into machines. Making sense of this vast amount of data has therefore become the key challenge for companies, including every company discussed at length in this book—Adobe, Amazon, GE, Goldman Sachs, Mastercard, the *New York Times*, and The Weather Company.

One powerful approach for leveraging massive amounts of data is through machine learning and artificial intelligence (AI). Today, AI is the force behind automation, and it creates fear and excitement at the same time. While some people, like Elon Musk, worry about the possibility of AI running amok, others feel that this technology will revolutionize every industry in the future. No matter which view you hold, there is no doubt that AI will have a dramatic impact on the future of work and the skills needed to thrive in the digital era. To understand the potential impact of AI on jobs, it is perhaps useful to understand what it is and how it might enable machines to perform many tasks that are currently done by people.

Origins of Artificial Intelligence

The idea of artificial intelligence dates back to a workshop held at Dartmouth College in the summer of 1956. The early attempts focused on creating rule-based "expert systems" in which a machine learned rules (e.g., how to play chess) from a human expert and then used its computational power to sift through millions of combinations to arrive at the best decision. In 1996, IBM used this approach for developing its chess supercomputer, Deep Blue, to play against reigning world champion Garry Kasparov. Deep Blue searched six, eight, sometimes even twenty moves ahead, processing two hundred million positions per second. This brute-force computational power allowed Deep Blue to win the first game against Kasparov, but Kasparov won the next three games and drew the remaining two.

Expert systems leveraged the computing power of machines, but the results, however impressive, were hardly "intelligent." Most practical situations, such as language translation, don't follow neat and well-defined rules the way chess does. As a result, interest in AI remained dormant for decades. It resurfaced with the availability of large data and the ability to detect patterns.

Big Data and Pattern Recognition

The term *big data* crept up into the business lexicon to represent the large amounts of complex data available today. Is big data a big deal or a big hype? After all, data has always formed the backbone of decision-making in business. What does a large amount of data allow us to do that we could not do before? In 2008, researchers at Google provided a glimpse of the power of big data. In a 2015 article, I described this research as follows:

> In November 2008, researchers at Google published an article in the journal *Nature* about Google Flu Trends (GFT)—a model that used hundreds of billions of US consumer searches on Google about influenza during the years 2003–2008 to predict the incidence of the flu. Google scientists claimed that no prior knowledge of influenza was used in building the model. Instead, they analyzed more than 50 million of the most commonly used search queries, and automatically selected the best-fitting search terms by estimating 450 million different models on candidate queries. The final model used a mere 45 search terms to predict rate of flu in several regions of the [United States]. The results of this model were compared with the actual incidence of influenza as reported by the Centers for Disease Control (CDC). The paper reported an incredible accuracy rate with correlations between actual and predicted influenza rates between 0.90 and 0.97.[5]

Suddenly it seemed that you didn't need domain expertise to predict the incidence of flu. Although the Google research came under some criticism later, it opened up the possibility of data and algorithms replacing experts.[6]

Rebirth of Artificial Intelligence

Most studies based on big data, including Google's flu research, use numerical data such as the number of queries of a search term. This is the kind of data that we are used to dealing with in business through an Excel spreadsheet or an econometric model. However, data now comes in many other forms—texts, images, videos—that don't fit neatly into the rows and columns of an Excel spreadsheet. How do you sort through thousands of your digital photos to identify only those pictures that show one of your children? This problem was the focus of ImageNet, a database of millions of images, which challenged scholars to build models to correctly classify images. In 2010, machines and software algorithms had an accuracy rate of 72 percent, whereas humans were able to classify images with an average accuracy of 95 percent. In 2012, a team led by Geoff Hinton, at the University of Toronto, used a novel approach, called "deep learning," which allowed them to improve the image-recognition accuracy to 85 percent. Today, facial-recognition algorithms based on deep learning have an accuracy rate of over 99 percent.[7]

Deep learning is based on artificial neural networks (ANNs), which are rooted in how the human brain works. An average human brain has 100 billion neurons, and each neuron is connected to up to 10,000 other neurons that allow it to transmit information quickly. When a neuron receives a signal, it sends an electric impulse that triggers other neurons, which in turn propagate the information to neurons connected to them. The output signal of each neuron depends on a set of "weights" and an "activation function." Using this analogy and massive amounts of data, researchers train an ANN by adjusting the weights and the activation function to get the desired output.

ANNs have been around for several decades, but the breakthrough came from a new method called "convolution neural net." Effectively, this approach shows that with a single "layer" of network you can identify only simple patterns, but with multiple layers you can find patterns of patterns. For example, the first layer of a network might distinguish an object from the sky in a photo. The second layer might separate a circular object from a rectangular figure. The third layer might identify a circular figure as a face, and so on. It is as if with each successive layer the image comes more and more into focus. Networks with twenty to thirty layers are now commonly used. This level of abstraction, dubbed deep learning, is behind the major improvement in machine learning and AI.

Training Machines to Learn

Instead of the rule-based or top-down approach used in the past, machine learning relies on a bottom-up, data-based approach to recognize patterns. Young children don't learn languages by memorizing the rules of grammar but instead by simply immersing themselves. Pattern recognition works best when there is a large amount of data, which is where the power of big data becomes apparent. There are several approaches for training machines to do tasks performed by humans today.

The first approach, called "supervised learning," is now used by Google to identify spam emails or translate a web page into over one hundred different languages. None of these activities involve the manual processing of data. How are machines able to do this automatically? How are computer scientists at Google able to translate one hundred different languages without any knowledge of them? Supervised learning involves using large amounts of "training" data, say emails, which are first classified or labeled by humans as spam or not spam. These emails are then fed to a machine to see if it can correctly identify spam emails. No rules are specified for identifying spam emails. Instead, the machine automatically learns which phrases or sentences to focus on based on the accuracy of its prediction. This trial-and-error process improves as more data becomes available.

Similarly, Google Translate would convert a sentence or a page from, say, English to Spanish and back and then measure its own accuracy, without any knowledge of either language. As more data becomes available, the machine learns and becomes more accurate. Today, Google Translate is so accurate that it is hard to distinguish its translations from those done by a linguist. Google can now automatically translate conversations in a different language in real time. Suddenly, language skills have become less critical. And this is not limited to languages. Machines can read X-ray or MRI images as well as or better than radiologists who have years of training and experience. Any repetitive task for which large amounts of data are available for training machines can and will be automated.

While supervised learning requires us to classify or label data to train machines, "unsupervised learning" involves no such guidance. This approach effectively asks the machine to go and look for interesting patterns in the data, without telling the machine what to look for.

This can be very useful in identifying cyberattacks, terrorist threats, or credit card fraud. But unsupervised learning is extremely difficult, and scholars struggled for a long time to find a way to make it work. The breakthrough came in 2011, when Quoc Le, a doctoral student of the leading AI scholar Andrew Ng, developed an approach that successfully detected cats from millions of unlabeled YouTube videos.[8] The findings, in what is fondly known as "the cat paper," were published in 2012, and they opened up the area of unsupervised learning, which is currently considered the frontier of machine learning.

In between supervised and unsupervised learning is "reinforcement learning." Here the machine starts with unsupervised learning, and when it finds an interesting pattern, a researcher sends positive reinforcement to the machine to direct its search. Another approach is "transfer learning," in which experts (e.g., in cybersecurity) transfer their knowledge to the machine instead of letting the machine start from scratch. Most of the current AI approaches are domain specific—for example, language or medicine. The next frontier of this research is to develop "generalized AI," which would be capable of synthesizing and finding patterns from multiple domains, just like the human brain does.[9]

Impact of Automation on Jobs

The ability to collect data and train machines to analyze and learn is transforming every industry, and it is going to have a major impact on jobs. In a highly cited 2013 study, Oxford University researchers examined 702 typical occupations and found that 47 percent of workers in the United States had jobs that were at risk of automation. The probability of automation varied by profession: 99 percent for telemarketers, 94 percent for accountants and auditors, 92 percent for those in retail sales, but only 0.3 percent for recreational therapists and 0.4 percent for dentists.[10] A 2017 study by McKinsey reported that while less than 5 percent of jobs have the potential for full automation, almost 30 percent of tasks in 60 percent of occupations could be computerized.[11] Even highly skilled and well-educated lawyers and radiologists are under threat from automation. Automation in the 1960s and 1970s replaced blue-collar jobs in factories, but the type of automation driven by AI is likely to replace many of the white-collar jobs. Effectively, jobs that are routine, repetitive, and predictable can be done by machines better, faster, and cheaper. The distinction is no longer between manual and cognitive skills, or blue-collar and white-collar work, but whether a job has large elements of repetition.

Automation creates anxiety among people and politicians because of the prospect of mass unemployment. It evokes scenarios where we won't have jobs and simply sit around watching Netflix all day. However, history shows that many of these fears are overblown. In the 1930s, John Maynard Keynes, the famous economist, predicted that technology would allow his grandkids to have a fifteen-hour work week—far from what we experience today.[12] ATMs were expected to end the careers of bank tellers, and while the number of bank tellers fell from twenty per branch in 1988 to thirteen in 2004, the number of bank branches increased by 43 percent over the same period. ATMs did not destroy jobs. They shifted the role of bank teller from one of simply dispensing cash to one of customer service.[13] The same type of shift is likely to happen with AI and the current wave of automation. Routine and repetitive parts of jobs will be automated, and people will need to retrain themselves for the nonrepetitive aspects of the job. While some jobs will be eliminated—as happened in the past, for instance, with elevator operators—new jobs will get created that require new skills.

Talent Management in the Digital Age

Not only are jobs changing, but the process by which firms recruit, develop, and manage talent is also undergoing dramatic change.

Recruiting

Technology is forcing firms to rethink who they hire and how they hire them. Goldman Sachs has automated many parts of its IPO process and replaced the majority of its traders with software engineers who write algorithms. GE Digital has over thirty thousand people with software and cloud-computing skills and those related to the internet of things. After becoming the CEO of Gap, Art Peck decided that instead of relying on the instincts and vision of his creative directors, the company should instead mine data from Google Analytics and its own sales and customer databases to come up with new designs. This increased focus on data is universal across companies and is leading them to hire people with skills in data analytics. Degrees in computer science and the ability to code are in great demand. The marketing function is also shifting, with greater emphasis on digital-marketing skills.

How firms hire is also undergoing radical change. The traditional approach of interviewing is subjective and can introduce bias. Additionally, it is time consuming and limits the number of candidates a company can screen. Some companies are even beginning to question the reliability of traditional data points, such as college degrees and academic records, for spotting the right talent. Catalyst DevWorks, a software-development company, evaluated hundreds of thousands of IT professionals and found no significant relationship between a college degree and success on the job.[14]

In 2003, Michael Lewis wrote a provocative book, *Moneyball*, which described how the Oakland Athletics used an analytics- and evidence-based approach, instead of the judgment of sport scouts, to assemble a powerful baseball team. Can firms use this approach for hiring? Guy Halfteck, founder and CEO of Knack, a startup based in Silicon Valley, believes that by using mobile games and analytics his company can do as well as or better than companies that use the traditional interview process for recruiting consultants, financial analysts, surgeons, or people of just about any skill.

How can a ten- or twenty-minute mobile game identify the right candidates? When I posed this question to Halfteck, he described how Knack works:

> Knack's games create an incredibly immersive and engaging digital experience. Playing a game involves up to 2,500

microbehaviors per game, or about 250 microbehaviors per minute. These include active and passive decisions, actions, reactions, learning, exploration, and more. Knack scores are computed from the patterns of how an individual plays the game, rather than how well they score on the game. From the raw data, our automated analysis distills within-game markers of different behaviors (e.g., how quickly the player processes information, how efficiently they attend to and use social cues like facial expressions of emotion, how they handle challenges, how they learn, how they adapt and change their behavior and thinking, and much more). These behavioral markers are articulated by a combination of machine learning and state-of-the-art behavioral science.

We then combine the behavioral markers to build and validate predictive models of psychological attributes, such as social intelligence, quantitative thinking, resilience, planning, and more. Each Knack score comes from one of these models. Having developed models ("Knacks") for 35 Human Model behavioral attributes, we predict real-world behavior, such as job performance, leadership impact, ideation, learning success, and more.[15]

Recognizing that identifying talent through mobile games is likely to elicit skepticism, Halfteck and his team embarked on a series of studies with universities, scholars, and companies to validate their approach. In a 2017 study, researchers at NYU Langone Medical Center asked 120 current and former orthopedic trainees to play Wasabi Waiter, one of Knack's games, and found that the data from the game was able to predict participants' performance on the Orthopedic In-Training Exam during their residency.[16]

Rino Piazzolla, head of human resources at AXA Group, one of the largest insurance companies in the world, with over $100 billion in revenue and 165,000 employees, is among the ardent fans of Knack. He described how he became a huge supporter and user of Knack:

We found out about Knack when we started looking at several startups to understand what innovations were happening in HR. We decided to test Knack to recruit for our call center, where we hire a large number of people. Then we followed the people we hired and did some back testing. We now have statistical evidence that by using Knack we are hiring people who are better fit for the job.[17]

This data-analytic and gamification approach to recruiting has won Knack many clients, including BCG, Citigroup, Deutsche Telekom, Nestlé, IBM, Daimler, and Tata Hotel and Resorts. In a recent talent-acquisition effort, BCG sent a link of Knack's mobile game to a large number of universities, many of which BCG did not visit in the past due to the time constraints of its own executives. Within a few weeks it obtained thousands of applicants. Without having the résumé or the background of applicants, Knack used its algorithms to analyze the data to identify the top 5 percent of candidates that would be a good fit for BCG.

Knack and its clients are not the only companies using this approach. Startups such as Gild, Entelo, Textio, Doxa, and GapJumpers as well as established firms such as Unilever, Goldman Sachs, and Walmart are also experimenting with the data-driven approach to spotting talent and broadening their pool of candidates. Typically, algorithms screen candidates in the early stages and face-to-face interviews happen only in the final phase. Unilever found that this approach was faster, more accurate, and less costly and that it increased the reach of the company to a pool of candidates that it had never interviewed before.[18]

Advances in analytics and AI have significantly improved the power and accuracy of "people analytics," the *Moneyball* approach described by Michael Lewis. This is even more important in the "gig economy," where many freelance workers are available for short periods of time for specific tasks and it would be too costly for a company to spend enormous resources in selecting these part-time employees.

Training and Development

Almost every company has online training courses and tools to help employees update their skills and learning. Using gamification that appeals to millennials, Appical, a Dutch startup, is helping companies onboard their young employees. The next step in this journey is to understand the specific needs of each employee and create customized training courses. While this idea is still in its early stages, it will be achieved by leveraging the knowledge of how firms customize content for their *customers* in real-time. Eyeview, a video marketing–technology company, can offer real-time customized video ads to consumers based on their past purchases and browsing behavior. Adobe is able to send specific learning content to users based on their current level of knowledge and potential needs. The same technology can be adapted to customize training content for employees.

Rino Piazzolla of AXA Group is now using Knack for executive development. This is how he described it:

> Knack originally positioned itself for recruiting, but I talked to Guy [founder of Knack] and said that if you can see my strengths, then you can also see my weaknesses, which could be valuable for assessment and development purposes. So I decided to be a guinea pig and play the game myself. Over my career at large companies like AXA, GE, and Pepsi, I have done—as well as received—a lot of executive assessment using traditional methods, so I was curious to see what Knack would come up with. Knack results were stunning, and its assessment was one of the best that I had seen in my long career in HR. Traditional assessment methods are usually contextualized and can create bias, but Knack knew nothing about me or my long career, and yet it came back with amazing results in a short period of time. So now we are using Knack for many of our executive-development programs, such as emerging-leaders development. We also used it in the [United States] for strategic workforce planning to gauge

what are our current skills and what skills we will need in the future. We asked, on a voluntary basis, all our US employees to play the Knack game. Over 30 percent of the people played the game, and that allowed us to create an inventory of our current human capital by function.

Rapid changes in technology also warrant continuous learning. Senior executives in a company may be familiar with Snapchat and WeChat, which their target customers are immersed in, but it is their junior employees who really know how millennials use and engage with these technologies. Recognizing this gap, Unilever instituted a "reverse mentoring" program, in which a senior executive is paired with a young employee. The junior person helps the senior colleague in understanding the role that new technology plays in young consumers' lives, and the senior executive mentors the junior partner about company strategy. The CEO of Coke in China told me a few years ago that he created a teen advisory board where he invited a few teenagers every quarter to help him get a deep understanding of their media consumption and buying behavior.

The need for continuous learning also raises important questions for our education system. Is the four-year college degree, which has been around for centuries, the right model today? Should universities and governments invest more in apprentice-based models, as Germany has done so successfully? Many countries, such as India, are investing heavily in skill-based education that needs to be constantly updated as the skill requirements change and evolve. For executives and universities, it means investing more in executive-development programs. According to Rino Piazzolla of AXA Group, the core competency employees will need in the future is the ability and desire to learn.

Performance Evaluation

Every company uses some version of a performance-evaluation system that includes 360-degree feedback and quarterly or annual reviews to set salary and bonuses and suggest improvements for the future.

This traditional approach has three major limitations. First, it is very time consuming. Deloitte found that it spends over two million hours per year to do performance evaluations for its 65,000 employees. This in itself may not be bad, because people are a major asset of an organization and spending time to measure and improve their performance is valuable. However, the second problem with the traditional approach is that it is often ineffective. One study examined how 4,492 managers were evaluated by their bosses, peers, and subordinates. It found that raters' perception accounted for 62 percent of the variance in ratings and that actual performance accounted for only 21 percent of the variance.[19] This biased approach leads neither to productivity improvement nor to employee engagement. The third limitation of the current approach is its batch mode, wherein employees often receive feedback only at the end of the year and not in the moment when it could help them improve their performance.

Digital tools and technology are now allowing firms to test new and faster ways to assess employees' performance. For its 300,000 employees, GE is in the middle of scrapping its decades-old annual reviews, which were notorious under previous CEO Jack Welch, and replacing them with an app, PD@GE, that allows workers to get real-time feedback from peers, subordinates, and bosses.[20] GE is also now developing an app that uses past employee data to help leaders do better succession planning and career coaching.[21] In April 2017, Goldman Sachs introduced Ongoing Feedback 360+, a system designed to let employees exchange real-time feedback with their managers. The system will also provide a dashboard that summarizes the feedback an employee has received throughout the year.[22] Impraise and DevelapMe are other examples of apps for real-time performance feedback.

Technology is not only useful in providing real-time feedback. The data-driven approach can also identify good performers without any bias inherent in rater-driven evaluations. When Hans Haringa, an executive at Royal Dutch Shell who runs a team that solicits, evaluates, and funds disruptive ideas from inside and outside the company, heard about Knack, he decided to see if it could help him with his task. He asked 1,400 people who had contributed ideas in the past to play Knack games. He then gave Knack information on how the ideas of three-quarters of these people had done in terms of seed funding or more. Using the game and performance data, Knack built a model, which was then used to predict the potential success of the remaining 25 percent of people. "Without ever seeing the ideas," Haringa noted, "without meeting or interviewing the people who'd proposed them, without knowing their title or background or academic pedigree, Knack's algorithm had identified the people whose ideas had panned out. The top 10 percent of the idea generators as predicted by Knack were in fact those who'd gone furthest in the process."[23]

Talent Retention

Retaining talented employees is a constant challenge for every organization. Often firms learn about imminent departures too late, when an executive has already secured another job and is ready to move on. If we can predict customer churn for a credit card or a wireless company using historical data of customers' past usage, why can't we use a similar approach to predict employee churn? This question has led to the development of new tools that are able to predict, well in advance, the likelihood of an employee leaving a firm. GE is currently testing such an application, to predict six months in advance if an employee is likely to leave, so that the company can design an appropriate intervention before it is too late.[24] Scores of academics are using their skills in customer-churn modeling to develop machine-learning algorithms for predicting employee churn.

Human resource decisions ranging from recruiting and training to evaluation and retention will be driven by data and machine-learning algorithms. Machines will not replace human judgment, but they will be major complementary assets to what we currently do to manage talent. The technology revolution is only going to accelerate in the future, and we better prepare and brace ourselves for it.

Notes

Introduction

1. Kasper Rørsted, interview by author.

Chapter 1

1. Theodore Levitt, "Marketing Myopia," *Harvard Business Review*, August 1960, 45–56.

2. Das Narayandas, Sunil Gupta, and Rachna Tahilyani, "Flipkart: Transitioning to a Marketplace Model," Case 516-017 (Boston: Harvard Business School, 2015, revised 2016).

3. Jeffrey Dastin, "Exclusive: Amazon's Internal Numbers on Prime Video, Revealed," Reuters, March 14, 2018, https://www.reuters.com/article/us-amazon-com-ratings-exclusive/exclusive-amazons-internal-numbers-on-prime-video-revealed-idUSKCN1GR0FX.

4. Ibid.

5. Tricia Duryee, "Amazon May Have up to 80 Million High-Spending Prime Members Worldwide," *GeekWire*, September 14, 2015.

6. Christian Camerota, "Amazon's Prime Opportunity," *HBS News*, July 14, 2015.

7. Kelly Liyakasa, "BMO Capital Markets: Amazon's 2017 Ad Revenue Could Top $3.5B," *AdExchanger*, April 28, 2017.

8. Jeff Dunn, "Netflix and Amazon Are Estimated to Spend a Combined $10.5 Billion on Video This Year," *Business Insider*, April 10, 2017, http://www.businessinsider.com/netflix-vs-amazon-prime-video-content-spend-estimate-chart-2017-4.

9. Sunil Gupta and Margaret L. Rodriguez, "Amazon in 2017," Case 514-025 (Boston: Harvard Business School, 2013, revised 2017).

10. Kelly Liyakasa, "Amazon's Q1 Sheds (More) Light on Ad Revenues," *AdExchanger*, April 23, 2015.

11. "Amazon Commands Nearly Half of Consumers' First Product Search," *PR Newswire*, October 6, 2015.

12. JP Mangalindan, "In Online Search War, It's Google vs. Amazon," *Fortune*, October 15, 2014, http://fortune.com/2014/10/15/in-online-search-war-its-google-vs-amazon/.

13. Spencer Reiss, "Cloud Computing. Available at Amazon.com Today," *Wired*, April 21, 2008, https://www.wired.com/2008/04/mf-amazon/.

14. Robert D. Hof, "Jeff Bezos' Risky Bet," *Bloomberg Businessweek*, November 13, 2006, 52–58.

15. "Quarterly Revenue of Amazon Web Services from 1st Quarter 2014 to 4th Quarter 2017," statista.com, https://www.statista.com/statistics/250520/forecast-of-amazon-web-services-revenue/.

16. Carol Hymowitz, "For Now, the Focus Is More on Innovation Than on Budget Cuts," *Wall Street Journal*, July 17, 2006.

17. John Deere Annual Report, 2014, http://www.annualreports.com/HostedData/AnnualReportArchive/d/NYSE_DE_2014.pdf.

18. Hymowitz, "Innovation," *Wall Street Journal*, July 17, 2006.

19. Ibid.

20. Matthew Cawood, "Streamlining Big Data Collection," *Farm Weekly*, July 6, 2015.

21. Michael E. Porter and James E. Heppelmann, "How Smart, Connected Products Are Transforming Competition," *Harvard Business Review*, November 2014, 64–88.

22. Adam Levy, "Netflix CEO Reed Hastings Just Told Cable How to Beat Netflix," *The Motley Fool*, November 22, 2015.

23. Michael E. Porter, "How Competitive Forces Shape Strategy," *Harvard Business Review*, March 1979, 137.

24. See YCharts, "The Cash Conversion Cycle," *Forbes*, March 10, 2012, http://www.forbes.com/sites/ycharts/2012/03/10/the-cash-conversion-cycle/, for the source of this data and discussion of cash conversion cycle.

25. Rohit Arora, "Another Industry Amazon Plans to Crush Is Small-Business Lending: Op-Ed," *CNBC*, June 16, 2017, https://www.cnbc.com/2017/06/16/amazon-plans-to-crush-small-business-lending.html.

26. Chuck Salter, "Kindle 2 Preview: Jeff Bezos on Why Amazon Works Backwards," *Fast Company*, February 6, 2009, https://www.fastcompany.com/1153395/kindle-2-preview-jeff-bezos-why-amazon-works-backwards.

27. Alastair Stevenson, "John Deere: Technology Vendors Need to Feed Agriculture's Big Data Needs," *V3*, June 5, 2014, https://www.v3.co.uk/v3-uk/news/2348372/john-deere-technology-vendors-need-to-feed-agricultures-big-data-needs.

28. Cawood, "Streamlining," *Farm Weekly*, July 6, 2015.

29. Mike Ramsey, "Ford Says It Will Focus More on Transportation-Services Sector," *Wall Street Journal*, January 5, 2016, B5.

Chapter 2

1. *Global Entertainment and Media Outlook 2016–2020: A World of Differences*, PwC Report, https://www.pwc.com.tr/tr/industry/entertainment-media/ outlook-global-entertainment-and-media-outlook-2016–2020.pdf.

2. The description of the Weather Company is based on personal interviews with David Kenny and his team. Additional sources include Rosabeth Moss Kanter, "The Weather Company," Case 314-083 (Boston: Harvard Business School, 2014) and Claire Suddath, "The Weather Channel's Secret: Less Weather, More Clickbait," *Bloomberg Businessweek*, October 9, 2014, https://www.bloomberg.com/news/articles/2014-10-09/ weather-channels-web-mobile-growth-leads-to-advertising-insights.

3. Kerry Close, "A Third of American Malls Will Close Soon," *Time*, May 12, 2016, http://time.com/money/4327632/shopping-malls-closing/.

4. Sunil Gupta, Michela Addis, and Ruth Page, "Eataly: Reimagining the Grocery Store," Case 515-708 (Boston: Harvard Business School, 2015).

5. Personal interview with Oscar Farinetti by the author.

6. Personal interview with Alex Saper by the author.

7. Phil Wahba, "Reinventing the American Mall," *Fortune*, December 15, 2016, 150.

8. Sarwant Singh, "The Future of Car Retailing," *Forbes*, February 5, 2014, https://www.forbes.com/sites/sarwantsingh/2014/02/05/ the-future-of-car-retailing/#7df822ce7d00.

9. Philips, "Philips Provides Light as a Service to Schiphol Airport," http:// www.philips.com/a-w/about/news/archive/standard/news/press/2015/20150416-Philips-provides-Light-as-a-Service-to-Schiphol-Airport.html.

10. "Washington Metro to Install Cost-Free LEDs," *Lux*, November 26, 2013, http://luxreview.com/article/2013/11/washington-metro-to-install-cost-free-leds.

11. Joris Van Ostaeyen, *Analysis of the Business Potential of Product-Service Systems for Investment Goods* (PhD thesis, KU Leuven, 2014).

12. Atlas Copco, "Mobile Air Compressors," https://www.atlascopco.com/ en-us/construction-equipment/products/Mobile-air-compressors.

13. Thomas Fischer et al., "Managerial Recommendations for Service Innovations in Different Product-Service Systems," in *Introduction to Product/ Service-System Design*, eds. Tomohiko Sakao and Mattias Lindahl (London: Springer, 2009), 237.

14. Mark Egan, "Deep Learning: New Subsea Service Model Helps Oil Drillers Limit Costs," *GE Reports*, February 24, 2016.

15. Thomas Fleming and Markus Zils, "Toward a Circular Economy: Philips CEO Frans van Houten," *McKinsey Quarterly*, February 2014.

16. *Horizons, Michelin's Letter to Its Shareholders*, November 2014.

17. Karim R. Lakhani, Marco Iansiti, and Kerry Herman, "GE and the Industrial Internet," Case 614-032 (Boston: Harvard Business School, 2014, revised 2015).

18. Martha Heller, "GE's Jim Fowler on the CIO Role in the Digital Industry Economy," *CIO*, March 29, 2016.

19. Heather Ashton and Jeffrey Hojlo, "IDC FutureScape: Worldwide Manufacturing Product and Service Innovation 2018 Predictions," IDC Report US43317317, December 2017.

20. Vivek Agarwal, Vinay Arora, and Kris Renker, *Evolving Service Centric Business Models: Quest for Profitability and Predictability*, Accenture Report, 2013.

Chapter 3

1. Smithers Pira, *The Future of Global Printing to 2020* (Surrey, UK: Smithers Pira, 2015).

2. Felix Oberholzer-Gee and Julie M. Wulf, "Alibaba's Taobao (A)," Case 709-456 (Boston: Harvard Business School, 2009).

3. "Benefits of Online Platforms," Oxera, October 2015, https://www.oxera.com/Latest-Thinking/Publications/Reports/2015/What-are-the-benefits-of-online-platforms.aspx.

4. Information shared with the author by Henrik Müller-Hansen.

5. For details see Das Narayandas, Sunil Gupta, and Rachna Tahilyani, "Flipkart: Transitioning to a Marketplace Model," Case 516-017 (Boston: Harvard Business School, 2015, revised 2016).

6. Catherine Shu, "Alibaba Group Starts Work on Massive Logistics Network to Provide 24-Hour Deliveries throughout China," TechCrunch, May 28, 2013, https://beta.techcrunch.com/2013/05/28/alibaba-csn/?_ga=2.12398516.144819195.1522769375-453968051.1501205451.

7. William Ruh, interview by author.

8. Thor Olavsrud, "GE, Pitney Bowes Team Up on Predictive and Prescriptive Analytics," *CIO*, July 14, 2015, https://www.cio.com/article/2947908/big-data/ge-pitney-bowes-team-up-on-predictive-and-prescriptive-analytics.html.

9. Thomas Kellner, "The Power of Predix: An Inside Look at How Pitney Bowes Is Using the Industrial Internet Platform," *GE Reports*, February 24, 2016, https://www.ge.com/reports/the-power-of-predix-an-inside-look-at-how-pitney-bowes-has-been-using-the-industrial-internet-platform/.

10. General Electric, 2015 Annual Report, http://www.ge.com/ar2015/letter/.

11. This section is based on Sunil Gupta and Sara Simonds, "Goldman Sachs' Digital Journey," Case 518-039 (Boston: Harvard Business School, 2017).

12. See Thales S. Teixeira and Morgan Brown, "Airbnb, Etsy, Uber: Acquiring the First Thousand Customers," Case 516-094 (Boston: Harvard Business School, 2016, revised 2018); and Michael Blanding, "How Uber, Airbnb, and Etsy Attracted Their First 1,000 Customers," *Harvard Business School Working Knowledge*, July 13, 2016.

13. Travis [Kalanick], "Chicago—Uber's Biggest Launch to Date?" Uber Newsroom, September 22, 2011.

14. Narayandas, Gupta, and Tahilyani, "Flipkart."

15. Geoffrey Parker and Marshall W. Van Alstyne, "Two-Sided Network Effects: A Theory of Information Product Design," *Management Science* 51, no. 10 (2005): 1494.

16. Elizabeth J. Altman and Mary Tripsas, "Product-to-Platform Transitions: Organizational Identity Implications," in *The Oxford Handbook of Creativity, Innovation, and Entrepreneurship*, eds. Christina E. Shalley, Michael A. Hitt, and Jing Zhou (Oxford: Oxford University Press, 2015), 379–394.

17. For an example of this see Clarence Lee, Vineet Kumar, and Sunil Gupta, "Designing Freemium: Managing Growth and Monetization Strategies," unpublished paper, July 2017.

18. "Global Mobile OS Market Share in Sales to End Users from 1st Quarter 2009 to 2nd Quarter 2017," Statista, https://www.statista.com/statistics/266136/global-market-share-held-by-smartphone-operating-systems/.

19. Nilson's Global Card Report 2015, *The Nilson Report,* April 2016, http://www.businesswire.com/news/home/20160509005108/en/Nilson-Report-Releases-Global-Cards-Report-2015.

20. Michael Wüertenberger, interview by author.

21. For a discussion on various degrees of openness, see Thomas R. Eisenmann, "Platform-Mediated Networks: Definitions and Core Concepts," Module Note 807-049 (Boston: Harvard Business School, 2006, revised 2007).

22. Erle Ellis, "Ecosystem," *The Encyclopedia of the Earth*, September 24, 2014, http://www.eoearth.org/view/article/152248/.

23. James F. Moore, "Predators and Prey: A New Ecology of Competition," *Harvard Business Review*, May–June 1993, 75.

24. Peter James Williamson and Arnoud De Meyer, "Ecosystem Advantage: How to Successfully Harness the Power of Partners," *California Management Review* 55, no. 1 (2012): 24.

25. Eamonn Kelly, "Introduction: Business Ecosystems Come of Age," *Deloitte Insights*, April 15, 2015. This article was part of Deloitte's Business Trends 2015 report.

26. Tim Cook, "September 2014 Live Event," webcast, Apple, Inc., http://www.apple.com/live/2014-sept-event/.

27. Sunil Gupta, Shelle Santana, and Margaret L. Rodriguez, "Apple Pay," Case 516-027 (Boston: Harvard Business School, 2015, revised 2016).

28. Wilko Stark, interview by author.

29. Mark Zuckerberg in a November 12, 2016, Facebook post, https://www.facebook.com/zuck/posts/10103253901916271.

30. Alvin E. Roth, "The Art of Designing Markets," *Harvard Business Review*, October 2007, 118–126.

Chapter 4

1. Paraphrased from NASA's ISS Longeron Challenge, https://www.nasa.gov/content/iss-longeron-challenge-0.

2. Mike Wall, "$30,000 NASA Contest to Boost Space Station's Power," Space.com, January 17, 2013, https://www.space.com/19315-nasa-contest-space-station-power.html.

3. Sylvain Zimmer, "Optimizing the ISS Solar Arrays, a Python Solution to the NASA Longeron Challenge," February 6, 2013, https://sylvainzimmer.com/2013/02/06/optimizing-the-iss-solar-arrays-a-python-solution-to-the-nasa-longeron-challenge/.

4. "NASA Tournament Lab: Space Poop Challenge," Hero[x], https://herox.com/SpacePoop.

5. Karim R. Lakhani et al., "Prize-Based Contests Can Provide Solutions to Computational Biology Problems," *Nature Biotechnology* 31, no. 2 (2013): 108–111.

6. Larry Huston and Nabil Sakkab, "Connect and Develop: Inside Procter & Gamble's New Model for Innovation," *Harvard Business Review*, March 2006, 58–66.

7. Eric von Hippel, "The Dominant Role of Users in the Scientific Instrument Innovation Process," *Research Policy* 5, no. 3 (1976): 212.

8. Eric von Hippel, *Free Innovation* (Cambridge: MIT Press, 2017).

9. Eric von Hippel, "Open User Innovation," *The Encyclopedia of Human-Computer Interaction*, 2nd ed., eds. Mads Soegaard and Rikke Friis Dam (Aarhus N, Denmark: Interaction Design Foundation, 2013).

10. Dietmar Harhoff and Karim R. Lakhani, *Revolutionizing Innovation: Users, Communities, and Open Innovation* (Cambridge: MIT Press, 2016).

11. Mike Helser, "The Future of Open Innovation," *Research-Technology Management*, January–February 2017, 35.

12. Henry Chesbrough, "The Future of Open Innovation: The Future of Open Innovation Is More Extensive, More Collaborative, and More Engaged

with a Wider Variety of Participants," *Research-Technology Management,* January–February 2017, 35.

13. Kevin J. Boudreau and Karim R. Lakhani, "Using the Crowd as an Innovation Partner," *Harvard Business Review,* April 2013, 60–69.

14. J. M. Bates and C. W. J. Granger, "The Combination of Forecasts," *Operational Research Quarterly* 20, no. 4: 451.

15. Sunil Gupta, "Big Data: Big Deal or Big Hype," *The European Business Review,* May–June 2015, 11.

16. Eliot van Buskirk, "How the Netflix Prize Was Won," *Wired,* September 22, 2009, https://www.wired.com/2009/09/how-the-netflix-prize-was-won/.

17. Von Hippel, "The Dominant Role of Users."

18. Dietmar Harhoff, "Context, Capabilities, and Incentives—The Core and the Periphery of User Innovation," in *Revolutionizing Innovation: Users, Communities, and Open Innovation,* eds. Dietmar Harhoff and Karim R. Lakhani (Cambridge, MA: MIT Press, 2016), 27–44.

19. Kate Linebaugh, "Citizen Hackers Tinker with Medical Devices," *Wall Street Journal,* September 26, 2014. This story was also highlighted by Eric von Hippel in his book *Free Innovation.*

20. Jeroen P. J. de Jong et al., "Market Failure in the Diffusion of Consumer-Developed Innovations: Patterns in Finland," *Research Policy* 44, no. 10 (2015): 1856.

21. Jon Fredrickson, interview by author.

22. John Davis, "InnoCentive—Oil Spill Cleanup Part 2—Meet the Solver," https://www.youtube.com/watch?v=5_ucQKWmxdk.

23. Karim Lakhani, interview by author.

Chapter 5

1. Matt Burgess and Amelia Heathman, "Samsung Opens Galaxy Note 7 Exchange after Battery Fire Problems," *Wired,* September 19, 2016, http://www.wired.co.uk/article/samsung-galaxy-note-7-exchange-uk-battery-fire.

2. Brian X. Chen and Choe Sang-Hun, "Why Samsung Abandoned Its Galaxy Note 7 Flagship Phone," *New York Times,* October 11, 2016.

3. Germany Trade & Invest, *Industrie 4.0: Smart Manufacturing for the Future* (Berlin: Germany Trade & Invest, 2014).

4. Willy Shih, "Building the Digital Manufacturing Enterprise of the Future at Siemens," Case 616-060 (Boston: Harvard Business School, 2016).

5. Siemens, "Defects: A Vanishing Species?" *Pictures of the Future: The Magazine for Research and Innovation,* October 1, 2014.

6. Rajiv Lal and Scott Johnson, "GE Digital," Case 517-063 (Boston: Harvard Business School, 2017).

7. James Manyika et al., "Unlocking the Potential of the Internet of Things," McKinsey Global Institute, June 2015.

8. "MX3D Bridge," MX3D website, http://mx3d.com/projects/bridge/.

9. "The First On-Site House Has Been Printed in Russia," Apis Cor, February 20, 2017, http://apis-cor.com/en/about/news/first-house.

10. Kaya Yurieff, "This Robot Can 3D Print a Building in 14 Hours," *CNN Tech*, May 2, 2017.

11. "3D Printing and the Future of Supply Chains," DHL Report, November 2016.

12. Marianna Kheyfets, "Could 'Westworld' Ever Be a Reality? This Doctor Is Already 3D Printing Tissues and Organs," *Circa*, February 3, 2017.

13. Tomas Kellner, "An Epiphany of Disruption: GE Additive Chief Explains How 3D Printing Will Upend Manufacturing," *GE Reports*, November 13, 2017.

14. Ibid.

15. Ibid.

16. "EOS and Airbus Group Innovations Team on Aerospace Sustainability Study for Industrial 3D Printing," Airbus Press Release, February 5, 2014.

17. Devindra Hardawar, "Mattel's New ThingMaker Is a $300 3D Printer for Toys," *Endgadget,* February 15, 2016.

18. DHL Report, 2016.

19. Nick Parkin, "Doctors Turn to 3D Printing to Source Medical Supplies in Earthquake-Recovering Nepal," *ABC News Australia*, March 5, 2017.

20. DHL Report, 2016.

21. Varun Bhasin and Muhammad Raheel Bodla, "Impact of 3D Printing on Global Supply Chains by 2020" (thesis, Massachusetts Institute of Technology, 2014).

22. Dave McNary, " 'Star Wars' Helps Licensed Merchandise Sales Grow to $251.7 Billion," *Variety*, June 21, 2016.

23. Daniel Cohen, Matthew Sargeant, and Ken Somers, "3-D Printing Takes Shape," *McKinsey Quarterly*, January 2014.

24. Ernst & Young, "How Will 3D Printing Make Your Company the Strongest Link in the Value Chain: EY's Global 3D Printing Report 2016."

25. MIT, "Self-Assembly Lab," http://www.selfassemblylab.net.

26. Lockheed Martin, "Collaborative Human Immersive Laboratory," http://www.lockheedmartin.com/us/products/chil.html.

27. Magid Abraham and Marco Annuziata, "Augmented Reality Is Already Improving Worker Performance," hbr.org, https://hbr.org/2017/03/augmented-reality-is-already-improving-worker-performance.

28. Ibid.

29. Haje Jan Kamps, "Touch Surgery Brings Surgery Training to Augmented Reality," *TechCrunch*, January 6, 2017.

30. Lucas Matney, "Walmart Is Bringing VR Instruction to All of Its U.S. Training Centers," *TechCrunch*, June 1, 2017.

31. "Virtual & Augmented Reality: Understanding the Race for the Next Computing Platform," Goldman Sachs Report, January 13, 2016.

32. James A. Cooke, "Kimberly-Clark Connects Its Supply Chain to Store Shelf," *Supply Chain Quarterly*, Q1 2013.

33. Stan Aronow, Kimberly Ennis, and Jim Romano, "The Gartner Supply Chain Top 25 for 2017," *Gartner Report*, May 24, 2017.

34. Hayley Peterson, "Amazon Is Getting Closer to Crushing America's Biggest Clothing Stores," *Business Insider,* January 14, 2017, http://www.businessinsider.com/amazon-becomes-the-biggest-clothing-retailer-in-the-us-2017-1.

35. "Demand Planning—The Catalyst for Higher Performance," Tecsys White Paper, 2016.

36. Jeremy Hill, "Inside Amazon's Hiring Spree at Its Massive Etna Warehouse," BizJournals.com, August 2, 2017.

37. Eilene Zimmerman, "Cheaper and More Nimble Than Amazon's Kiva Robot," *Forbes*, January 11, 2016, https://www.forbes.com/sites/eilenezimmerman/2016/01/11/cheaper-and-more-nimble-than-amazons-kiva-robot/#4b510933cb32.

38. Mark Roberti, "How Tiny Wireless Tech Makes Workers More Productive," *Wall Street Journal*, August 16, 2016.

39. Ibid.

40. "UPS Fact Sheet," UPS, https://pressroom.ups.com/pressroom/ContentDetailsViewer.page?ConceptType=FactSheets&id=1426321563187-193.

41. Mathieu Dougados et al., "The Missing Link: Supply Chain and Digital Maturity," Capgemini Consulting, December 16, 2013, https://www.capgemini.com/consulting/resources/the-missing-link-supply-chain-and-digital-maturity/.

42. Steven Rosenbush and Laura Stevens, "At UPS, the Algorithm Is the Driver," *Wall Street Journal*, February 16, 2015.

43. Dakin Campbell, "Goldman Set Out to Automate IPOs and It Has Come Far, Really Fast," *Bloomberg*, June 13, 2017, https://www.bloomberg.com/news/articles/2017-06-13/goldman-set-out-to-automate-ipos-and-it-s-come-far-really-fast.

44. Sunil Gupta and Sara Simonds, "Goldman Sachs' Digital Journey," Case 518-039 (Boston: Harvard Business School, 2017).

45. Singapore Academy of Law, *Legal Technology Vision: Towards the Digital Transformation of the Legal Sector* (Singapore: Singapore Academy of Law, 2017).

46. Zach Abramowitz, "More Evidence That Software Is Eating the Legal Industry: An Interview with LawGeex CEO Noory Bechor," *Above the Law*, June 2, 2015.

47. Singapore Academy of Law, *Legal Technology Vision*.

Chapter 6

1. This discussion is based on Sunil Gupta and Eren Kuzucu, "Enpara.com: Digital Bank at a Crossroad," Case 518-030 (Boston: Harvard Business School, 2017).

2. This discussion is based on Robert J. Dolan and Leslie K. John, "Kiehl's Since 1851: Pathway to Profitable Growth," Case 514-044 (Boston: Harvard Business School, 2013, revised 2015).

3. Ibid., page 2.

4. This discussion is based on Jill Avery, Chekitan S. Dev, and Peter O'Connor, "Accor: Strengthening the Brand with Digital Marketing," Case 316-103 (Boston: Harvard Business School, 2016).

5. Nick Vivion, "Accor Is Now AccorHotels and Fights OTAs with Open Enrollment for Independents," *Tnooz*, June 3, 2015.

6. "AccorHotels Opens Its Distribution Platform to Independent Hotels," *Hospitality On*, June 6, 2015, http://hospitality-on.com/en/news/2015/06/03/accorhotels-opens-its-distribution-platform-to-independent-hotels/.

7. Nicole Spector, "Retailers Are Making It Easier for You to Return Gifts—and Buy More," *NBC News*, January 3, 2017.

8. Cliff Kuang, "Disney's $1 Billion Bet on a Magical Wristband," *Wired*, March 10, 2015.

Chapter 7

1. Gregory Karp, "Millennials, Nontraditional Travelers Chase the Sapphire Reserve," *NerdWallet*, April 5, 2017, https://www.nerdwallet.com/blog/credit-cards/chase-sapphire-reserve-millennials-travel-trends/.

2. Jennifer Surane and Hugh Son, "Dimon Says New Sapphire Card Cuts Profit by up to $300 Million in Quarter," *Bloomberg*, December 6, 2016.

3. Ibid.

4. "J.P. Morgan Chase Strategy Update," Marianne Lake, Chief Financial Officer, February 27, 2018, https://www.jpmorganchase.com/corporate/investor-relations/document/3cea4108_strategic_update.pdf.

5. Justina Perro, "Mobile Apps: What's a Good Retention Rate?" Localtyics.com, March 21, 2017, http://info.localytics.com/blog/mobile-apps-whats-a-good-retention-rate.

6. Corrie Driebusch and Eliot Brown, "Blue Apron Serves Up an Insipid Offering," *Wall Street Journal*, June 28, 2017, https://www.wsj.com/articles/blue-apron-prices-ipo-at-10-a-share-1498688019.

7. Robert S. Kaplan, "Elkay Plumbing Products Division," Case 110-007 (Boston: Harvard Business School, 2009, revised 2010).

8. For details, see Sunil Gupta and Joseph Davies-Gavin, "BBVA Compass: Marketing Resource Allocation," Case 511-096 (Boston: Harvard Business School, 2011, revised 2012).

9. Kevin Roberts, *Lovemarks: The Future beyond Brands* (Brooklyn: Power-House Books, 2015).

10. Jim Lecinski, "Winning the Zero Moment of Truth," Google report, June 2011, https://www.thinkwithgoogle.com/marketing-resources/micro-moments/zero-moment-truth/.

11. David Court et al., "The Consumer Decision Journey," *McKinsey Quarterly*, June 2009.

12. Glen L. Urban et al., "Morphing Banner Advertising," *Marketing Science* 33, no. 1 (2013): 27.

13. John R. Hauser, Guilherme Liberali, and Glen L. Urban, "Website Morphing 2.0: Switching Costs, Partial Exposure, Random Exit, and When to Morph," *Management Science* 60, no. 6 (2014): 1594.

14. Garrett A. Johnson, Randall A. Lewis, and Elmar I. Nubbemeyer, "Ghost Ads: Improving the Economics of Measuring Online Ad Effectiveness," *Journal of Marketing Research* 54, no. 6 (2017): 867.

15. Anja Lambrecht and Catherine Tucker, "When Does Retargeting Work? Information Specificity in Online Advertising," *Journal of Marketing Research* 50, no. 5 (2013): 561.

16. Mark Borden, "The Mekanism Guarantee: They Engineer Virality," *Fast Company*, May 1, 2010.

17. Carla Marshall, "How Many Views Does a YouTube Video Get? Average Views by Category," *TubularInsights,* February 2, 2015.

18. Sharad Goel, Duncan J. Watts, and Daniel G. Goldstein, "The Structure of Online Diffusion Networks," *Proceedings of the 13th ACM Conference on Electronic Commerce*, 623. See also Derek Thompson, "Why It's a Lot Harder to 'Go Viral' on the Internet Than You Think," *Time*, February 17, 2017.

19. Duncan Watts and Jonah Peretti, "Viral Marketing for the Real World," *Harvard Business Review*, May 2007, 22–23.

20. Felix Oberholzer-Gee, "Buzzfeed—The Promise of Native Advertising," Case 714-512 (Boston: Harvard Business School, 2014).

21. Ibid.

22. Jonathan Ringen, "Point Man," *Fast Company*, July/August 2017, 85.

23. John Deighton and Leora Kornfeld, "The Ford Fiesta," Case 511-117 (Boston: Harvard Business School, 2011).

24. Sinan Aral, "What Would Ashton Do—and Does It Matter?" *Harvard Business Review*, May 2013, 25–27.

25. Eytan Bakshy et al., "Everyone's an Influencer: Quantifying Influence on Twitter," *Proceedings of the Fourth ACM International Conference on Web Search and Data Mining*, 65.

26. Oberholzer-Gee, "Buzzfeed."

27. Carl F. Mela, Sunil Gupta, and Donald R. Lehmann, "The Long-Term Impact of Promotion and Advertising on Consumer Brand Choice," *Journal of Marketing Research* 34, no. 2 (1997): 248.

28. Michael Lewis, "Customer Acquisition Promotions and Customer Asset Value," *Journal of Marketing Research* 43, no. 2 (2006): 195.

29. Julian Villanueva, Shijin Yoo, and Dominique M. Hanssens, "The Impact of Marketing-Induced Versus Word-of-Mouth Customer Acquisition on Customer Equity Growth," *Journal of Marketing Research* 45, no. 1 (2008): 48.

30. Philipp Schmitt, Bernd Skiera, and Christophe Van den Bulte, "Why Customer Referrals Can Drive Stunning Profits," *Harvard Business Review*, June 2011, 30.

31. Donald Ngwe and Thales Teixeira, "Improving Online Retail Margins by Increasing Search Frictions," working paper, Harvard Business School, Boston, 2017.

32. "37 Cart Abandonment Rate Statistics," Baymard Institute, January 9, 2017, https://baymard.com/lists/cart-abandonment-rate.

33. Bill Carmody, "Freemium Is About Marketing & Innovation, Not Pricing," *Inc.*, April 14, 2017.

34. Uzi Shmilovici, "The Complete Guide to Freemium Business Models," *Techcrunch*, September 4, 2011, https://techcrunch.com/2011/09/04/complete-guide-freemium/.

35. Clarence Lee, Vineet Kumar, and Sunil Gupta, "Designing Freemium: Strategic Balancing Growth and Monetization," working paper, Harvard Business School, Boston, 2015, https://papers.ssrn.com/sol3/papers.cfm?abstract_id=2767135. See also Sunil Gupta and Carl Mela, "What Is a Free Customer Worth?" *Harvard Business* Review, November 2008, 102–109; and Vineet Kumar, "Making 'Freemium' Work," *Harvard Business Review*, May 2014, 27–29.

36. Kaifu Zhang et al., "Content Contributor Management and Network Effects in a UGC Environment," *Marketing Science* 31, no. 3 (2011): 433.

Chapter 8

1. Andrew Rice, "Does BuzzFeed Know the Secret?" *New York*, April 7, 2013; http://nymag.com/news/features/buzzfeed-2013-4/.

2. Tobi Elkin, "Survey Finds 90% of People Skip Pre-Roll Video Ads," *MediaPost*, June 8, 2016.

3. Yuyu Chen, "More Than 60 Percent of Snapchat Users Skip Ads on the Platform," *Digiday*, February 13, 2017.

4. "The State of the Blocked Web: 2017 Global Adblock Report," PageFair.

5. Mary Meeker, "Internet Trends 2017—Code Conference," Kleiner Perkins, May 31, 2017.

6. Daniel G. Goldstein et al., "The Economic and Cognitive Costs of Annoying Display Advertisements," *Journal of Marketing Research* 51, no. 6 (2014): 742.

7. https://en.wikipedia.org/wiki/E-mart#cite_note-6.

8. "Tesco Builds Virtual Shops for Korean Commuters," *The Telegraph*, June 27, 2011, https://www.telegraph.co.uk/technology/mobile-phones/8601147/Tesco-builds-virtual-shops-for-Korean-commuters.html.

9. Anaheeta Goenka and Abhijit Panicker, "Kan Khajura Station: From the 'Dark' to Connectivity," *Warc*, 2014, https://www.warc.com/NewsAndOpinion/News/34990.

10. "HUL Opens Up Kan Khajura Tesan," *Warc*, June 29, 2015, https://www.warc.com/NewsAndOpinion/News/34990.

11. This discussion is based on Sunil Gupta, Srinivas K. Reddy, and David Lane, "Marketing Transformation at Mastercard," Case 517-040 (Boston: Harvard Business School, 2017).

12. Drew Neisser, "Clorox CMO's Five Building Blocks of a Better Brand," *AdAge*, March 8, 2017.

13. Thales S. Teixeira, "When People Pay Attention to Video Ads and Why," hbr.org, October 14, 2015.

14. "Moment Marketing Tool Kit," 2006, *Warc*.

15. "Your Guide to Winning the Shift to Mobile," Google, September 2015, https://www.thinkwithgoogle.com/marketing-resources/micro-moments/micromoments-guide-pdf-download/.

16. Sunil Gupta, "In Mobile Advertising, Timing Is Everything," hbr.org, November 4, 2015.

17. Allison Mooney and Brad Johnsmeyer, "I-Want-to-Buy Moments: How Mobile Has Reshaped the Purchase Journey," Google, May 2015, https://www.thinkwithgoogle.com/marketing-resources/micro-moments/i-want-to-buy-moments/.

18. Gupta, "Mobile Advertising."

19. See company website for Home Connect: https://www.dbs.com.sg/personal/loans/mortgage-resources-tools/property-guide-app.

20. Forrester Research, "Moments That Matter: Intent-Rich Moments Are Critical to Winning Today's Consumer Journey," July 2015.

21. Robert D. Hof, "Marketing in the Moments, to Reach Customers Online," *New York Times*, January 17, 2016, https://www.nytimes.com/2016/01/18/

business/media/marketing-in-the-moments-to-reach-customers-online.
html?_r=0.

22. Consumers in the Micro-Moment, Wave 3, Google/Ipsos, U.S., August 2015, as reported in Google's *Micromoment Guide to Winning Mobile*.

23. See Brandy Shaul, "Report: Average App Session Length Is Around 5 Minutes," *Adweek*, November 22, 2016; and "One-Third of Mobile App Engagements Last Less Than One Minute," Swrve.com, July 17, 2014, https://www.swrve.com/company/press/one-third-of-mobile-app-engagements-last-less-than-one-minute.

24. *Micromoment Guide to Winning Mobile*, Google, September 2015.

25. Daniel An, "Find Out How You Stack Up to New Industry Benchmarks for Mobile Page Speed," Google, February 2018, https://www.thinkwithgoogle.com/marketing-resources/data-measurement/mobile-page-speed-new-industry-benchmarks/.

Chapter 9

1. Chris Anderson, "The End of Theory: The Data Deluge Makes the Scientific Method Obsolete," *Wired*, June 23, 2008.

2. Jeremy Ginsberg et al., "Detecting Influenza Epidemics Using Search Engine Query Data," *Nature* 457 (2008): 1012.

3. David Lazer et al., "The Parable of Google Flu: Traps in Big Data Analysis," *Science* 343 (2014): 1203.

4. Andrew Lipsman et al., "The Power of 'Like': How Brands Reach (and Influence) Fans through Social-Media Marketing," *Journal of Advertising Research*, March 2012, 40.

5. Leslie K. John et al., "Does 'Liking' Lead to Loving? The Impact of Joining a Brand's Social Network on Marketing Outcomes," *Journal of Marketing Research* 54, no. 1 (2017): 144. See also Leslie K. John et al., "What's the Value of a Like?" *Harvard Business Review*, March–April 2017.

6. Nicholas A. Christakis and James H. Fowler, "The Spread of Obesity in a Large Social Network over 32 Years," *New England Journal of Medicine* 357 (2007): 370.

7. Rob Stein, "Obesity Spreads in Social Circles as Trends Do, Study Indicates," *Washington Post*, July 26, 2007.

8. Ethan Cohen-Cole and Jason M. Fletcher, "Detecting Implausible Social Network Effects in Acne, Height, and Headaches: Longitudinal Analysis," *British Medical Journal* 337 (2008): 2533.

9. Russell Lyons, "The Spread of Evidence-Poor Medicine via Flawed Social-Network Analysis," *Statistics, Politics and Policy* 2, no. 1 (2011): 2151.

10. Cosma Rohilla Shalizi and Andrew C. Thomas, "Homophily and Contagion Are Generically Confounded in Observational Social Network Studies," *Sociological Methods and Research* 40 (2011): 211.

11. Sinan Aral, Lev Muchnik, and Arun Sundararajan, "Distinguishing Influence-Based Contagion from Homophily-Driven Diffusion in Dynamic Networks," *Proceedings of the National Academy of Sciences* 106, no. 51 (2009): 21544.

12. Catherine Tucker, "Identifying Formal and Informal Influence in Technology Adoption with Network Externalities," *Management Science* 54, no. 12 (2008): 2024.

13. Joseph P. Davin, Sunil Gupta, and Mikolaj Jan Piskorski, "Separating Homophily and Peer Influence with Latent Space," working paper 14-053, Harvard Business School, Boston, 2014. http://www.hbs.edu/faculty/Publication%20Files/14-053_f72cd431-8b9c-4991-8ea4-6ab5209f11a1.pdf.

14. Dean Eckles, René F. Kizilcec, and Eytan Bakshy, "Estimating Peer Effects in Networks with Peer Encouragement Designs," *Proceedings of the National Academy of Sciences* 113, no. 27 (2016): 7316.

15. Thomas Blake, Chris Nosko, and Steven Tadelis, "Consumer Heterogeneity and Paid Search Effectiveness: A Large-Scale Field Experiment," *Econometrica* 83 (2014): 155.

16. Mark Sweney, "Google Keyword Advertising Is Waste of Money, Says eBay Report," *The Guardian*, March 13, 2013.

17. Weijia (Daisy) Dai and Michael Luca, "Effectiveness of Paid Search Advertising: Experimental Evidence," working paper 17-025, Harvard Business School, Boston, 2017. See also "Do Search Ads Really Work?" *Harvard Business Review,* March–April 2017, 26.

18. Sunil Gupta and Joseph Davies-Gavin, "BBVA Compass: Marketing Resource Allocation," Case 511-096 (Boston: Harvard Business School, 2012).

19. For recent examples of research on attribution, see Pavel Kireyev, Koen Pauwels, and Sunil Gupta, "Do Display Ads Influence Search? Attribution and Dynamics in Online Advertising," *International Journal of Research in Marketing* 33, no. 3 (2016): 475; Hongshuang (Alice) Li and P. K. Kannan, "Attributing Conversions in a Multichannel Online Marketing Environment: An Empirical Model and a Field Experiment," *Journal of Marketing Research* 51 (2014): 40; and Anindya Ghose and Vilma Todri-Adamopoulos, "Toward a Digital Attribution Model: Measuring the Impact of Display Advertising on Online Consumer Behavior," *MIS Quarterly* 40, no. 4 (2016): 889.

20. Jim Lecinski, *Winning the Zero Moment of Truth* (Palo Alto: Think with Google, 2011), 25.

21. For details see Kireyev, Pauwels, and Gupta, "Do Display Ads Influence Search?"

22. "TV and Digital Are in a Dead Heat for US Media Dollars," *eMarketer*, October 4, 2016.

23. https://www.statista.com/statistics/187439/share-of-e-commerce-sales-in-total-us-retail-sales-in-2010/.

24. https://www.facebook.com/business/success/general-motors-onstar.

25. Thorsten Wiesel, Koen Pauwels, and Joep Arts, "Marketing's Profit Impact: Quantifying Online and Off-line Funnel Progression," *Marketing Science* 30, no. 4 (2010): 604.

26. Isaac M. Dinner, Harald J. Van Heerde, and Scott A. Neslin, "Driving Online and Offline Sales: The Cross-Channel Effects of Traditional, Online Display, and Paid Search Advertising," *Journal of Marketing Research* 51, no. 5 (2014): 527.

27. Prasad Naik and Kay Peters, "A Hierarchical Marketing Communications Model of Online and Offline Media Synergies," *Journal of Interactive Marketing* 23, no. 4 (2009): 288.

Chapter 10

1. http://investors.nytco.com/investors/investor-news/investor-news-details/2018/The-New-York-Times-Company-Reports-2017-Fourth-Quarter-and-Full-Year-Results/default.aspx.

2. Sunil Gupta and Lauren Barley, "Reinventing Adobe," Case 514-066 (Boston: Harvard Business School, 2014, revised 2015).

3. Michael Corkery, "Adobe Buys Omniture: What Were They Thinking?" *Wall Street Journal*, September 16, 2009, https://blogs.wsj.com/deals/2009/09/16/adobe-buys-omniture-what-were-they-thinking/.

4. Gupta and Barley, "Reinventing Adobe."

5. Shantanu Narayen, interview by author, April 2017.

6. Sunil Gupta and Sara Simonds, "Goldman Sachs' Digital Journey," Case 518-039 (Boston: Harvard Business School, 2017).

Chapter 11

1. Discussion in this section is based on Sunil Gupta and Eren Kuzucu, "Enpara.com: Digital Bank at a Crossroad," Case 518-030 (Boston: Harvard Business School, 2017).

2. Ibid.

3. Ibid.

4. Interview conducted by author.

5. Nicholas Wade, "Your Body Is Younger Than You Think," *New York Times*, August 2, 2005, http://www.nytimes.com/2005/08/02/science/your-body-is-younger-than-you-think.html.

6. Discussion in this section is based on Sunil Gupta and Sara Simonds, "Goldman Sachs' Digital Journey," Case 518-039 (Boston: Harvard Business School, 2017).

Chapter 12

1. "The Future of Agriculture," *The Economist*, June 11, 2016.

2. Ibid.

3. Sunil Gupta and Sara Simonds, "Goldman Sachs' Digital Journey," Case 518-039 (Boston: Harvard Business School, 2017).

4. "10 Key Marketing Trends for 2017 and Ideas for Exceeding Customer Expectations," IBM report, 2017, https://www-01.ibm.com/common/ssi/cgi-bin/ssialias?htmlfid=WRL12345USEN.

5. Sunil Gupta, "Big Data: Big Deal or Big Hype?" *The European Business Review*, May 25, 2015.

6. David Lazer et al., "The Parable of Google Flu: Traps in Big Data Analysis," *Science* 343, no. 6176 (2014): 1203.

7. "The Return of the Machinery Question," *The Economist*, June 25, 2016.

8. Quoc V. Le et al., "Building High-Level Features Using Large Scale Unsupervised Learning," *Proceedings of the 29th International Conference on Machine Learning*, 2012, 507.

9. "Machinery Question," *The Economist*.

10. Carl Benedikt Frey and Michael A. Osborne, "The Future of Employment: How Susceptible Are Jobs to Computerisation?" working paper, University of Oxford, Oxford, 2013, http://www.oxfordmartin.ox.ac.uk/downloads/academic/The_Future_of_Employment.pdf.

11. James Manyika et al., "Harnessing Automation for a Future That Works," McKinsey Global Institute, January 2017, http://www.mckinsey.com/global-themes/digital-disruption/harnessing-automation-for-a-future-that-works.

12. Arwa Mahdawi, "What Jobs Will Still Be Around in 20 Years? Read This to Prepare Your Future," *The Guardian*, June 26, 2017.

13. "Automation and Anxiety: Will Smarter Machines Cause Mass Unemployment?" *The Economist*, June 25, 2016.

14. Susan Lund, James Manyika, and Kelsey Robinson, "Managing Talent in a Digital Age," *McKinsey Quarterly*, March 2016.

15. Interview conducted by author.

16. Kenneth A. Egol et al., "Can Video Game Dynamics Identify Orthopaedic Surgery Residents Who Will Succeed in Training?" *International Journal of Medical Education* 8 (2017): 123.

17. Interview conducted by author.

18. Kelsey Gee, "In Unilever's Radical Hiring Experiment, Resumes Are Out, Algorithms Are In," *Wall Street Journal*, June 26, 2017.

19. Marcus Buckingham and Ashley Goodall, "Reinventing Performance Management," *Harvard Business Review*, April 2015, 40–50.

20. Max Nisen, "How Millennials Forced GE to Scrap Performance Reviews," *The Atlantic*, August 18, 2015, https://www.theatlantic.com/politics/archive/2015/08/how-millennials-forced-ge-to-scrap-performance-reviews/432585/.

21. Steven Prokesch, "Reinventing Talent Management," *Harvard Business Review*, September–October 2017, 54.

22. Jennifer Surane, "Goldman Sachs Introduces Real-Time Employee Performance Reviews," *Bloomberg*, April 21, 2017, https://www.bloomberg.com/news/articles/2017-04-21/goldman-sachs-introduces-real-time-employee-performance-reviews.

23. Don Peck, "They're Watching You at Work," *The Atlantic*, December 2013, https://www.theatlantic.com/magazine/archive/2013/12/theyre-watching-you-at-work/354681/.

24. Prokesch, "Reinventing Talent Management."

Index

Acknowledgments

I have always been fascinated by technology. The dawn of the internet era, in the 1990s, created a new sense of excitement for me as I saw its dramatic impact on consumers, firms, and society. A startup like Amazon was taking on the retailing giant Walmart, and eBay was reducing consumers' transaction costs, which, according to Nobel Prize–winning economist Ronald Coase's "theory of the firm," are the reason why we work for a firm instead of being freelance workers. The birth of Google (1998), the emergence of Facebook (2004), and the launch of the iPhone (2007) further piqued my curiosity and led me to embark on a ten-year journey of research into digital technology and its impact on consumer behavior and firm strategy.

During this period I studied three groups of companies. The first group consisted of startups that were disrupting incumbents by inventing new business models and services. I had the privilege of talking with and learning from the founders of many amazing startups—Jennifer Hyman and Jennifer Fleiss of Rent the Runway (who discussed their startup idea with me when they were my students at Harvard Business School), Will Dean of Tough Mudder (also an HBS student of mine), Steve Kaufer of TripAdvisor, Jason Kilar of Hulu, Chad Hurley of YouTube (one of its founders), Vijay Shekhar Sharma of Paytm (a mobile-payment company in India), Mikael Hed of Rovio (of Angry Birds fame), Hyung-Chul Joo of Cyworld (a Korean social-network company), Oscar Farinetti of Eataly (an innovative Italian grocery chain), Sachin and Binny Bansal from Flipkart (an Indian online retailer like Amazon), Naveen Tewari of InMobi (a global mobile-advertising-network company), Ritesh Agarwal of OYO (an online marketplace for hotel rooms in India), and Guy Halfteck of Knack (a people-analytics company). Several other founders and VCs, many of them HBS alumni, were also very generous with their time, helping me understand the mindset of disruptors. Our California Research Center, under the direction of Allison M. Ciechanover and her excellent staff, and our India Research Center, under the direction of Anjali Raina and her superb staff, especially Rachna Tahilyani, were extremely helpful in organizing my numerous trips to meet with and learn from these entrepreneurs.

The second group of companies I studied consisted of "digital giants" like Amazon, Apple, Facebook, and Google—companies that grew up with a digital DNA but are now large enough that they have to deal with established companies as well. For example, Facebook and Google have to understand the advertising goals and practices of P&G and Coke. I am indebted to several executives at these firms for their time and guidance. I am especially thankful to Shuvo Saha of Google for sharing Google's view on digital marketing, and Eddy Cue and Jennifer Bailey of Apple for helping me understand the thinking behind launching Apple Pay.

The third group of companies in my research consisted of the incumbents—large, established firms that are being threatened by digital technology. I learned about the opportunities and challenges of digital transformation from the leaders of these companies. Ajay Banga showed me how he is leading Mastercard by creating a platform for digital innovation, and Raja Rajamannar explained the marketing transformation at the firm. David Kenny told me how he transformed The Weather Company, and how that experience is guiding him as he leads the Watson group at IBM. Hubert Joly highlighted how he is leading Best Buy even as it faces tremendous pressure from Amazon. From Kasper Rørsted I learned the challenges of digital transformation at Henkel and Adidas. Marty Chavez outlined the digital journey of Goldman Sachs. Shantanu Narayen described the amazing transformation of Adobe, which produced a sevenfold increase in the company's stock price in five years. Ömer Aras described the creation of a digital bank as a separate entity from the parent Finansbank in Turkey.

As part of my research I interviewed dozens of other executives who were instrumental in shaping my thinking. I am especially grateful to our Europe Research Center, under the direction of Vincent Dessain and his skilled team, especially Daniela Beyersdorfer, Emilie Billaud, and Tonia Labruyere for arranging interviews with Dr. Josef Reiter and Michael Wuertenberger of BMW, Thomas Romieu of LVMH, Wilko Stark of Daimler Group, Patrice Bula of Nestlé, Paul Van Arkel of Novartis, Antonia McCahon of Pernod Ricard, Luis Di Como and Laura Misselbrook of Unilever, and Dr. Hans Langer of Electro Optical Systems. Esel Çekin and her team at our MENA Research Center were also helpful in connecting me with many executives in Turkey and the Middle East.

As I learned from these interviews and developed my ideas, my HBS colleagues were a great resource for helping me refine my thinking. My special thanks to Bharat Anand, Doug Chung, John Deighton, Anita Elberse, Vineet Kumar, Rajiv Lal, Henry McGee, Donald Ngwe, Felix Oberholzer-Gee, Kash Rangan, and Thales Teixeira. I also got valuable input from my other academic colleagues and coauthors, especially Don Lehmann, Carl Mela, Raghu Iyengar, Puneet Manchanda, Aurélie Lemmens, Clarence Lee, Joseph Davin, Pavel Kireyev, Michela Addis, Koen Pauwels, Leslie John, Misiek Piskorski, and Srinivas Reddy.

I have always learned a lot from my MBA and executive students. My sincere thanks to the more than one thousand participants of our General Management Program (GMP) with whom I shared my ideas for the last five years. I am also grateful to hundreds of executives who attended our one-week executive program on Driving Digital Strategy and who provided suggestions to improve the content of this book. Thanks are also owed to hundreds of our alumni and MBA students for their constructive feedback, especially Zach Clayton (MBA 2009) and Kristin Armstrong (MBA 2009), who helped me in the early years of my research in this area.

The real testing ground of my ideas centered on the companies that were going through the digital transformation. When my presentations based on the ideas in this book resonated with executives around the world, I was ready to write the book. I want to thank the people who provided me this opportunity. Søren Røssel, head of PwC's executive education in Europe, gave me the forum to speak to hundreds of PwC executives in Norway and Finland. I want to thank Søren and his excellent team, especially Line Lüthje and Fie Gottschalck, for their support during these programs. Thanks also to Håvard Abrahamsen of PwC Norway and Mikko Nieminen of PwC Finland. I am grateful, in addition, to executives of Abu Dhabi Investment Authority, Adidas, Autotrader, Bertelsmann, *CTO Forum*, Franklin Templeton, Heineken, Henkel, IBM, Jyske Bank, KLP, LVMH Asia, Novartis, T-Mobile, Turkcell, and Unilever for giving me the opportunity to share my work.

A research journey that spans ten years requires the help of many people, and I have been fortunate to get the support of several superb research associates and administrative assistants. Sara Simonds was my first RA when I embarked on this journey, and coincidentally she was also my last RA as I finished this book. In between I had the excellent support of Kavita Shukla, Dharmishta Rood, and Margaret Rodriguez. This book would not have been possible without their tremendous enthusiasm and support. Heather McNeil, Steve Church, and Elise Clarkson have been amazing administrative assistants during these years.

I worked with an incredible team at Harvard Business Review Press whose help and guidance have been crucial for the completion of the book. Tim Sullivan guided me during the early phases of the book, and later Kevin Evers took over Tim's role and gave me excellent suggestions for positioning and improving the book. Jon Zobenica spent enormous time to copyedit the manuscript. Allison Peter and Anne Starr were extremely helpful in a variety of ways, including copyediting, composition, and copyright permissions. Kenzie Travers worked hard to get endorsements for the book. My sincere thanks to the global sales and marketing team of HBR Press including Sally Ashworth, Julie Devoll, Lindsey Dietrich, Brian

Galvin, Vinay Hebbar, Keith Pfeffer, Jon Shipley, and Felicia Sinusas for their ongoing effort in promoting the book.

Finally, my deepest gratitude is to my family—my parents for instilling in me a deep sense of curiosity; my wife, Kamal, for her love and support, which never waned, even when I was deeply engrossed in my research and neglected things at home; and my sons, Tarun and Kunal, for their love and affection, which inspire me every day.

About the Author

SUNIL GUPTA is the Edward W. Carter Professor of Business at Harvard Business School, where he is the chair of the General Management Program and cochair of the executive program on Driving Digital Strategy.

As an expert in digital strategy, Gupta has conducted seminars and consulted with numerous companies around the world. He has published two books and over ninety articles, book chapters, cases, and notes, and his research has won many national and international awards. Gupta sits on the board of US Foods and on the advisory board of several startups.